ALL IN THE MIND

A Farewell to God

Ludovic Kennedy

Hodder & Stoughton

Copyright © Ludovic Kennedy 1999

Extract on p.23 reproduced with kind permission from *The Spectator*

First published in Great Britain in 1999
by Hodder and Stoughton
A division of Hodder Headline PLC

The right of Ludovic Kennedy to be identified as the Author of
the Work has been asserted by him in accordance with the
Copyright, Designs and Patents Act 1988.

10 9 8 7 6 5 4 3 2 1

British Library Cataloguing in Publication Data
A CIP catalogue record for this title is available
from the British Library.

ISBN 0 340 68063 6

Typeset by Palimpsest Book Production Limited,
Polmont, Stirlingshire
Printed and bound in Great Britain by
Clays Ltd, St Ives plc

Hodder and Stoughton
A division of Hodder Headline PLC
338 Euston Road
London NW1 3BH

For Doubters everywhere

When I was a child, I spake as a child, I understood as a child, I thought as a child; but when I became a man, I put away childish things. (1 Corinthians 13:11)

The study of theology, as it stands in Christian churches, is the study of nothing; it is founded on nothing; it rests on no principles; it proceeds by no authorities; it has no data; it can demonstrate nothing; and it admits of no conclusion. (Thomas Paine: *The Age of Reason*)

The quest for God may be likened to a blind man in a darkened room looking for a black cat that isn't there. (Anon)

Religion is a dream of the human mind which projects on to an illusory God the higher human ideals and aspirations. (Feuerbach)

We're here because
We're here because
We're here because
We're here.   (Popular song)

Contents

Part Two: Disbelief

List of Illustrations

Cicero, marble bust portrait, Wellington Museum (*E. T. Archive*)
Pierre Charron, engraving by W. de Launay (*Mary Evans Picture Library*)
Denis Diderot, unnamed engraver (*Mary Evans Picture Library*)
Baron D'Holbach, engraving by Robinson after Latourt (*Mary Evans Picture Library*)
David Hume by Allan Ramsay (*Scottish National Portrait Gallery*)
P.B. Shelley by Amelia Curran, 1819 (*National Portrait Gallery, London*)
Charles Darwin by George Richmond (*E. T. Archive*)
The Rev Sir Leslie Stephen by Sir William Rothenstein, 1903 (*National Portrait Gallery, London*)
Charles Bradlaugh, M.P. unnamed artist, 1880 (*Mary Evans Picture Library*)
Sigmund Freud (*Mary Evans/Sigmund Freud Copyrights*)
Winwood Reade from *The Martyrdom of Man*
Bertrand Russell (*Camera Press Ltd*)
Dr Margaret Knight and Mrs Jenny Norton, 1955 (*Paul Popper*)
Sir Julian Huxley (*Camera Press Ltd*)
The Rt Rev David Jenkins by Jane Bown (*Camera Press Ltd*)
The Rev Don Cupitt (*SCM Press*)

Introduction

I have wanted to write this book all my life because all my life I have found myself at odds with the Christian religion. Having recently entered what Dylan Thomas would call my eightieth year to heaven, I realise I have left it rather late. But when I was younger, I did not have the knowledge, the experience or indeed the courage to set down in print what I have come to believe with such certainty today; and even if I had, I doubt if the social climate would have been conducive to a favourable reception.

On the other hand it could be that the moment has passed; and that what I had originally envisaged as a radical scenario may now be thought to be old hat. Timing in life, whether striking a deal, hitting a ball or making love, is all; and I shall not know until after publication whether on this occasion I have got the timing right. All I can say, as Winwood Reade said of *The Martyrdom of Man* a hundred years ago, is that whatever reception does await this book, it has done me good to write it: I have unburdened myself of something that has been simmering in my system for too long.

I have chosen the title *All in the Mind* to emphasise what I think the orthodox are in danger of forgetting, that the god whom they worship and see as a powerful, independent, looming, if also loving, figure, is entirely a creature of their imaginations, fashioned to fulfil a need, as he and other gods have been for countless millions through the ages. Arguments therefore as to whether God does or does not exist are futile: the truth of the matter is that the idea of God exists in some people's minds and not in others';[1] and now that it is generally accepted that, for many, religion is no longer the mainspring of morals, proponents of whatever beliefs, Christians, Humanists, atheists, are none the better or worse for being so, a point which the poet Shelley was always keen to emphasise.

The basic doubts that I have expressed in these pages about the Christian religion can also be applied to the much simpler faiths of Judaism and Islam, but to have included them too would have made the book top-heavy. I have always thought that one reason why Stephen Hawking's incomprehensible *A Brief History of Time* sold millions of copies worldwide was the word 'brief'. Readers imagined that they were going to get the whole history of the universe in 190 pages which to some degree they did, even if they barely understood a word. This book is neither brief nor, I hope, overlong; and I make no apologies for restricting it to a survey of what has been the dominant faith in western Europe these past 2,000 years.

Many writers admit that one reason they write is not in the first instance to tell anybody anything but to find things out for themselves. That is especially true of this book. In the course of researching it, I have gained many fresh insights: the false claims put forward by the authors of the gospels that the alleged prophecies made in the Old Testament, often hundreds of years earlier, *proved* that Jesus's life and death had long been predicted, and that he had been chosen by God to be the Saviour of the world; the inflated importance given to Jesus's birth as a consequence of Luke's and Matthew's nativity stories embellished by idealised Renaissance paintings of Mother and Child – in fact there is no reason to suppose there was anything unusual about his birth at all; the unlikelihood of Bethlehem being the place of birth and of Herod massacring all the babies there without confirmation from other sources; the cruelty of the Roman Catholic Church over many centuries in its killing of infidels and heretics, and its obsession even to this day with its championing of celibacy and disapproval of sex; and atheism making its mark in western Europe much earlier than I had imagined. I realise however that my interpretation of events may well not be shared by others. We all have to find our own way to spiritual fulfilment and mine, which I have outlined in the last chapter, 'Touching the Transcendent', is not the Christian one.

Two subjects I have not embraced. The first is whether, in view of the decline of Christian worship in this country, the Church of England should be disestablished, i.e. should the reigning monarch continue to hold the titles bestowed on Henry VIII and his successors of Supreme Governor of the Church of England and Defender of the (Christian) Faith. Prince Charles is on record as saying that when he becomes king he would like to be thought of as Defender of *all* faiths – a friendly gesture to British Jews, Moslems and Hindus (though naturally he did not add 'and of none'). Many clergy as well as lay people think that the time for disestablishment has come, that the Church should be free to run its own show and appoint its own bishops, free of political interference. This apart, it seems to me that religious preferences or lack of them today are (unlike yesterday) an essentially private matter. If the British head of state were a president rather than a monarch, it would plainly be absurd to stipulate that he or she should have to adhere to a particular faith or sect.

The other matter which I have not touched on is the religious situation in the United States where the numbers of regular church-goers (more Nonconformist than Episcopalian, I gather), representing some 75 per cent of the population, are in inverse proportion to their numbers here. Why should this be? First, as Raymond Seitz, the former US Ambassador here has reminded me, the country was founded on the Puritan ethic; and it is well to remember that when successive waves of European immigrants uprooted themselves from everything familiar and dear to seek a better life across the sea, they were obliged to leave behind almost everything except what was most precious to them: belief in a power they imagined to be greater than themselves who would safely see them through whatever adversities lay ahead. And nowhere was this belief more sustained than among the pioneers who made the great nineteenth-century push westwards, across terrain unfriendly to lumbering wagons and where native Indians, vivid in the imagination if not always in reality, lurked behind each passing bush. In those times a god, however illusory, was a very present help in trouble.

Other relevant factors are that many Americans have a stronger sense of local community than we do, the local church and its Reverend still commanding a respect and affection which used to be the norm here but is now more the exception. The fact that the Church of America is not institutionalised but free and democratic has been held out to me as another, attractive reason for belief; though if ever the Church of England, in England, did become disestablished, I doubt if it would result in a regeneration of faith and the filling of empty pews: we have lived beyond the pale now for too long.

I have many to thank; once again Professor Peter Jones, Director of the Institute for Advanced Studies in the Humanities at Edinburgh University for renewing my Fellowship there, together with the assistance of staffs of the Edinburgh University Library, the National Library of Scotland, the Scottish Record Office and, in London, of the always helpful London Library. Peter Jones, the writer Ian Gilmour, David Berman, Professor of Philosophy at the University of Dublin, the biblical scholar Karen Armstrong, the writer and former psychiatrist Dr Anthony Storr and Nicolas Walter, director of the Rationalist Press Association, were all kind enough to read the completed manuscript and collectively have saved me from many errors. Others who have given me assistance or advice of one kind or another are David B. Barrett, Claude Conyers, the Very Rev. Hugh Dickinson, Dr David Edwards, Ruth Gledhill, Neiti Gowrie, Michael Grant, Michael Holroyd, Phil Jefferson, the Rt Rev. David Jenkins, Paul Johnson, Robin Lane-Fox, Erika Langmuir, Dr Patrick Moore, Kevin Myers, Dr C.C. Pond, the Rt Rev. Hugh Sebag-Montefiore, Raymond Seitz, the Rev. Professor W.P. Stephens, Peter Troughton, the Rev. Gavin Williamson, Ian Wilson and Will Wyatt, to all of whom I express grateful thanks. My editor at Hodder, Roland Philipps, has proved a rigorous but fair and percipient taskmaster, Anne-Marie Ehrlich has been responsible for the admirable illustrations, my agent Gill Coleridge has given me unstinted support from the conception of the idea, my secretary

INTRODUCTION

Deryn Wilcox has printed out impeccably successive drafts of the manuscript too numerous to mention, while my wife Moira, now a critic in her own right, has been a wise counsellor throughout. To my nephew Richard Calvocoressi and his wife Francesca and their delightful children I am again much indebted for comfort and companionship when enjoying the hospitality of their house in Edinburgh.

Ludovic Kennedy

PART ONE – BELIEF

Chapter One

THEN

My first introduction to religion was my mother telling me that God made the world and everything in it including us; and every night I was instructed to kneel by my bed and say a prayer to him, as morning and evening I had seen my father do. Later I was taken to church for the first time, and when I asked my mother what church was for, she said it was the house where God lived and we were going to say prayers and sing hymns to him. I understood from this that we were actually going to meet God and say hello to him and was disappointed when my mother said he would not be there in person, only in spirit. She tried to explain to me what 'in spirit' meant but it was beyond me and, I guess, beyond her too. Another puzzlement on reaching church was to find that God had nowhere to sleep or wash. I mentioned this to my parents over lunch and it naturally caused much merriment. Yet who were they to laugh, for most people have always thought of God, if not as an entirely flesh and blood being, as a Being of some sort with human attributes and understanding, like ourselves only better?

Was God watching us pray? I asked my mother. She hesitated before replying but then said, Yes, she was sure he was. All of us, I asked, and all at the same time, and the people in the other church in the village as well? Yes, my mother said, but not all that convincingly. How did he manage that, I said, did he have a thousand pairs of eyes and ears? Ah, said my mother, that was one of the wonderful things about God, he could do things that human beings couldn't do. And the hymns chosen in church seemed to support her. 'My God, how wonderful thou art', we sang, 'Thy Majesty how bright/How beautiful thy mercy-seat/In depths of burning light', and it went on, 'Oh, how I fear Thee, Living God/With deepest, tenderest fears/And worship Thee with trembling hope/And penitential tears.' Another hymn whose tune I liked (I found most hymn tunes very melancholy) began, 'Immortal, Invisible God only wise/In light inaccessible hid from our eyes'. All this was a great puzzle. If he was as wonderful and important as people said, why did he make himself invisible and inaccessible? And if he was both, how could anyone know if he was wise? He was said to be merciful too. Where did his wisdom and mercy show itself? Once again I asked my mother for an explanation, but by this time she had had enough. 'Listen, Ludovic,' I remember her saying, 'there are many things about religion that are hard to understand, but you'll come to them in time.' Something in her voice prompted me to ask, 'Do you understand them?' Desperate to avoid further quizzing, she was quite frank. 'No,' she said, 'I can't say I do. Not entirely anyway.'

So as a child my doubts came early. In our household religion was never discussed, which was probably true of most households in the country. Parents were too embarrassed to discuss it, if for no other reason that they did not know what, if anything, they believed. Most people in those days took an uncritical view of religion, apart from a few intellectual left-wingers whose views were regarded by the majority as blasphemous, and which were seldom reported in the national press. People spoke of a godless society with abhorrence and of a God-fearing one with approval: it was that, they believed, that gave societies stability, continuity and cohesion. I do not know how much my parents feared God or even thought about him – I would say very little, but their general attitude, like that of most upper-middle-class people, was to take the Christian religion as read; and they paid their dues to it by attending Sunday morning church service once or twice a month and Holy Communion once or twice a year. This enabled them to see and be seen by their neighbours and to gossip with them on local matters when the service was over. In short, their commitment to church was almost entirely social: its principal function, as they saw it, being the organisation of christenings, confirmations, weddings and funerals.

In time I was packed off to prep school and there and at Eton for the next ten years I was subjected to services in chapel each day and twice on Sundays, amounting in all, I calculated, to some 1,300 hours. I had to learn a new vocabulary and come to terms with words like Advent, Atonement, Assumption, Ascension, Epiphany, Eucharist, Redeemer, Salvation, Trinity, Transfiguration, with very little success. Every Sunday we had to kneel together and say with the priest:

> Almighty and most merciful Father; We have erred, and strayed from thy ways like lost sheep. We have followed too much the devices and desires of our own hearts. We have offended against thy holy laws. We have left undone those things which we ought to have done; And we have done those things which we ought not to have done. And there is no health in us. But Thou, O Lord, have mercy upon us, miserable offenders.

Even as a schoolboy I found this demeaning and untrue. I had no idea what holy law I was supposed to have offended against and I objected strongly to being likened to a lost sheep and having to declare publicly that I had been a miserable offender. Worse than this though was the Apostles' Creed which was considered so important that we had to turn towards the altar to recite it. This said that Jesus had been conceived by the Holy Ghost and born of a virgin, that after his death he had descended into hell and three days later had come back to life and ascended into heaven. I did not know then and I do not know now what all this meant.

Another puzzlement was the assertion in sermon after sermon that Jesus had died for our sins. Although my mother had proved something of a broken reed in my previous enquiries, I decided to tackle her again. For whose sins, I asked? She looked pole-axed. 'Well,' she said after a long pause, 'everybody's, I suppose.' I said, 'Yours and mine?' and my mother said, 'Well, yes,' so then I said, 'What would you say yours were?' She gave a little embarrassed laugh, a pause for thought and then with an air of triumph said, 'As you know, I'm very unpunctual.' I said, 'That's hardly a sin,' but my mother insisted it was. 'You see, it's being very inconsiderate of other people, making them wonder if you're coming or not.' I said, 'Hardly something Christ died for?' She looked deflated. 'No,' she had to agree, 'I suppose not.' And as she presumably had no major sins in her locker like defrauding the railways or grievous bodily harm, and wasn't going to admit to any other minor ones, that really was that.

Neither at prep school nor at Eton where I let the Creed and the self-deprecatory prayers wash over me, did I find any schoolfellows who shared my doubts about the things we said or sang in chapel; indeed they seemed as reluctant to talk about it as my father and mother. The staff, highly educated teachers, ought to have known better; yet in all my time there, no master, tutor or chaplain considered it part of my education to be told that many, if not most, of the claims made for Christianity were either based on speculation or were contrary to the laws of nature. Henry Ford's assertion that history was bunk was itself bunk: theology seemed to me a much better candidate. Yet so entrenched was the Christian religion in people's minds at that time, so universally taken for granted, that to challenge it in any way was to invite incredulity and bewilderment. So I kept my misgivings to myself.

When I was about fifteen, I was asked if I would like to be prepared for Confirmation in order to be accepted as a fully communicating member of the Church of England, culminating in a ceremony in college chapel to be performed by the Bishop of Lincoln. Afterwards I would be entitled to take Holy Communion. For a public schoolboy in those days Confirmation was more or less automatic, like joining the Officers' Training Corps, and to have made a public statement by refusing would have stamped me as something of a freak (few people today can have any idea of the force of conformity then). In any case I wasn't bothered about it one way or the other. Like logarithms and Milton it was just another burden to be borne.

So a small group of us gathered together and for six or seven weeks attended Confirmation classes given by the junior chaplain. He explained that the purpose of Confirmation was to confirm the promises made by our godparents at our baptism. These were, he said (reading from prayer book), 'To renounce the devil and all his works, the vain pomp and glory of the world with all covetous desires of the same and the carnal desires of the flesh, so that we would not follow or be led by them and to keep God's holy will and commandments.' After our godparents had made these promises, said the chaplain, our local priest would have asked God to sanctify the water in the font, some of which he would then have poured on our heads for the mystical washing away of sin (and we just a few months old!).

Did we have any questions? asked the chaplain. On the whole we didn't because we were conscripts rather than volunteers. I did have questions, not about Confirmation, which was relatively straightforward, but about the Atonement and the Assumption and all that, but I sensed that this was not the time or the place to ask: perhaps there never would be.

The great day arrived and some twenty-five or thirty of us filed into college chapel and stood in a line before the bishop, an imposing figure in mitre and vestments. Then we knelt and the bishop laid his hands on each of our heads and asked God to defend us with his holy grace that we might continue his for ever.

'The Lord be with you,' said the bishop when my turn came.

'And with thy spirit,' I replied as instructed.

Now came the moment for our first communion. An acolyte of the bishop handed him a goblet of red wine and a tray of wafers and when they had both consumed a wafer and taken a sip of the wine, they progressed down the line of kneeling boys. Like fledgling sparrows in a nest, we opened our mouths for the bishop to place a wafer on each of our tongues. This, said the bishop, was the body of Christ. 'Take and eat this in remembrance that Christ died for thee, and feed on him in thy heart by faith with thanksgiving.' Then he proffered each of us the goblet, having first hygienically wiped the rim of it. 'Drink this in remembrance that Christ's Blood was shed for thee and be thankful.'

Although in years to come I would regard this ritual of symbolically eating the flesh and drinking the blood of the Christian God as archaic, it was not like that at the time. It had been a solemn and impressive ceremony and, whatever my uncertainties, I felt bound to respond. But how? I did not consider myself a great sinner. I did not steal or bear false witness. I did not covet my neighbour's ox or ass: I proffered a few alms from time to time. But I was vulnerable in one area of my affirmation, as whoever had drafted it knew that any normal, healthy fifteen-year-old boy would be. Covetousness, falsehoods, envy, greed, I might have been able to dispose of, but not the one frailty the drafter had so cunningly singled out – the carnal desires of the flesh.

I would be telling a lie if I did not admit that, like many of my schoolfellows, imprisoned for weeks at a time without the company of women (as we were in those far-off monastic days), it was on the carnal desires of the flesh that, for long stretches at a time, my mind dwelt. And not only with women. *Faute de mieux* I was also susceptible to the charms of younger boys and at the time that Confirmation classes were in progress was enjoying a mild affair with one. On two or three evenings a week we would repair to one of the downstairs cubicles for a little mutual kissing and fondling. There was nothing more to it than that, for it was an idealised, romantic sort of attachment and it never struck me or, I think, him, that what we were doing might be wrong; not until I had to confront this stipulation about the carnal desires of the flesh; and such was the force of Christian propaganda that I felt a sense of guilt that was quite foreign to me. You may laugh at this in view of what I have written, but I had a strong sense that, as with Adam and Eve in the garden, God had seen what we had been doing and was displeased. So one night before going to bed, I knelt down to apologise to God and promised not to offend again. Yet I knew in my heart I was deceiving myself, and that what I had really wanted to say to God was what St Augustine of Hippo had said to him a thousand years earlier: 'Make me chaste, O Lord, but please, not yet.' So I laid off visits to the cubicle for a whole week until the old Adam proved stronger than the newly found God. My friend was puzzled by the break, and I very much minded that I could not tell him the reason.

Although that was the only time in my life that what the Church calls the living God – or rather my notion of him – entered my consciousness, from that moment on I never ceased to be amazed by the view people had of him. First of all, the mind-boggling claim that out of nothing he had made the universe and everything in it; not just our planet earth but all the billions of galaxies and stars existing in outer space and stretching from here to eternity. How had he done that? No one in the Church or outside it could begin to say. It was a matter of faith, they said, to me an inadequate explanation. 'God moves in a mysterious way,' the hymn ran, 'His wonders to perform.'

It seemed to me that to posit a Creator was one thing, because it was only by seeking causes and making discoveries that man had advanced at all; and the cause of the cosmos was the greatest unsolved mystery there was; yet by endowing this imagined Creator with supernatural powers and human attributes the Church had gone much further. He was said to be superhuman in that he was able to keep an eye on all peoples at all times and being omnipotent he could do with them what he willed (but where was the evidence?). The Church preached that God had made us in his likeness, but more and more it seemed to me that men and women saw him in *their* likeness, a sort of celestial Santa Claus, dispenser of mercy, love and justice (but in a world full of cruelty, injustice and hate, where again was the evidence?). Bishops and others preached in chapel that whatever we had done wrong, God would forgive us, that God loved a sinner who was repentant even more than someone who hadn't sinned in the first place. They talked in an airy way about God's will and that even if things went badly for us, God had a reason for it, though we might not see it at the time. We took the *Daily Mirror* in the house library and I once saw a headline: I WANTED TO JOIN FIRE BRIGADE BUT GOD WANTED ME TO BE A PRIEST, SAYS VICAR. Whatever he may have thought, did he not make the decision himself?

And so my doubts and uncertainties went to and fro and my disbeliefs grew. And yet one reservation always held me back from ditching Christianity completely. *What if I was wrong?* Wherever I turned, to teachers, newspapers, the radio, archbishops and field marshals, lord chancellors and prime ministers, not to mention the King and Queen, it was clear I was the odd man out. Did they know something I didn't? I had already suffered one dent in the fragile armour of my self-confidence because of my poor relationship with my mother which, I had come to believe, was my fault. Was it not also my fault that I could not bring myself to jog along with Christianity when so many others did? Were they deluded in their beliefs, or was I?

The gospel of St Mark tells the parable of the sower and the seed. Some of the seed fell by the wayside and was devoured by the fowls of the air, some fell on stony ground, and some was choked by thorns; but other seed fell on fertile ground and yielded fruit. According to Jesus the seed was the word of God, and the fowls of the air, stony ground and thorns aspects of Satan who did not want the word of God to flourish. On this issue I was half with Satan, finding the word of God to be as much of a problem as he did. Yet mine was a long-term affair, an elaborate jigsaw puzzle in which some pieces doggedly refused to fit, and it wasn't until my life was moving towards its close that they all came together and the puzzle was solved.

One of its pieces fell into place sooner than I had expected. A year after I left Eton the war broke out. My father, who had retired from the navy as a captain in 1922, now rejoined it, and at the age of sixty was given command of a converted passenger liner, HMS *Rawalpindi*, flying the White Ensign and armed with ancient six-inch guns. I too joined the navy as a midshipman and went to a variety of establishments for training. At one I found a prayer book containing prayers I had never heard before, some quite eccentric in their solicitations and all displaying expressions of self-abasement.

There were prayers for Times of Dearth and Famine ('grant that the scarcity and dearth which we now most justly suffer for our iniquity, may through thy goodness be mercifully turned into goodness and plenty . . .'), for Times of Plague and Sickness ('O Almighty God who in thy wrath didst send a plague upon thine own people in the wilderness for their obstinate rebellion against Moses and Aaron . . . have pity upon us miserable sinners . . .'), prayers for the protection of the Houses of Parliament, the King and Queen and other members of the royal family. 'Ask and ye shall receive,' Jesus had said, and that is just what these prayers were doing, pleading for specific requests to be met.

In a different category altogether was the prayer for the navy, crafted in beautiful and moving language and without a trace of grovel:

> O Eternal Lord God, who alone spreadest out the heavens and rulest the raging of the sea; who hast compassed the waters with bounds until day and night come to an end; Be pleased to receive into thy Almighty and most gracious protection the persons of us thy servants and the Fleet in which we serve. Preserve us from the dangers of the sea and from the violence of the enemy . . . that we may be a security for such as pass on the seas upon their lawful occasions . . .

I knew for certain that whatever other prayers my father and his ship's company would be hearing on Sunday morning church service as *Rawalpindi* patrolled the wild seas off Iceland, the navy's prayer would be one of them; and I also knew that morning and evening he would drop to his knees to offer up his own personal prayers as he had done all the days of his life.

And what happened to him? On the afternoon of 23 November 1939, as it was growing dark, two warships were reported approaching from astern. Assuming they were British, my father altered course towards them; and only realised his mistake when one of them flashed a false identification signal. They were the fast German battleships *Scharnhorst* and *Gneisenau*. My father turned *Rawalpindi* towards the darkening western horizon and increased to full speed. But the Germans were twelve knots faster and after an hour's chase caught up. In that hour most of those in *Rawalpindi* knew they were about to die. Within fifteen minutes the enemy shells had reduced the old passenger liner to a blazing wreck, and when she sank she took to the bottom my father, all his officers and more than 200 of his crew.

At the time of my father's death I was too overcome by the trauma of it (for I loved him dearly) to consider it objectively. But when, soon afterwards, I attended a church service in my own ship and heard again the navy's prayer with its plea to preserve us from the violence of the enemy, it sounded depressingly hollow. It was, I had to admit, absurd of me to think that prayers to the Almighty could have any influence on the outcome of events which could not be predetermined.

Intelligent Christians must know that prayers go unanswered. If it were otherwise, every non-believer in the land would convert to Christianity tomorrow. Why then do Christians continue to pray? Largely, I suspect, because their ministers preach endlessly about the *power* of prayer and, however illusory, prayer deludes them into thinking that they are in touch with someone or something greater and wiser than themselves. Open your hearts to God, the priests say, and he will respond, though not necessarily in the way you expect. And so prayers and incantations continue.

As for myself, I developed an attitude of *Che sera sera*, whatever will be will be; and whatever it turned out to be was the result of chance or fate, not the work of God or any other agent. E.M. Forster had said about human relationships, 'Only connect'. My philosophy was, and is, 'Only accept' – that is, the universe and all that is in it.

And yet, just because God was indifferent to people's prayers, even assuming he ever heard them, that was still no reason to jettison him entirely. At least not yet. The weight of 2,000 years of Christian teaching, Christian art, Christian wars lay heavily upon me. In the years ahead I needed to read all I could about Christianity and other religions too, open my mind so that any truths they contained might be revealed to me, as they had been to so many millions; or else conclude that they had come into being to meet a need which was not my need and perhaps never would be.

Chapter Two

NOW

In the fifty and more years that have since gone by, I have learned many things, and one of the most valuable has been that what some people call Christian values are in fact human values, and it is a mistake to think that religion and morality are synonymous and that atheists and agnostics must be somehow less moral than believers. 'It is an insult,' writes the Humanist Nicolas Walter, 'to suggest that we are inferior to the majority or responsible for any decline in behaviour.' Another Humanist, Derek Hunt of Ludlow, echoes him: 'We have no knowledge of God. We have some knowledge of human behaviour, and moral guidance of how we should act arises from this knowledge.' These views are coming to be generally acknowledged, with the result that the Christian Churches of Europe seem to have entered into a period of sharp decline, whether terminal or not it is too early to say.

For objective confirmation we can begin with a book published in 1982 by the Oxford University Press and called *The World Christian Encyclopaedia*. This traces the global rise of secularism or non-belief from a base of almost nil in 1900 to more than 20 per cent in 1980 and continuing to rise thereafter at the rate of more than 8 million a year. And this rise is posited not just on the decline of Christianity but of all faiths, world-wide.

As you might expect, the growth of secularism has been least

15

marked in Islamic countries. The Christian Churches of the west have experienced an opposite trend, secularism having grown from a nil base in 1900 to an average 7.3 per cent in 1980 with Britain well above the average. In Britain in the year 1901 there were more than 22,000 paid Anglican clergy; in 1965 there were just over 14,000; today there are fewer than 11,000 and the numbers continue to decline.

Coincidentally there has been a massive fall in church attendances. A report in the *Freethinker* of May 1998 says of the position in Britain: 'The rate of decline in Roman Catholic attendance appears even more dramatic when compared with the other churches. In the 20 years from 1980 to 2000 (extrapolated) the number of adults attending English churches will reduce by 20%, but within this figure R.C. attendances will have dropped by nearly 40%. Baptist, Methodist and United Reformed churches jointly fell by 23% and Anglicans by 14%. The same has been true of Church of Scotland attendances, though the tiny, Evangelical Alliance with its joyful, clap-happy services, has shown a modest rise.

In the same O.U.P survey the question was put to people in thirteen western countries: 'Do you believe in God?' (it was presumably not put in 1900 as being considered not only blasphemous but absurd). In all the countries canvassed the majority answer was *yes*, ranging from 95 per cent in the USA to 52 per cent in Sweden. This was surprising when you consider the steep fall in church attendances, and that many churches have been pulled down or converted into warehouses, electricity sub-stations, bingo halls, or whatever. Yet although in all countries and denominations Church membership and ceremonies have declined, there would seem to be no correlation between belief in God and church attendance. In England recently a book was published called *Religion in Britain since 1945* with the subtitle *Believing without Belonging* which confirmed the figures in the Oxford survey of more than 70 per cent of Britons affirming belief in God but not as churchgoers.

What is the explanation for this apparent discrepancy? I suggest that for an ordinary, perhaps not well-educated person, the unexpected appearance of a total stranger carrying a clipboard and wanting to know whether he or she believes in God must be a worrying experience, almost as worrying as being asked in similar fashion in pre-war Germany if one believed in Hitler. Who were those being canvassed to say they didn't believe in God when so many people of importance clearly did? And even if they felt they didn't believe, wasn't there a possibility they might be wrong and if so, what view would God take and – worse – what punishment might God inflict on them for having denied him? Far better to play safe; and, heartened by the result of the poll, those of the true faith who had come to think their boat was sinking, found it righting itself.

But their boat is sinking. To all intents and purposes we already are a secular society in which Christian faith and practices have become largely moribund. Take the teaching of Christianity in schools. The reader will recall from the first chapter the years of indoctrination my generation had to endure at school, with no teacher telling us that many people, as educated and intelligent as themselves, disagreed profoundly with what we were being taught. Today the situation is that every state school is obliged by the 1988 Education Reform Act to hold a daily assembly 'of a broadly Christian character', but there is no compunction for any child to attend whose parents object.

Because so many teachers these days are not religious themselves, the occasion often becomes less a specifically Christian event than a Humanist one, with stress being laid on such human virtues as truth, beauty, love, unselfishness, patience and courage. The 'worship' side of it tends to be ignored, because many teachers feel that to worship an imaginary god is to worship a human construct and is therefore a non sequitur. In addition all secondary schools have to set aside an hour a week for the teaching of religious education to children between the ages of eleven and sixteen. In my own county of Wiltshire the syllabus is extraordinarily thorough, embracing not only the Old and New Testaments but also the main tenets of Islam, Hinduism and Buddhism. For fourteen - and fifteen-year-olds the syllabus is surprisingly catholic, subjects included being: Theism, Atheism, Humanism, Marxism, Freud, Christian Myth, Darwin, the Big Bang.

Secular teachers working under less liberal educational authorities have less cause to rejoice. Robert Shayler, now retired, was one such:

> Over the years I have learned to sit, albeit uneasily, sharing in the conspiracy of silence with other atheists but also Baptists, Catholics, High/Low churchgoers, Jews, all of whom from time to time had to participate in a process of imparting to pupils religious dogma which was different from theirs.
>
> Particularly in primary church schools, but also in many county schools, the tenets of the Christian faith and the presumption of Christian teachers to use their position of power in class and assembly to propagate their faith not only are endemic but are assumed to be morally correct and desirable. As such, they are not to be questioned, challenged or presented to pupils as just one option within a multi-faith perspective. In this context it is not the job of the professional teacher, nor is it expedient, to rock the boat in which he or she earns his or her living.

There is also one anomaly to which Humanists strongly object; and that is the government, or rather the taxpayer, having to subsidise the costs of running denominational schools. If parents wish to inculcate their children with religious beliefs they can do so at home, as do the Americans – a far more religious-oriented country than ours.

If the practice of subsidising denominational schools is regrettable, in Northern Ireland it is catastrophic. Catholic schools are funded by the taxpayer to teach the Catholic version of events, while the state schools teach the Protestant version. If, say, twenty-five years ago, all (rather than a few) schools in Northern Ireland had been integrated, then the divisiveness of the two communities might have been lessened, the hatred the thug elements of both sides had for one another would not have found the climate in which to fester, peace might have come, and lasted, earlier.

Another indication of secularism in Europe has been the growth of Humanist associations which used to be regarded as fringe activities but which have now gained a new lease of life. Nicolas Walter, who has taken part in numerous school and college debates on Christianity versus Humanism, has spoken of past occasions when he won the argument but lost the vote, but now finds he is winning the vote as well; while a poll of 15,000 school children undertaken by Trinity College, Carmarthen, found that one-third described themselves as agnostics and one-quarter as atheists.

Recognising the human need for ritual in matters of union (as the Soviets did under Communism when, in lieu of churches, they set up secular marriage parlours with flowers, piped music and bridal attendants) and of death, both occasions once the exclusive province of the Church, British Humanists have devised their own; and Humanist weddings and funerals have doubled in recent years. They have also devised Humanist prayers (addressed not to God but to fellow humans) and graces. Here is a Humanist prayer:

> May those who are sick find peace where there is pain, comfort where there is sorrow, courage where there is fear, and may we find the goodness in our hearts to offer friendship, love and help to those in need, whenever we can.

And here is a grace: 'For what we are about to receive, let us be thankful and at the same time mindful of others less fortunate than ourselves.' (When asked to whom we should be thankful, the composer of the grace replied, 'The chef'!) The greatest Humanist success story comes from Norway where in a country of only 4½ million, Humanist membership has already reached 50,000 and by the turn of the millennium hopes to claim 100,000. The largest single reason for this increase has been the attraction for the country's youth of the Humanist coming-of-age ceremony which has a parallel in the Jewish Bar Mitzvah but none in the Protestant religion.

On a wider front secularism has affected our lives in a variety of ways. In the past the most important charities were nearly all conducted by Christian bodies. Today they are mostly secular, as, for example, Oxfam, Shelter, the Red Cross. Then, until quite recently, historians used the prefix BC, 'Before Christ', to indicate the years pertaining to the ancient world and AD, 'Anno Domini' (the year of Our Lord) for all the years since. But in a global context there are millions reluctant to accept the arbitrary intrusion into the calendar of a religious figure not their own, and so today AD has become CE ('The Common Era') and BC has become BCE ('Before the Common Era').

Again in western Europe the biblical injuction, 'Remember the Sabbath day to keep it holy', was for many centuries strictly observed. My own country, Scotland, had a history of Calvinist repression against those who lifted a finger on a Sunday in the cause of work or play. Things eased a bit, but even in the early 1930s I recall Sundays when the doors of golf clubs and public houses were closed all day and fishing, even up in the hills where I could not be seen, was considered out of order. Later, on Sundays in France or Italy I remember waking to the sound of church bells; and yet it was the Roman Catholic countries, popularly thought to be among the most devout, which were the first to relax the laws, recognising it as the one day in the week which gave an opportunity for people to watch or take part in sports – a trend which may be said to have started in the sixteenth century by the Archbishop of St Andrews enjoying a round of golf after officiating at Sunday morning service. In time came the introduction of continental Sunday shopping, many shops that used to be closed on a Sunday taking Monday off instead. In Britain we were slower to follow suit, thanks or rather no thanks to the Lord's Day Observance Society which was quick to urge the prosecution of offenders, and was supported by several Christian Members of Parliament. But we have caught up since and are now in line with most of the rest of Europe.

Another sign of the changing times has been society's attitude to the disposal of its remains. A person who a hundred years ago would have been deeply distressed to be told that his body would not be laid to rest in consecrated ground, today and in the knowledge that many cemeteries in urban areas are displaying full house signs, is perfectly content to let the flames of the local crematorium dispose of his remains instead; and thus ensure for self and family a finality denied to those left to moulder in a coffin six feet below ground.

The churches themselves have seen many changes. In the old days, when the office of ministers of religion commanded respect and authority, many country parishes could support both parson and curate, and two services a day plus Holy Communion on Sundays were considered routine. Today a single priest has to minister to three or sometimes more churches, taking them in rotation. In few can he expect more than a handful of worshippers; and the language of the hymns they sing, many in the mournful minor key, has all the mustiness of a bygone age.

> *Praise to the Holiest in the Height*
> *And in the depths be praise,*
> *In all his words most wonderful,*
> *Most sure in all his ways.*

A stranger from another planet might well ask of whom they were speaking; and where his wisdom lay.

The present Archbishop of Canterbury, Dr George Carey, said recently that the Anglican Church was in danger of becoming fossilised, which some believe it already is. He did not add that the cause of this fossilisation was that to many the principal teachings of the Church are no longer credible; further that senior members of the Church were publicly admitting that they no longer found them credible themselves. And yet, although the Church is withering on the vine, although one writer has compared its remaining adherents to an infant sucking on a dry breast and another has likened Christianity to a rock in a stream with the rushing water of Humanism sweeping by it, the virus (as Dr Richard Dawkins calls it) is still alive. Jehovah's Witnesses show up at the door from time to time. The Evangelical Alliance distributes a pamphlet called *Ultimate Questions* telling whoever reads it that they are debased sinners and that unless they repent hell awaits them, but also that God loves them and it is not too late to be saved. All over the country are bill posters saying JESUS (dead these 2,000 years) SAVES; other signs proclaim JESUS LIVES, yet do not add that the same goes for Michelangelo, Shakespeare, Bach.

At the memorial service for Lord Home, a former Prime Minister, at St Giles's Cathedral in Edinburgh, a passage was read from his autobiography where he claimed that his love of art and beauty and justice were gifts from God (and not, as Sir Julian Huxley would say, because of the altruistic traits which are endemic in human nature and pertain to peoples of all faiths and none). A recent newspaper reported that Roy and Sheila Hartle had been thrown out of the Scouts and Guides movements after twenty-six years of joint service because the Chief Scout, name of Garth Morrison, would not accept their commitment to Humanism as an alternative to 'duty to God'. And in a recent book of memoirs, a former pupil at a Roman Catholic convent has told how she was forced by the nuns to write right-handed because the left-handedness which came to her naturally was the mark of Satan.

In the west it is the Roman Catholic Church that holds the most rigid and illiberal religious beliefs. However, even here there are signs of dissension within the ranks. A recent opinion poll in France has revealed that in all ethical judgements 83 per cent of Catholics rely on their consciences and only 1 per cent on Church teachings, while a poll in Germany showed that support for the Pope among Catholics had slipped from 79 per cent in 1980 to a bare 16 per cent ten years later. And in Catholic Belgium, secularism has now been recognised by a ruling that from the ages of six to eighteen children must attend 'philosophical' classes which may be either religious or non-religious at parental choice; and all children are abjured to solve moral problems without reference to an imaginary transcendent authority.

Perhaps nowhere in the world has the Catholic Church taken more of a tumble than in Ireland, once the most Catholic-oriented and priest-ridden country in Europe, where schools and hospitals and residential colleges are funded by the government but run by the Church. What led to the undoing of the Catholic Church in Ireland was its insistence that its priests observe the harsh rule of permanent bachelorhood and celibacy, a burden which most young clerics with normal sexual drives found impossible to follow. Kevin Myers, a columnist on the *Irish Times*, wrote about the problem in the *Spectator*:

> Celibacy is what makes the priesthood the hardest of callings. In Ireland the priesthood combines a great deal of parish work with vast amounts of emotional solitude. Celibate, alone, physically untouched through the decades of manhood, prey to unrequitable sexual urges, many of these men had been selected for the Church from infancy by mothers who loathed carnality, and whose social standing would be hugely enhanced by *their son the priest*.

He goes on:

> Many Irish priests still seem frozen in a state of adolescence. They giggle easily. They love lavatory jokes. A joke with the word 'fuck' in it will reduce them to hysteria. Those who were not among the brightest were probably never taught to confront intellectual issues. They were mere freighters of doctrine, not questioners, which they unloaded in unquestioned dribs and drabs around their parish.

In the early 1990s the bubble burst:

> A Norbertine priest, Brendan Smyth, was imprisoned in Northern Ireland after a horrifying career of pederasty reaching back into the 1940s, much of it in the Republic and involving scores of children . . .
>
> This was only the start of the horror show. Dog-collar after dog-collar appeared sheepishly over the dock as their owners were charged with sodomising young boys, though courts in Ireland still tended to protect the Church as much as they could – one court ordered the press to name neither a priest who buggered a dozen young boys, nor his religious order, the boarding school where he worked nor even the county where he toiled. Many other child abuse stories still wait to be processed. And this bitter joke did

the circuit: 'What do Catholic priests hand round after dinner?'
'The Under-Eights.'

Other clerical delinquents, according to Kevin Myers, were Bishop
Casey of Galway who embezzled diocesan funds to pay hush money
to the mother of his illegitimate child, Father Michael Clery, Dublin's
most famous priest who was found after his death to have fathered
three children by two different women, and an elderly unnamed
priest 'who dropped dead among the giggles and slaps of a homo-
sexual sauna'.

The effect of all this on recruitment for the Church was shattering.
Applications for the priesthood fell by 85 per cent. In 1967, 537 girls
applied for enrolments in convents; in 1992 the number was forty-two
and few stayed even for a year. Applications for teaching orders such
as the Christian Brothers dried up almost completely: in 1965 there
were 179 applications, in 1992 just three. Yet although Ireland like
the rest of Europe has been moving towards secular values, with
homosexuality and divorce no longer illegal and information on
contraception and abortion no longer unobtainable, the effect on
churchgoing has been minimal:

> Over 80 per cent of Catholics still go to Mass once a week,
> regardless of what they were doing the night before. I know
> so many people who think nothing of spending Saturday night
> in revelry with a stranger or two but who will stagger out of
> bed on Sunday to attend Mass and maybe even Communion.
> Vatican II seems to have done a perfectly splendid job of ridding
> the Catholic Church in Ireland, as elsewhere, of a sense of sin or a
> belief in hell . . . Is Mass attendance some gregarious manifestation
> of a still not understood need for bonding unique to Irish life?

In other countries too there is evidence that the Roman Catholic
Church and its leader Pope Paul II have been adamant in making no
concessions to the Church's traditionally rigorous rules on marriage,
chastity, procreation and sex. In a way, it is understandable, as for

him to have done so would have been an admission that the early Fathers, St Augustine, St Thomas Aquinas and their successors, had been in error. Indeed on many occasions he has reinforced them, as when he approved of periods of marital chastity which, he said, 'in no way detracts from married love, but rather lends it a higher human value'. As a married man of nearly fifty years, I do have to ask what a presumably lifelong bachelor knows about married love. And he continued to repeat the myth about Jesus's mother being a virgin when he wrote in *Redempotoris Mater* in 1987 that Mary 'preserved her virginity intact'. Was he ignorant of the mistranslation[1] of the prophecy in Isaiah 53 which led to 'virgin' being substituted for 'girl' or 'young woman' in Luke and Matthew and which in any case referred to an event some seven hundred years earlier? Or did he know about it and after 2,000 years of Mariolatry lack the courage to correct it?

Yet if John Paul II could hardly find reverence enough for Christ's mother, the same could not be said for other women. He epitomised his Church's traditionally dismissive attitude towards women when in 1986 he leaned on the doctrine of papal infallibility that women priests would have no place in the Catholic Church, not only in his lifetime but *for ever*, though presumably some future Pope, also claiming infallibility, could rescind it. (Papal infallibility was introduced by Pius IX in 1870 and had been exercised only once before when in 1950 Pius XI had decreed as a matter not to be contradicted the bizarre claim that after her death Christ's mother had been bodily transported to heaven.)

One of the shortest reigning, yet most loved Pope of our times, Angelo Giuseppe Roncalli, Pope John XXIII, felt the strictures about relations with women early on. As a fourteen-year-old boy he wrote in his diary: 'I must avoid having dealings, playing or joking with women – regardless of what condition, age or degree of friendship', while in 1966 theological students at a German seminary voiced the same sort of unease. One wrote that they were forbidden to say hello to the girls who dusted the corridors. Another complained, pathetically, 'We were left entirely without guidance on the subject of celibacy; for the most part we were advised that the best way to conduct ourselves was to run away from women.'

Yet the most distasteful example of Catholic bigotry in matters of sex occurred in 1982 when a German newspaper reported the case of two young handicapped people, both Catholics, who wished to marry in a Catholic church in Munich. She was almost blind. He suffered from muscular atrophy which meant that he was unable to raise an erection and therefore procreate; and on the traditional grounds that the purpose of marriage was not sex but procreation, the Catholic priest refused to marry them; and a Protestant pastor, with no such scruples, married them instead. When they heard of the affair, Munich's Youth Union protested to the office of the local archbishop that the so-called 'penis test' had been 'a violation of humanity and an infringement of human dignity'.

The German Roman Catholic theologian Uta Ranke-Heinemann, to whose book *Eunuchs for the Kingdom of Heaven*[2] I am grateful for much of this information, has summed up her views on it:

> Recently Catholic moral theology has lost much of its prestige. With its contrived elaborations it stands today, practically speaking, facing the ash-heap. It is a folly that poses as religion and invokes the name of God, but has distorted the consciences of countless people. It has burdened them with hair-splitting nonsense and has tried to train them to be moral acrobats, instead of making them more human and kinder to their fellow men and women . . . Its theology is no theology and its morality is no morality. It has come to grief on its own stupidity.

As Avedon Carol has pointed out in her book *Nudes, Prudes and Attitudes: Pornography and Censorship* the more religiously repressive an upbringing, the greater the likelihood of moral deviancy, especially in relation to sexual violence.

Reading all this and regarding it as incontrovertible that religion was beginning to lose its hold on people, I decided to find out where and when religion first began, what were the forces that sustained it and what others more recently had contributed to its long decline.

Chapter Three

EARLY MYTHOLOGIES

'Out of ignorance came fear, out of fear came gods.' It requires no great effort of the imagination to recognise the fears instilled in early man by natural causes. We know, or if we don't know we can look it up, that a flash of lightning is caused by an electrical charge strong enough to overcome the resistance of air and which generates several hundred million volts, and that the thunder that accompanies it is the result of the rapid expansion of hot air forming a compression wave. Early man knew nothing of this; and the combination of the two followed by torrential rain must have scared him out of his wits. Other phenomena such as floods and forest fires and earthquakes must have been equally alarming and given the impression that some hostile unseen force was showing its displeasure. Add to this his more immediate concerns such as long winter nights with the baying of wild animals coming from the darkness beyond the circle of the campfire; whether the warming sun which he had seen go down in the evening would rise again next morning (on days of low cloud it didn't); which berries and fungi were edible and which harmful (which could only be discovered by testing); and the ever-present fear of creatures which might attack him when sleeping. Then, as Hobbes said, life was solitary, poor, nasty, brutish and short.

Throughout history one of man's most distinguishing characteristics has been his compulsion to seek causes and explanations: it is that which has brought him from a ragged, bearded cave-dweller carrying a club and draped in skins to the world of lasers and computers, space rockets and superhighways. In the thunder and lightning that so frightened him he recognised a power infinitely greater than himself, which gave no warning of its intentions and struck, it must have seemed to him, when it had a mind to. This power had to be revered and, where possible, appeased; thus, out of need, gods were born. Other gods followed: those of river and sky, sea and forest. There were spirits and ghosts too which took him in his dreams to unknown places and thus had a life of their own, independent of the body. Some of these spirits he incarnated in fish and birds and animals, in plants and bushes and trees, even in inanimate objects like rocks. Some he regarded as well disposed, others as malevolent; so that when a rock did him harm, his reaction was like that of a modern child who, hurt by running into a table, smacks it soundly with a cry of '*Naughty* table!' It is this concept of the spirit world, what one might describe as the otherness in man, that over the millennia has become transmogrified into what we call 'the spiritual' of which today's religions claim to be exclusive guardians. The ghosts too of long ago were the progenitors of what used to be called the Holy Ghost, the third person of the Trinity, and today is more commonly known as the Holy Spirit.

Another belief of early man has also partly survived, that of life after death. In graves of the Palaeolithic period have been found flintstones (to create warmth?) and necklaces buried beside the skeletons of corpses, the skeletons themselves showing sprinklings of red ochre, the symbol of blood and therefore of continuing life. Some skeletons have been found in a trussed-up position (which must have been arranged soon after death to pre-empt *rigor mortis*); though whether the position being analogous to that of a foetus in the womb is indicative of a rebirth or whether done to prevent the corpse wandering around and being a nuisance to the living is impossible to say.

The only other evidence that still survives of the people of that time are the magnificent rock paintings and engravings in the caves of, among others, Altamira in Spain and Lascaux in France, both of which I once visited in the course of the same day. The reason that some of the best of these paintings and engravings were not discovered until the twentieth century is because they are situated literally in the bowels of the earth and reached only by narrow fissures or holes in the ground. The purpose of this was not secrecy but preservation: had the paintings been made on rocks above ground, the soluble red ochre and black manganese with which many of them were drawn would have been obliterated by the rain. Paradoxically the refrigerated atmosphere of the caves which kept the paintings preserved for 20,000 years has in recent years been threatened by corrosion from the hot breaths of thousands of tourists, as a result of which some caves have had to be closed and access to others restricted.

In both Altamira and Lascaux the paintings are depictions of the animals which the people of that time hunted, and are wonderfully vivid. Altamira is dominated by what Geoffrey Grigson calls 'a medley of bisons, some bulls some cows, in red, black, yellow, brown, violet; and on each flank of the herd a wild boar drives inward, as much in movement as the bisons are still'. There are bisons at Lascaux too, black bulls humped and massive with their members erect, and a huge red cow in calf, superimposed on animals of another species. There are horses with black manes and yellowy brown bodies, one of them upside down, perhaps tumbling over a cliff, another in flight, its side pierced by darts or lances. Paintings of ox, ibex, mammoth and what is said to be a woolly rhinoceros are also preserved at Lascaux, though what I remember most from my visits are the disembodied necks and antlers of five red deer who look to be swimming a river. Grigson thinks that all the Lascaux paintings were executed by one hand, the work of a talented artist. They are the more remarkable when you consider that the caves are without natural light and the only illumination afforded to the artist must have come from some primitive wick or taper. What the purpose of the paintings was, no one knows for certain. One view is that the artist wanted to express the kinship his people felt for the beasts they hunted for food and so absorb something of their strength, fleetness and courage. Others interpret them magically. 'By drawing the animals successfully hunted,' says Ninian Smart, 'they would in fact *be* successfully hunted.'

In the past there was a widely held view – still held by some today – that it was polytheism (the cult of many gods) that paved the way to monotheism (the cult of one); but there is evidence to show that some primitive tribes fashioned a Supreme Being who existed conjointly and had power over lesser gods; and that they endowed these Supreme Beings with some sense of morality. 'It is certain that savages,' wrote Andrew Lang, 'when first approached by curious travellers and missionaries have again and again recognised our God in theirs.' If there was an element of wishful thinking in this, there was some evidence. In Australia in the nineteenth century an aborigine told a traveller named Howitt that when he was a boy and before the white man came to Melbourne, his grandfather took him out one night to look at the stars. 'You can see Bunjil up there,' he said, 'and he can see you and all you do down here.' Bunjil was the Supreme God of several aboriginal tribes who claimed that he approved of respect for the aged, avoidance of adultery and other sins, and settling differences by peaceful means. The Andaman Islanders invented a great god called Puluga. 'He was never born, and is immortal. By him all things were created except the powers of evil.' What angered him, declared the Andamese, was *yubda*, i.e. falsehoods, theft, assault, murder, adultery. To those in pain or distress he was said to have pity and would sometimes give relief. He was the judge of souls and led men to believe that those who had transgressed in this life might 'to some extent' expect punishment in a future state. The first missionaries who went to Greenland assumed that the Eskimos had no notion of a Supreme Being but found otherwise. 'Thou must not imagine,' one of them told a missionary, 'that no Greenlander thinks about these things. There must be a Being who made all these things. He must be very good too. Ah, did I but know him, how I would love and honour him.'

The idea of a great sky god, omniscient and omnipresent, was prevalent in many parts of Africa (where man first surfaced) from earliest times. The explorer Dr Richard Livingston found that the

Bakwain tribe, before any contacts with whites, 'had a tolerably clear conception of good and evil, God and the future state'. The Zulus called this god Ukqili, the wise one, while the Ganda of Uganda believed that his great eye never blinked and nothing escaped him: even today the Yoruba of Nigeria are agreed that Olodumare the Creator sees the inside and outside of men.[1] The fables naturally differed, said Andrew Lang, 'but their ethical, benevolent, admonishing and creative aspects were the same'. In short, the tribes attributed to these omnipotent sky gods rules for human behaviour to which they themselves aspired; rules which in time to come the supporters of Judaism, Islam and Christianity were to confer on their supreme gods too.

Alongside belief in a unitary sky god many of the tribes also believed in lesser gods and spirits inhabiting trees and rocks, in the magic practised by witch doctors or healers, above all in ancestor worship. When missionaries arrived from Europe they regarded such practices as idolatrous nonsense and set about preaching the gospel of Jesus Christ. This alien seed, planted among people of a quite different temperament and culture, did not always take. It not only confused them but, according to one authority, 'effectively destroyed the social fabric of traditional morality based on their tribal beliefs, causing much subsequent turbulence'.

Elsewhere in the world, from the days when man ceased to be exclusively a hunter/gatherer and became an agriculturist, lesser gods multiplied. Fertility at that time was symbolised by woman in whose body seed grew, and earth mothers and corn goddesses were conjured up to bring about a successful harvest. In one guise or another this goddess was to be found in areas from the Indian Ocean to the Baltic. In Babylon she was known as Ninlil, in Greece as Gaia, in Scandinavia as Freya. Effigies of her showed her heavy with child, with wide hips and huge breasts. Later she was given a sacred cow as an attendant.

Yet if the growth of seed in a woman was analogous to the seed planted in the ground, it was the great life force of the universe, the sun, that succoured both; brought the earthly seed to fruition which in turn gave sustenance to man and woman, allowed man to impregnate and woman to conceive. H.L. Mencken called the sun 'spectacular, lordly, dramatic, brilliant, its caress shared by all, even the beasts'. Accordingly all over the agricultural world sun gods were created in huge numbers. In Egypt he was known first as Horus and later Ra, and the Pharaohs claimed to be his children. A hymn to one of the Pharaohs ran: 'Thou hast the form of thy father Ra. When he rises in the heavens, thy rays penetrate all the lands of earth.'

At this time the belief that when the sun sank out of sight at night and the air was dank and evil spirits were abroad, it might not rise in the morning, was common to many cultures. The Pueblo Indians of New Mexico believed that it was only their closely observed religious rites that ensured the supposed daily transit of the sun across the sky. As his children, declared the Pharaohs, they would guarantee that he would rise in the morning. Elsewhere in the Middle East the Jewish sun god was known as Shamash, while the devout Parsees made their way, and still do, to the seashore to pray to its rising and setting. Mediterranean man created another sun god named Mithra, so powerful that at one time he challenged both the old Roman gods and the newly born Christianity. His birthday was 25 December, the same as that given to Jesus, and the Mithraic celebration of the vernal equinox was later paralleled by the Christian celebration of Easter. The day of the sun, Sun-day, was chosen as the first day of the Christian week, while European peasants would light fires on midsummer's eve to boost the powers of the waning sun.

In Japan the people adopted the belief that the Mikado was descended from their sun goddess by making an emblem of the rising sun their national flag. In the New World the Mayan sun god was called Kinichahau, the Inca sun god Inti, the Aztec one Tonatiah, the last so powerful he was sometimes referred to as Teotl or God; and to him were offered appalling human sacrifices, men, women and children murdered (and some eaten) in their thousands.

There was also a widespread belief that sun gods could become the fathers of mortal children or of children by mortal mothers. In

Fiji chiefs used to shut up their virgin daughters so that the sun could not see them. The Incas put their daughters in convents; if one conceived she was put to death unless the priests believed her claim that the sun was her father which allowed her to be accepted into the reigning family.

When and how priests first started is lost to history. Mencken posits a situation whereby early dwellers in a river valley saw to their alarm the floodwaters beginning to rise and threaten the caves in the valley hillsides where they lived. He envisaged various members of the community urging the waters to recede without effect, and eventually one more fortunate than the rest seeing his entreaties or commands seemingly obeyed. Henceforth he was accepted by his fellows as having magical powers and when future catastrophes loomed he was called on to intervene. There must have been times when he failed in this, but was invariably forgiven, for it was believed that where he had succeeded once, he had the power to succeed again. In time he was joined by others who had impressed their fellows for similar reasons. And so began the priestly caste: they wore different garments as they do today, devised incantations and prayers and were generally acknowledged by the tribe to have access to the invisible, ineffable forces that shaped and governed men's lives. From this it was but a logical extension of their duties to become keepers of the community's morals and to declare that by living a socially acceptable life here on earth they might escape the wrath of the gods in the life to come, for death held terrors for all. Thus they became humanity's first law-makers; and to enforce obedience to themselves and their teachings they insisted on gifts of money and burnt offerings to sweeten the mood of the gods.

Everywhere priests multiplied. In ancient Babylon, it was said, 'their numbers swelled almost beyond belief and were a crushing burden on the community'. In sophisticated Rome there were so many that Cato wondered how one could pass another in the street without laughing. In Egypt they had to do service at the temples in rotation. And they had vast revenues: at the shrine of Amon the chief priest took 20 per cent of the temple's income and divided the remaining 80 per cent equally among his eighty assistants. Whenever a bull was sacrificed the priests ate it; when beer or wine was offered to the gods they drank it. For casting out demons, determining lucky days, praying for the dead, etc., they charged special fees, and their wives were paid salaries too. So many young men wanted to enter the priesthood for its perks that ordinations had to be restricted to the sons of priestly families. Well-to-do Egyptians sent their children of four and five to be educated by the priests and instructed in their duties to the gods: copying religious texts had a high place in the curriculum. Later the Jesuits were to claim that as long as they could educate the children of Roman Catholics up to the age of seven they would be God's for life.

It was the corruption of the Roman Catholic clergy in medieval times that paved the way for the Reformation. When Henry VII came to the throne in England there were between 30,000 and 40,000 priests in a population of 3 million, or about one priest to every hundred people. Many were almost illiterate and spent much of their time drinking and fornicating, as did some of the nuns. And there was a good trade to be done in the matter of selling to the gullible what were called indulgences, absolution for the remission of sins; so that when the Reformation came, its impetus was as much economic as theological. During these times it was the unchristian practice of most priests to preserve the status quo by backing the king and nobles. Only later did the Christian Church come to heed Jesus's call to care for the poor and dispossessed.

Again from the earliest times priests have introduced ritual of all kinds to emphasise the solemnity of their practices. It is far less common today but in my youth I remember many occasions when the officiating priest developed a 'holy' voice, shifting gear from natural to artificial speech which was thought to be more agreeable to God. If the Reformation was to bring the word nearer to the common people, it failed in that the new translation of the Bible was constructed in archaic language, dominated by thees and thous, phrases such as 'And it came to pass', 'Verily, verily, I say unto you' and 'Woe unto the Philistines', all very sonorous and impressive, but now quite dead. Some sects called in aid bells and chantings, cries and refrains, holy oil and candles, rosaries and perfumes. Incense has been much used in many religions: the Andaman Islanders employed it to ward off demons, the Moslems to scare *djinns* during Ramadan, while in China it was ordered up to fumigate the dead.

Posturing and genuflections have also been adapted as a means of grace and hope of glory. On entering a church the Roman Catholic drops to one knee and makes the sign of the cross. The Evangelical Protestant prepares for prayer by rising, throwing back his head, folding his hands and closing his eyes. At the Wailing Wall in Jerusalem the Orthodox Jew nods his head towards the wall like a puppet. Preparatory to each of his five prayers a day the Moslem washes face, hands, arms and feet, then on his prayer mat and facing Mecca he puts his hands on the ground in front of his knees and bends forward until his head is also on the ground and posterior in the air. Whether the practitioners of these several examples of self-abasement do it to please their gods or to show solidarity with their fellow believers or just to make themselves feel good is hard to say.

The cross as a religious icon is not exclusive to Christianity, though Christians have more direct reasons for paying homage to it than most. (Once in Amman, having been asked to buy a crucifix for a friend, I was offered by a young Arab shop assistant two kinds: 'These ones are plain, but these have an interesting feature, a little man on the front.') In Assyria the cross was a symbol of the sun god, in Scandinavia it was the hammer of Thor, among the Egyptians and Aztecs it represented life, while to the Chinese it symbolised the four corners of the earth. In prewar Germany the crooked cross or swastika was, appropriately, the logo of the Nazi Party. Today in many countries macho young men wear crucifixes slung from their necks in the belief that it increases their sex appeal; and they may well be right.

Nor was the ceremony of the Eucharist exclusively Christian. It stems from the ancient rite of sacrificial cannibalism and the eating of totem animals; for example Red Indian tribes who held the buffalo to be sacred used to kill and eat one once a year in order to absorb its strength. Among the Aztecs a huge image of the corn god Huitzilopochtli was set up, made of dough and the blood of infants which by a process of trans-substantiation became the god himself and was eaten. Later Huitzilopochtli became a god of war and his followers came to believe that by eating his body and blood they were gaining courage in battle. At the annual feast to celebrate another Aztec god, Tezcatlipoca, a victim was chosen to be his surrogate and ritually killed. His arms and legs were eaten by the principal chiefs of the nation, and the rest distributed among the people. In a similar way the early Christians celebrated the Last Supper not to obtain remission for the forgiveness of sins, but to gain eternal life. The body and blood of Christ were said to be eternal, so they would be made eternal by consuming them symbolically.

The gods invented by the ancient Greeks are in a class of their own, different from the gods of most other religions in two ways. While most religions predicate their gods as being of an altogether higher order to ourselves, remote from earth and its sinful inhabitants and conveying a moral message, Zeus and his fellow gods entrenched on Mount Olympus, far from being a great moral force, were themselves practitioners of the sins – deceit, fraud, adultery, incest, murder – common to mankind. And if all religions to some degree anthropomorphise the gods they create – it would be almost impossible for them not to – the ancient Greeks did it more than most; even fashioning statues of them in human form, many of outstanding beauty and dignity, as imagined by Praxiteles and others.

As in many societies of the time, every town and community in Greece had adopted its own local gods from as far back as could be remembered and these were celebrated at regular festivals by sacrifices of cattle, sheep and goats. Just when the activities of the Olympian gods first came into circulation is uncertain, but it is known that from around 1100 BC the stories of their adventures were being handed down orally from generation to generation. First to leave a recorded account of them was the poet Homer around 750 BC with his two great epics, the *Iliad* about the siege of Ilium or Troy during the tenth year of the Trojan War and, in the same year, the *Odyssey*, an account of the departure of Odysseus from Troy and his subsequent travels in many lands. After Homer and the *Homeric Hymns* came Hesiod and his two epics, *Theogony* (the birth and genealogy of gods) and *Works and Days*. Hesiod's account of the union of Father Sky (Uranus) and Mother Earth (Gaia) is paralleled by the beliefs of many early societies such as the Maoris of New Zealand, the Kumana of South Africa, the Navajos of North America and the Ewe of Togoland, and opposed only by the Judaeo-Christian-Islamic view that one supreme god created them both. The last progeny of this union was Cronus who castrated his father Uranus and in turn was overcome by his own son Zeus. Later Aeschylus, Euripides and Sophocles would continue the story of the gods begun by Homer and Hesiod.

Zeus, most historians are agreed, was the nearest thing to monotheism in Greek mythology. 'Zeus is the air, the earth and the sky,' wrote Aeschylus. 'Zeus is everything and all that is more than these.' The Orphic hymns describe him as being the breath of all things, the sun and the moon, the roots of the sea. Half of his fellow gods, Zeus fathered: Athene, patron goddess of Athens who sprang fully armed from her father's head, and was so angered by Arachne's tales of the lusty doings of the gods that she turned her into a spider; the nine Muses; Apollo the sun god representing harmony and order and his twin sister, the many breasted but virginal Artemis, huntress and dancer and goddess of childbirth; Dionysos[2], Apollo's opposite, the great liberator, god of wine and song, the only god to be born of a mortal mother and, after his marriage to Ariadne, the only one to remain faithful to his wife; the earth goddess Demeter whose daughter Persephone was kidnapped by Hades, Zeus's brother and the eponymous guardian of the underworld, and condemned to spend a third of her life there; and Hermes, the winged messenger, a lover of the faithless Aphrodite and whose *herm* or effigy of himself as patron of roads and travel, accompanied by a giant phallus, was to be seen in courtyards and at staging posts all over ancient Greece.

Nor did Zeus stop there. Metamorphosis was a running theme in the canon of Greek myths and Zeus changed himself into a bull and then an eagle to ravish Europa, into a shower of gold to penetrate Danae and beget Perseus, into a swan to couple with Leda whose golden egg produced Helen, into Amphitryon to seduce his wife Alcmena and father Hercules.

As well as Hades, Zeus had another brother, Poseidon, god of the sea and of storms and earthquakes, whose son Proteus, an exemplar of metamorphosis, gave us the word to indicate change of appearance or character. Then there was Hera, Zeus's sister and another of his wives, at first quarrelsome and obsessive, who struck the hermaphrodite Tiresias blind for saying that women enjoyed sex nine times more than men. Two of the three sons Hera conceived on her own were Ares, the god of war, and the club-footed Hephaistos, god of the workplace. Hephaistos married Aphrodite, goddess of beauty and unashamed sexuality (hence aphrodisiac), but when he caught her in bed with his brother Ares he spread a net over the pair and called on the other gods to come down from Olympus to witness their discomfort. To complete the Pantheon another sister of Zeus, Hestia, goddess of the hearth and centre, was much revered in Roman times as Vesta in whose temple the sacred flame was tended by the Vestal virgins. And then there were the legends, in some of which the gods played a part, in others not: those of Daedalus and Icarus, Theseus and Ariadne, Perseus and Andromeda, Philemon and Baucis, Cupid and Psyche, Hero and Leander.

For a thousand years, says Michael Grant, the Greek myths were the greatest unifying and civilising factor in Greek and Graeco-Roman history. To the ancients of those times Zeus and his fellow gods were as real as Yahweh, Moses and Abraham were to the early Jews, as Jesus, John the Baptist and Judas Iscariot were and are to the Christians. Alexander the Great loved the *Iliad* so much that on his eastern conquests he took a copy with him in a jewelled casket; and when he had travelled as far as he intended to go, he left a shrine dedicated to all the Olympian gods.

In Homer's marvellous poems the concept of the hero, as portrayed by Achilles and Odysseus, is introduced into western literature for the first time, an icon for others to admire and attempt to follow, yet not, as Anthony Storr says, a hero in the English mould, 'controlled, courteous, reluctant to show emotion, honest and straightforward' but more representative of Mediterranean culture, 'a man of many wiles, a trickster who would not shun deceit, who would use guile to defeat his enemies and would not disdain a show of emotion if the occasion warranted it'. This hero must go on a journey, fight battles with monsters and others, endure hardship with stoicism and patience, seek that which has been lost and find it, be united with his loved one at journey's end. To Greek and Roman peasants these tales of derring-do were wonderful entertainment; mighty deeds and supernatural interventions which, as Michael Grant says, 'gave an escape from the dull routine of his life, eased the drabness of a winter's night and the tedium of the road'. Centuries later Freud and Jung reinterpreted the myths in a new way, envisaging the gods not as external beings but as warring elements in the human psyche, inhabiting a world where the horrors of Hades mirrored the horrors of nightmares, and the dragons that challenged him on his travels were mother or father figures which he had to overcome if ever he were to grow up and become free; in which the tensions between flesh and spirit, reason and emotions, Apollo and Dionysos jostled for dominance, and the ultimate goal was the reconciliation of opposites leading to psychological integration. The Greek myths, said Jung, sprang from the collective unconscious and were similar to those told by the brothers Grimm and Hans Andersen and others, occurring everywhere, not rooted in time or place. In 1904 the Polyphemus myth in the *Odyssey* was found to have 125 global variants, some as distant as Lapland.

You do not hear the Greek gods much spoken of today because, as the German theologian Rudolf Bultmann said, we are living in a non-mythical or post-mythical age. But when the Greek and Roman classics were part of a European education, the impression their stories made on an artistic imagination was so vivid that there was hardly a painter or writer in the last 2,000 years who did not celebrate them on canvas or in prose or verse; among them Titian, Tintoretto, Veronese, Michelangelo, Botticelli, Leonardo,

Piranese, Brueghel, Dürer, Tiepolo, Goya, Turner, Blake, Renoir, Rossetti, Matisse, Braque, Kokoschka, Dali, Picasso; and among the writers Marlowe, Chaucer, Shakespeare, Dante, Calderon, Goethe, Tennyson, Wordsworth, Shelley, Keats, Byron, Wilde, Arnold, Poe, Whitman, Joyce, Cocteau, Sartre, Eliot, Pound. The planets have been graced with their Roman names (Mars, Saturn, Venus, Mercury, Jupiter, Uranus, Neptune, Pluto) while Britain's navy used to name its ships after them, such as *Argonaut, Neptune, Bellerophon, Leander, Ariadne*; two of them, *Ajax* and *Achilles*, were cruisers whose action with the German pocket battleship *Graf Spee* in 1939 led to her subsequent scuttling at the mouth of the River Plate. Even today the names of some endure; although few who speak so knowingly about the Apollo spacecraft or the Poseidon missile could tell you of the source from which they stem.

As the millennium before Christ moved towards his birth, the idea that instead of Hades awaiting you after death there could be Elysian fields began to take hold. 'There is a land,' said Proteus to Menelaus, 'where no snow falls, no strong winds blow and there is never any rain, but day after day the west winds' tuneful breeze comes in from the ocean to refresh its folk.' Then in the sixth century BC the myth of Demeter seeking her daughter Persephone in the underworld was acted out each autumn and sometimes spring in the ceremony of the Eleusinian Mysteries. 'Happy is he among men upon earth who has seen these Mysteries,' says one of the Homeric hymns, because of its promise to the initiated of a blissful afterlife. This concept, quite foreign to those conditioned only to the idea of Hades, had come about with the notion, already subscribed to in ancient Egypt, that if a successful harvest was the result of seeds and roots lying dormant in the earth all winter, was it not reasonable to suppose that the dead who were also lying buried in the earth might enjoy a resurrection too. Yet according to Aristophanes and Pindar the 'initiated' meant only those who had led a sober and righteous life; the uninitiated must still endure the torments of Hades: the idea would be given further impetus by the cult attributed to the legendary poet and singer Orpheus, which preached that the soul of man was a fallen god or demon imprisoned in an alien body and due for reincarnation; and that salvation could only be achieved through righteousness.

Little by little the idea of morality as an ideal which should be propagated was pushing its way into the highways and byways of pagan Greece. Xenophon of Colophon was one of the first to condemn some of the acts perpetrated by the gods which, if done by humans, would be considered disgraceful:

Homer and Hesiod fathered on the gods' divinity
All deeds most blameful and shameful that here on earth there be –
Yea, thieving and deceiving and adultery.

He went on to dispute the idea that the gods must be like ourselves:

If oxen or lions or horses had hands like men, they too,
If they could fashion pictures or statues they could hew,
They would shape in their own image each face and form divine –
Horses' gods like horses, like kine the gods of kine.
'Snub-nosed are the Immortals and black', the Ethiops say:
But, 'No' the Thracians answer, 'red-haired with eyes of grey'.

And so the way was open for Critias to write in his tragedy *Sisyphus* in the fifth century BCE the reasons that caused man to create gods. As a summary, succinct and to the point, it has seldom been bettered:

> There was a time when the life of man was disordered, and like that of wild beasts controlled by brute strength. There was then no reward for the good nor any punishment for the bad. Next, men conceived the idea of imposing laws as instruments of punishment, so that justice may be sole ruler and hold violence in check. If any erred, he was punished.
>
> Then, since the laws only prevented the commission of deeds of *open* violence, men continued to commit secret crimes. At this point it is my belief that some far-seeing and resolute man saw

the need for a deterrent which would have effect even when *secret* deeds were done or contemplated. So he introduced the idea of divinity, of a god always active and vigorous, hearing and seeing with his mind . . . all that men say or do.

Chapter Four

JUDAEO-CHRISTIAN MYTHOLOGIES

1. The Old Testament

E ducation syllabuses change. Until at least the beginning of the twentieth century no boy was considered to be truly educated unless he had a smattering of Greek and Latin; but in the first half of the century these subjects gradually fell into desuetude. As an integral part of general education, the Old Testament of the Bible, which purports to chronicle the doings of the Jews or Israelites during the millennium before Christ, has lasted longer; but today, apart from academics and students, it is no longer read.

There are those who find this regrettable, just as there were those who thought the omission of Greek and Latin from the syllabus regrettable. I guess that my generation must have been among the last to have been taught routinely the rudiments of Latin and Greek and also the Old Testament. From Latin I learned a lot about the origins of many English (and French) words, always beneficial to a writer, while many of the stories in the Old Testament made a powerful impression on a youthful imagination. My favourites were Moses in his ark of bulrushes; the dramatic parting of the Red Sea to let the Israelites escape; Samson pulling down the pillars of the prison house; Solomon's facile judgement on the dispute between the two whores as to which was the living baby's mother; Jael, the wife of Heber the Keenite, driving a nail through the forehead of the sleeping Sisera; and Shadrach, Mesach and Abednego being cast by King Nebuchadnezzar into the burning, fiery furnace. Yet however stimulating to the imagination these tales might be, we were never taught what relevance, if any, they were supposed to have to our own lives (unless we happened to be Jewish); and I have scarcely thought about them since.

Both in times past and present literally hundreds, maybe thousands, of books have been written by divines (as they used to be called) and academics on the subject of Old Testament exegesis. The great majority are directed at fellow scholars and existing believers, not the general reader, and many of those I have read are poorly written and deeply boring. The readers of this book will be relieved to hear that I have neither the scholarship nor the interest to add to them.

The Old Testament itself, which I read recently in the Authorised Version, is little better. There are too many places where, as one plods along, one finds the eyes glazing over and the head nodding on the chest. But contained within it, like diamonds on a dowdy dress, are passages or phrases of such striking beauty and imagery that I jotted down in a notebook those that delighted me most:

> And they heard the voice of the Lord God walking in the garden in the cool of the day.

> Sun, stand thou still upon Gibeon; and thou, Moon, in the valley of Ajalon.

> Tell it not in Gath, publish it not in the streets of Askelon; lest the daughters of the Philistines rejoice, lest the daughters of the uncircumcised triumph.

> There ariseth a little cloud out of the sea, like a man's hand.

> Are not Abana and Pharpar, rivers of Damascus, better than all the waters of Israel?

★   ★   ★

When the morning stars sang together and all the sons of God shouted for joy.

I am black but comely, O ye daughters of Jerusalem, as the tents of Kedar, as the curtains of Solomon.

A bundle of myrrh is my well beloved unto me; he shall lie all night betwixt my breasts.

Take us the foxes, the little foxes, that steal the vines.

O my son, Absalom, my son, my son, would God I had died for thee, O Absalom, my son, my son!

Rise up, my love, my fair one, and come away. For lo, the winter is past, the rain is over and gone; the flowers appear on the earth; the time of the singing of birds is come, and the voice of the turtle is heard in our land.

I shall go softly all my years in the bitterness of my soul.

By the waters of Babylon we sat down and wept.

But there is another darker side to the Old Testament, especially the earlier books; tales of treachery and betrayal, incest and adultery, killings on a massive scale which crowd one another with sickening regularity. Referring to what he called 'the obscene stories, the cruel executions and unrelenting vindictiveness with which more than half the Old Testament is filled', Thomas Paine, writing at the end of the eighteenth century, said it was more consistent with the word of a demon than the word of God. 'A history of wickedness,' he concluded, 'that has served to corrupt and brutalise mankind.'

Some of the atrocities stick in the mind longer than others: Moses instructing the children of Israel in their war against the Midianites to 'kill every male among the little ones, and kill every woman who hath known a man by lying with him. But all the women that have not known a man by lying with him, keep alive for ourselves'; Joshua and the children of Israel killing 12,000 of the people of Ai, *all* the men, the rest women: 'Only the cattle and spoil of that city Israel took for themselves. And the king of Ai Joshua hanged on a tree until eventide'; Jephthah burning his only daughter alive to keep a vow relating to a victory (Judges 11:30–9); Elijah having witnessed the triumph of his god in a contest with Baal the god of storm and fertility, ordering 450 priests of Baal to be killed 'and let not one escape'; Saul, jealous of David, telling him he wants a hundred foreskins of the uncircumcised Philistines in place of a dowry for his daughter, hoping that David will perish in the attempt, but David goes one better and returns to camp with *200* foreskins; and David himself, allegedly a forebear of Christ, seducing and impregnating Bathsheba, wife of Uriah the Hittite, then placing Uriah in the front line of battle in the hope that he will be killed, which he is. The baby dies but David and Bathsheba have another who is Solomon. And in addition to all this, godly approval for dashing babies against the stones (Psalms 137:9), stoning to death disobedient children and brides found not to be virgins (Deut. 21:18–21 and Deut. 22:21), and for those who have transgressed, parents eating the flesh of their children (Lev. 26:29).

Yet my quarrel with some books of the Old Testament is less with their brutalities than their irrelevance. I and many of my generation were taught that these books were history – or to be fair we were not taught that they were not history. If by history is meant accurate accounts of past events supported by evidence, they are certainly not that. They are mythological folk tales, prose poems written at unknown times by unknown authors to glorify the alleged escape of the Jews from Egypt and their subsequent adventures en route to the promised land.

They contain accounts of miracles far more numerous and far-fetched than those allegedly performed by Jesus, and in some of the books are passages which Christians claim foretell the coming of Jesus, although, as we shall see, today's scholars say this is not so:

'they predict nothing'. Some passages are contradictory such as the two versions of the flood in Genesis. Nor is there any confirmation in Egyptian or Mesopotamian records that some of the most familiar of Old Testament characters like Moses, Joshua, David and Solomon ever existed; and since nothing in the Pentateuch (the first five books of the Old Testament) is based on primary sources, as history it is valueless.

Yet in this survey of the worldwide creation and abandonment of gods since the earliest times, there is one important aspect in which the Old Testament is relevant today, and it is this. The Jews were the first significant group of people in the world to abandon the plethora of minor gods with which most societies saddled themselves, and to leave written records of their substitution by a new, single, all-embracing god such as many in both east and west still subscribe to; a Being or Spirit who created the world and everything in it and kept a sharp eye on the comings and goings of his (as they believed) chosen people. In about 2000 BC there was an epic poem called the *Enuma Elish* current among the peoples of Babylon and Canaan (the promised land) which told of the victory of the gods over chaos and fostered a sense of the numinous or holy for which many hungered. According to the *Enuma Elish* the gods emerged in pairs from a formless, watery waste, gods of the sky and sea, of the rivers and lakes, of earth and heaven. Among them was their sun god Marduk and also Baal. The god that superseded these minor gods (although for a time they continued to be worshipped in tandem) was called Elohim or, more commonly, Yahweh whose name was spelt YHWH as there were no vowels in ancient Hebrew scripts. He came into existence to fulfil a need arising from the collective unconscious. No likenesses of him were permitted to be made in stone or wood, as later with Allah the god of Islam, which was just as well, as there was no agreed idea of what they looked like. By the end of the first millennium after Christ, Yahweh, Allah and the Christian God who was said to be the father of Jesus Christ were all well established, the three greatest fictional characters in history.

Fictional Yahweh may have been but to the Jews he was very

real, very powerful. The experience of Jeremiah was not untypi-
cal:

> Yahweh, you have seduced me, and I am seduced,
> You have raped me and I am overcome . . .
> I used to say, 'I will not think about him,
> I will not speak his name any more.'
> Then there seemed to be a fire burning in my heart,
> Imprisoned in my bones.
> The effort to restrain it wearied me,
> I could not bear it.

Even today, to those for whom the Old Testament was not
primarily written, it is hard not to be seduced by Yahweh, not
to believe in him as an external being, so forcefully are accounts
of him written, so real are the human attributes – anger, jealousy,
vengeance, disappointment, mercy – which the leaders of the children
of Israel bestowed on him. He dominates the Old Testament, giving
the children of Israel instructions in what to do in every situation
from the right way to dress a burnt offering to how to isolate cases
of leprosy, issuing them with a set of moral commandments as a rule
of thumb to live by and threatening dire punishments if they fail to
follow them ('And your children shall wander in the wilderness forty
years and bear your whoredoms until your carcasses be wasted in the
wilderness'), frequently blowing his own trumpet ('And the earth shall
be filled with the glory of the Lord'), exhorting the children of Israel
to kill their neighbours ('Now go and smite the Amalekites and utterly
destroy all they have and spare them not; both man and woman,
infant and suckling, ox and sheep, camel and ass'), and then later in
the Psalms to acquire the ingratiation necessary to sing his praises:

Not unto us, O Lord, not unto us, but unto thy name give glory
Even from everlasting to everlasting thou art God.
O Lord, our Lord, how excellent is thy name in all the earth.

The effect on a reader of a thousand pages devoted to Yahweh is overpowering. Matthew Arnold wrote of them affecting him 'with indescribable force' and others have spoken of their immense power. It is this force and power that make it difficult for us, and impossible for the children of Israel, to resist the conclusion that Yahweh was an independent entity, existing outwith the minds of men and women and whether the world was peopled or not.

And yet if it is the truth we are after, we have to remind ourselves constantly that all gods including Yahweh are human constructs, the end product of a need felt deeply in ancient days and markedly less so today. Some religious writers cannot accept this. Jack Miles, for instance, a distinguished American biblical scholar, former Jesuit and accomplished Middle Eastern linguist, has written a book called *God: A Biography*, in which he sees the Old Testament Yahweh as entirely unattached, independent, autonomous. 'The Bible,' he tells us, 'is not just words *about* God, but also the word *of* God.' Some idea of what he has in store for us lies in the – for once accurate – blurb. 'We see God torn by conflicting urges. To his own sorrow he is by turn destructive and creative, vain and modest, subtle and naïve, ruthless and tender, lawful and lawless, powerful yet powerless, omniscient yet blind.'

Miles begins by telling us, as countless others have done, that God made humans in his own image; this despite the opinions of anthropologists that throughout history humans have created gods in theirs. Nor does Miles tell us what he thinks God's image is. Here are some of the ways in which he sees God:

> a male being who has no parents, wife or children and no sexual relations of any kind . . . never been loved by his mother or father . . . has no friend but Moses,
>
> seems to have made human beings because he wanted company;
>
> began without a history but has now acquired a tremendous history and knows himself better as a result of it;
>
> if he has a private life or even, we might say, a divine social life among other gods, he isn't admitting us to it.

Miles is also obsessed with genitalia:

> [God] may even be said to have male genitalia, but they are without genital function . . . angels also have male genitalia;
>
> the fact that the Lord wants to be seen only from behind may suggest he is concealing his genitalia from Moses;
>
> the men of Lot's town have demanded access to God's genitals just as, in the circumcision episode, God demanded access to Abraham's genitals.

There is one curious omission in Miles's eccentric thinking. He fails to criticise God for never attempting to explain or justify the atrocities he orders the Israelites and others to perform. A more serious and fundamental criticism of his approach, however, is his failure to see that God, like all other gods in the pantheon, is not autonomous but the brainchild of those who invented him. He admits to visualising God as a literary character like Hamlet, but shies away from its corollary that Hamlet's life and development is the work of his progenitor Shakespeare. He is likewise blind to the undisputed fact that the idea of the God of the Old Testament was the work of different writers who visualised him at different periods in different ways. It is astonishing to me that so eminent a scholar as Miles should fail to see this and to have produced a work so arid, uninformative and, in the end, pointless.

If Jack Miles's book is the most extreme example I have seen so far of an author regarding God as an autonomous being rather than a human construct, he is by no means the only one. My library is awash with books bearing such titles as *The Mind of God*, *The Biology of God*, *The Enigma of God*, *The Quest for God* (which quest A.N. Wilson has called the biggest wild-goose chase in history, though he was once on the goose chase himself).

And we are all aware of lesser clerical fry, cosy vicars in country churches giving us their own views of God's life and times, speaking of him as though he and they were on the most intimate terms, the oldest of old friends, not a frightening deity at all but one to whom you could turn in time of trouble. Thus to the waverers as well as to the committed is given comfort and joy.

But do we still need that sort of medicament today?

2. The False Prophecies

After Jewish mythology, Christian mythology; after the Old Testament, the New; and any writer wanting to take a fresh look at the four gospels that cover the life of Jesus Christ is at once beset by problems. As with the Old Testament, the first is that thousands of other writers have already walked this way and inevitably doubts will be raised whether a newcomer has anything fresh to say. Secondly the name of Jesus Christ has for millions of people past and present become so revered, so holy, that there must be a danger not only of causing offence but of one's views being dismissed out of hand. However, it was Jesus himself who said (or is said to have said) that the truth can make us free; and even if my assessment of the truth does not coincide with his, so be it. After all, the imperious, vengeful figure of Yahweh, the god of Moses and Isaac and Abraham whom Jesus inherited, becomes in his teaching and preaching a different sort of father figure.

Our knowledge of the instigator of the Christian religion is, I find, strictly limited, being contained principally in the four gospels of the New Testament, in the Acts of the Apostles and the letters of Paul and others, marginally in the non-canonical gospels of Thomas and Philip and almost nowhere else. He is mentioned in passing by the Roman historians Tacitus and Seutonius, also by the Jewish historian Josephus, but it is now accepted that the bulk of his comments are a later Christian interpolation. All four gospels are believed by most scholars to have been published first in Greek in the order Mark, written in Rome about AD (or CE for Common Era) 70, or some forty years after Christ's death, while the others are thought to have been completed between then and CE 100. Thus Mark's gospel was available to Matthew[1] and Luke who also made use of a source not known to Mark and called Q (for *Quelle*, the German word for source, which has long disappeared). No one knows who the author of each of the gospels was, though it is generally agreed that whoever wrote Luke (allegedly a medical man) also wrote Acts. The gospel of John begins later in the life of Jesus than the three Synoptics; its style is literary and dramatic, it shows first-hand knowledge of small historical details and contains many passages of striking beauty. Jesus himself left no record of his ministry, so that all the words he is reported as uttering have been put into his mouth by the gospel writers – with what degree of accuracy we simply do not know; a practice that has always been condemned when employed in dialogue passages in non-fiction books of today.

According to the times in which we live, there are two ways of interpreting the gospel stories: how they struck the Christians of the first century and for centuries after; and the very different impression they make on many of us living in a more advanced culture today. One can well understand the impact that the gospels made on the primitive communities of the time and, once they had been accepted, on more sophisticated ones later, for they describe the course of a human tragedy whose resonances are with us still. Yet however powerfully these stories may affect us, it is important to remember that they are not history, not based on undisputed facts, but for the most part stories masquerading as fact, what in television terms today is labelled docu-drama. Gospel truth is imaginative truth: an amalgam of art, artifice and sheer invention, and clothed overall, at least in the Authorised Version, in some of the most memorable English prose ever written.

What was it then about the gospel stories, both individually and collectively, that so captivated the minds of the early Christians? Foremost, I think, the allegedly supernatural events of Jesus's birth, life, death and resurrection. First, at least chronologically, is the claim in Matthew and Luke of Christ having been conceived without the impregnation of his mother by human sperm. There follows a succession of miracles performed by Jesus in the course of his brief ministry, some of healing the sick, others of exorcising evil spirits, two of raising the dead. To the people of those times and earlier, when tested and proven evidence was not the yardstick of belief that it is today, the idea of miracles was credible. The Old Testament is chock-full of miracles: Yahweh parting the waters of the Red Sea to allow the children of Israel to escape from Egypt, Moses striking a rock with his rod to produce water to ease their parched throats, Lot's wife being turned into a pillar of salt, Jonah living for three days and nights in the belly of a fish. After the hideous death of Christ on the cross (a sacrifice and redemption, it was later claimed, for the sins of mankind), came the most astonishing miracle of all: the resurrection of Jesus and his reappearance to a variety of people at different times and places, in one account (1 Corinthians 15:6) showing himself to 500 of his followers at once and in another (Acts 1:3) continuing to show himself *for forty days* after his death. Finally the Ascension (Acts 1:9–10) when Jesus was seen to float upwards towards heaven. And binding all this together the doctrine that Jesus preached and the authority with which he preached it: to love one's neighbour, and forgive one's enemies, and to look forward, after leaving this vale of tears (and assuming one had believed), to everlasting life in the company of God and his angels. These were messages which had not been proclaimed before, at least not with such persistence and passion.

Taken together, the prophecies referred to in the Old Testament scriptures and those made by John the Baptist and Jesus in the gospels are beguilingly persuasive, indicating as they do a planned tragedy like that of *Romeo and Juliet* or *Tess of the d'Urbervilles* or *The Secret Battle*, its end in its beginnings, its beginnings in its end. Add to that the magnetic and authoritarian personality of Jesus himself. Healer, prophet, moralist extraordinary, there is little wonder that he attracted the following he did, both then and thereafter, and led people to believe, first that he was the long-promised Messiah, later that he was the only begotten son of the Father.

But let us now consider the whole story with a rather more critical eye. Firstly the birth of Jesus. Over the centuries and after Christendom had accepted that Jesus was God, scores of gifted Renaissance artists almost fell over themselves in depicting both the Nativity (such as the breathtaking della Robbia at San Sepulcro) and the Virgin and Child, among them several by Leonardo and others (Michelangelo, Titian, Correggio, Cimabue, Giotto, Raphael, Botticelli, Fra Filippo Lippi, van Eyck, Fra Angelico, Bellini, Mantegna). They had one object: to show that *at the time* the birth of Christ was an event of great significance. In my view it was nothing of the kind, though collectively the splendours and detail of the paintings have led countless viewers to think so. No one in the district had any reason to suppose that Jesus's arrival heralded anything unusual. It was just one birth among many, and Jesus was not to become known, even locally, for another thirty years.

It also seems unlikely, despite long-held traditional belief, that the birth took place in Bethlehem. The only evidence (if it can be called evidence) for this are Matthew and Luke writing more than fifty years after the event on hearsay (Mark and John wisely avoid any mention of it); and Luke's choice of Bethlehem rests on his belief that Joseph and Mary went there to pay tax *because Joseph's ancestor David had lived there a thousand years earlier*, which is plainly absurd. Far more likely, if they had to pay tax, they would have done so in their home town of Nazareth where most probably Jesus was born; and the only reason that Matthew and Luke indulged in their fanciful imaginings about three unexpected strangers from the east with presents of gold, frankincense and myrrh following a rogue star which travelled at the speed of a camel, frightened shepherds in the freezing fields being comforted by an angel, a full house at the inn, the manger (actually a crib) and the farm animals was that *knowing the conclusion of the story in Jesus's death and resurrection* they felt as obliged as Leonardo, della Robbia and the rest to make its beginning as significant and momentous as its end.

What then was the true reason for Matthew and Luke choosing Bethlehem as the place where Jesus was born? The short answer – and Matthew at 2:4–5 freely admits it[2] – is that while scouring through the scriptures of the Old Testament for any indication of the coming of the Messiah who would free Israel from Roman rule, the gospel writers found what they were looking for in Micah 5:2 written 700 years before: 'But thou, Bethlehem, though thou be little among the thousands of Judah, yet out of thee shall he come forth unto me that is to be ruler in Israel.' This, they decided, must be Jesus; as Karen Armstrong puts it, Bethelehem was a better address. Similarly, having discovered in Isaiah 60:6 a reference to people coming from the eastern spice centre of Sheba bearing gold and frankincense, they transferred these gifts, along with myrrh, to three imaginary wise men (or kings) seeking the birthplace of Jesus. In any case and however wise the Wise Men, they could hardly have foreseen the imminent arrival of a baby quite unknown to them and of whose future they would also have been ignorant.

For much the same reason we can, I think, discount the improbable story of Herod massacring all the babies under two in Bethlehem, and the holy family, getting wind of it, fleeing to Egypt. Aside from the birthplace of Jesus being other than Bethlehem, aside from the fact that if Herod had committed so monstrous an act we should have heard of it from Mark or John or Josephus, he would have had no knowledge of Jesus's arrival and therefore no reason to fear it. But once again the gospel writers saw an opportunity of linking an Old Testament passage with Jesus's birth and the mythical massacre in Bethlehem; Matthew 2:18 ('In Rama there was a voice heard, lamentation and weeping and great mourning, Rachel weeping for her children and would not be comforted because they are not') conforming to Jeremiah 31:15 which says almost exactly the same thing. And the flight of the holy family to Egypt and subsequent return was, I think, another invention to fulfil Hosea 11:2: 'Out of Egypt have I called my Son.'

There are two other Old Testament 'prophecies' linking the scriptures with the conception and birth of Jesus. In the first both Matthew and Luke were let down by their translators. Isaiah 7:14 says, 'Behold, a virgin shall conceive and bear a son and shall call his name Immanuel,' which Luke accepts at 1:27 and Matthew *in toto* at 1:23 as referring to Jesus. Yet as already stated, there is no mention of a virgin in the original Hebrew. The word *almah* meaning a girl or young woman is used. In the translation of the passage into Greek, however, in which the gospels were first published, the word *parthenos* was used which does have implications of virginity. From this mistranslation the whole bizarre cult of the virgin unspotted arose and is with us to this day; as is its equally bizarre corollary, that Jesus, born out of wedlock, was fathered by the Holy Ghost.

The first popular writer to throw doubts on the virgin birth, now disbelieved by many churchmen, was the deist Thomas Paine, writing in Paris at the end of the eighteenth century:

> When also I am told that a woman called the Virgin Mary said or gave out, that she was with child without any co-habitation with a man, and that her betrothed husband Joseph said that an angel told him so, I have a right to believe them or not; such a circumstance requires a much stronger evidence than their bare word for it; but we have not even this – for neither Joseph nor Mary wrote any such matter themselves; it is only reported by others they said so – it is hearsay upon hearsay, and I do not choose to rest my belief upon such evidence.

Matthew and Luke however wanted to have their cake and eat it; for having declared that it was not Joseph but the Holy Ghost who had begat Jesus, they then give us a contradictory list of Joseph's ancestors (in Matthew twenty-five, in Luke forty-one) to prove that through Joseph Jesus was descended from David.

The second reference is Isaiah 9:6: 'For unto us a child is born, unto us a son is given . . . and his name shall be called Wonderful, Counsellor,' which is claimed by Luke, quite wrongly, to find fulfilment in his gospel at 2:11 ('For unto you is born this day in the city of David a Saviour which is Christ the Lord').

The gift of prophecy, or foretelling the future, is one that has always fascinated human beings and which many, perhaps most of us, have a predisposition to believe (hence the age-old and irrational obsession with astrology). The gospel stories are shot through with so-called prophecies linking the Old Testament to the New, it being the objects of their authors to show that the coming of Jesus had been planned by God from the very beginning, part of his grand scheme for the redemption of sinful mankind. But people the world over are gullible; and there is no doubt at all, as we shall see later, that it was the erroneous belief in this theory of the Old Testament foretelling the New that led so many early Christians to believe. We should heed the words of Robin Lane-Fox and other scholars that the passages in the Old Testament scriptures refer only to the people and events of that era: they and the gospels are separated by aeons of time and the attempts to link them are entirely artificial.

To continue with them then, for we cannot ignore them, Isaiah 40:3: 'The voice of him that crieth in the wilderness, make straight in the desert the highway for our God,' is said to find fulfilment in John the Baptist at Mark 1:3: 'The voice of one crying in the wilderness, prepare ye the way of the Lord, make his paths straight.' Again, Malachi 3:1 says: 'Behold, I will send my messenger and he shall prepare the way before me,' which Matthew at 11:10 has Jesus quoting to the crowd as proof of John the Baptist foretelling his coming ('For this is he of whom it is written, Behold, I send my messenger before thy face, which shall prepare thy way before thee'). The temptation in the wilderness is also claimed to have had its antecedents. When the gospel writers reported Jesus as saying to Satan, 'Thou shalt not live by bread alone', 'Thou shalt not tempt the Lord thy God' and 'Thou shalt worship the Lord thy God', they were paraphrasing what had been said in the sixth and eighth chapters of Deuteronomy.

John the Baptist and Jesus are alleged also to have made prophecies, and although they were accepted as genuine and impressive by early believers, they can now be seen as flawed. Prophecies of future events, when couched in sufficiently vague and general terms, can be credible but not those which are specific. For instance, Mark has John the Baptist say at 1:7: 'There cometh one mightier than I after me, the latchets of whose shoes I am not worthy to stoop down and unloose,' as part of the long build-up for Jesus. But at the time Jesus had not yet begun his ministry and John, so far as we know, had no reason to suppose he was about to. But by putting these words into John's mouth, Mark was giving another example of what he saw as God's grand design.

The same sort of criticism can be made of Jesus's prophecies. When on his way to Jerusalem he tells two disciples to go to the village where they will find a donkey and a colt and to bring them to him, the question arises as to how he knew they would be there? Christians would say, as they do of John the Baptist's prophecy, that both men were divinely inspired, which can explain anything. My own guess is that the gospel writers were so obsessed with the need to fulfil Zechariah 9:9: 'Behold thy King cometh unto thee . . . lowly and riding upon a donkey and upon a colt, the foal of a donkey,' that they put the instructions about fetching the donkey and the colt into Jesus's mouth. Christians have always maintained that Jesus chose to ride into Jerusalem on a donkey to show his humility. But it is not the most dignified way to travel, the rider being so much larger than the donkey, with his feet brushing the ground. Traditionally pilgrims entered Jerusalem on foot, as a mark of respect, so whether in fact a donkey and colt were found and fetched and whether or not Jesus entered Jerusalem riding on them must remain debatable. Either the prophecy created the event, suggests E.P. Sanders in *The Historical Figure of Jesus*, or (as so often) the prophecy created the story and the event never happened.

Again, take Jesus's saying to the disciples at Luke 18:32–3 that 'he shall be delivered to the Gentiles and be mocked and spitefully entreated and spitted on and be scourged and put to death'. As I said earlier this sort of prophesying in early times must have been seductively persuasive: 'What a remarkable man, he foretold exactly what was going to happen to him!' But how did he know the details, the mocking, the spitting, the scourging, his death? The answer is he couldn't and didn't; and the conclusion must be that once again the gospel writers *who knew the end of the story* put, with hindsight, the words into Jesus's mouth. A further example of this sort of deception, designed to prove Jesus's powers of prophecy, was their allowing him to make (in Matthew 24:1–3, Mark 13:1–4 and Luke 21:5–7) his predictions about the destruction of the Temple, seen as an apocalyptic event. But, most scholars agree, at the time the gospels were written, the Temple had already been destroyed, so they were making him prophesy an event that had already occurred. The more one studies the gospels, the more clear it is that their authors were great tellers of tales.

Or, take Mark 9:9 where, after Jesus's disciples had witnessed the Transfiguration (one of the first ever ghost stories?) he instructs them to tell no man what they have seen *until the Son of man* (i.e. himself) *is risen from the dead*. The disciples, baffled, didn't know what he meant, 'questioning one with another what the rising of the dead might mean'. As well they might, for they had never seen anyone rise from the dead, and they were pretty sure no one else had either. Later in the same chapter when he repeats what he had said about his rising on the third day, Mark says: 'They understood not that saying and were afraid to ask him.'

In the accounts of the crucifixion, we find there is an artificial Old Testament parallel for almost every event described. Mark 15:28 says of Jesus: 'And the scripture was fulfilled which saith, And he was numbered among the transgressors.' Here Mark, foraging around in the scriptures, lit on Isaiah 53:12 ('And he was numbered among the transgressors') to persuade his fellow Jews to believe that Isaiah foretold Calvary, which is nonsense. Then there is the passage in Matthew 27:34, when Jesus is thirsty, 'they gave him vinegar to drink' which replicates Psalm 69:21: 'In my thirst they gave me vinegar to drink.' And what is undoubtedly one of the most heart-rending things Jesus is said to have said, 'My God, my God, why hast thou forsaken me?' is a straight crib from Psalm 22:1: 'My God, my God, why hast thou forsaken me?', so one does have cause to wonder if he ever said it. Finally there is the passage in John 19:32–3 where the soldiers break the legs of the two criminals on the cross to hasten death, but do not break Jesus's legs because he is already dead, and this was said to be a fulfilment of Psalm 34:20: 'He keepeth all his bones. Not one of them is broken.'

Some scholars have said that these sayings and actions attributed to Jesus show his intimate knowledge of the Old Testament scriptures, though others think he was not highly educated. Whether or not, I have to say that I find the evidence of the gospel writers having attributed to Jesus sayings and actions which he most probably did not say or do, of having created for their own purposes an inflated picture of Jesus, is overwhelming. He was unique enough without their fabrications: he remains unique despite them.

3. The Alleged Miracles

Next the miracles. These may be divided into two classes: the healing miracles of the sick or of those with unclean spirits which needed to be exorcised, both then thought to be the consequence of sin; and those other miracles which relied on nature changing its course. As for the healing miracles, I have for a long time believed that certain people are endowed with a gift of natural healing and indeed have had some experience of it.

Many years ago I came to know an outstanding healer by the name of Bruce Macmanaway. Bruce told me he had discovered his gift during the war when he had gone out on the battlefield to comfort and, if possible, rescue a wounded soldier who was in great pain. 'When I touched him,' Bruce told me, 'he said that the pain had left him, but that when I took my hand away, it came back.' Once Bruce tried to relieve discomfort in my back, and when he put his hands on my spinal cord, I felt an extraordinary sensation of heat, as if he were using a blowtorch. I was later operated on for a tumour there. I had an even more surprising experience when the BBC sent me to interview a well-known healer of the time, Harry Edwards. After the interview I mentioned, rather casually, that my sinuses had been blocked for years so that I now had almost no sense of smell: could he help? He leaned forward and placed his fingers lightly on either side of my nose. Presently I not only felt *but heard* the congestion in the sinuses breaking up. The 'cure' didn't last more than two years before the condition returned, but I was amazed that he had been able to effect one at all.

My attitude to the healing miracles is therefore sympathetic, and has been reinforced by something that Ian Wilson wrote in *Jesus: The Evidence*. Referring to Jesus's healing at the pool of Bethesda of the man who had been paralysed for thirty-eight years, and recorded in John 5:8, he says this:

> As is well known medically, some paralyses are 'hysterical' in origin, that is, they have a mental rather than physical cause, usually as a result of some severe emotional stress. There would have been no shortage of causative stresses in Jesus's time. Besides paralysis, hysteria can induce disfiguring skin conditions, blindness, apparent inability to hear or speak and all manner of symptoms of mental illness. An important feature of hysterical disorders is that the patient has no conscious awareness of feigning such symptoms. To him or her they are all too real, and they may last for many years. But unlike a physical condition with a non-reversible cause, hysterical disorders can be cured by the original, debilitating emotional problem being reached and released, today usually via drugs, psychotherapy or hypnosis. When effected the 'cure' can be dramatically sudden, and many so-called 'faith-healings' may be explained by this process, the trigger essentially being a form of hypnosis induced by the so-called 'faith-healer'.

On the other hand one must draw a line somewhere and one can only conclude that the account of the unclean spirits which Jesus released from the madman who lived in the tombs transferring themselves to a herd of some *two thousand pigs* so that they all ran down a hill and drowned in the sea (Mark 5:13) is but one example of the gospel writers' graphic imaginations. As for the two stories of his raising people from the dead, I can just about accept the resurrection of the twelve-year-old daughter of Jairus because Jesus himself said at Mark 5:39: 'the damsel is not dead but sleepeth.' But the account at

John 11:1–46 of the raising of Lazarus has no such qualifications. At 11:14 we read: 'Then said Jesus unto them plainly, Lazarus is dead,' and this was confirmed by Martha and Mary, Lazarus's sisters. Indeed, when Jesus approached Lazarus's tomb, Martha warned him crudely, 'Lord, by this time he stinketh; for he hath been dead four days.' Nothing daunted, Jesus commanded Lazarus to come forth, which he did, 'bound hand and foot with grave clothes and his face covered in a napkin', though whether stinking is not recorded. This is a further example of how, in their apotheosis of Jesus, the gospel writers sought to persuade people to believe that Jesus was so remarkable that there was nothing he could not do.

Other extraordinary claims included his walking on the water (the notion has since become a music-hall joke), commanding a storm to cease, turning water into wine, feeding 5,000 people with five loaves and two fishes and having twelve basketfuls over, later feeding 4,000 people with seven loaves and a few little fishes and having seven basketfuls over. Some have tried to explain away these claims by suggesting that Jesus was not actually walking on the water but in the shallows, that the guests at the wedding feast at Cana were tricked by hypnosis into thinking that the water they were drinking was wine, that the 5,000 and the 4,000 had been persuaded to share their picnics with others, and so on. But the fact remains that for centuries afterwards and even today people believed that these alleged events actually happened, and were proof of Jesus's divinity.

The great Cicero, however, writing in *De Divinatione* in the century before Jesus about other so-called miracles, was not one of them:

> For nothing can happen without cause; nothing happens that cannot happen, and when what was capable of happening has happened, it may not be interpreted as a miracle. Consequently there are no miracles. We therefore draw this conclusion: what was incapable of happening never happened and what was capable of happening is not a miracle.

And so we come to the last great miracle of all and one I believe to be quite incapable of happening, Jesus's alleged resurrection, of which St Paul wrote: 'If Christ be not risen, then our faith and yours is in vain', a view endorsed by a former Archbishop of Canterbury, Michael Ramsey, when I talked to him in 1957. Various paltry explanations have been put forward, such as the shock of his death was so numbing and the force of his personality so great that the visions they had of him were hallucinations – because they longed to see him again, they did. As a supporter of Cicero's (and Matthew Arnold's) beliefs that miracles don't happen and of the poet Swinburne's line, 'Dead men rise up never', I cannot subscribe to that. In the whole of human history there is no record of any such similar happening. So what is the explanation? In the gospels Jesus refers on many occasions to his resurrection three days after his death. Were the gospel writers to say, as in truth they would have to, that this prophecy never happened, that would have been a denial of Jesus worse than Peter's, would knock the bottom out of their whole story, indeed ensure in the long run (though this they would be unaware of) that the Christian religion would be stillborn. They knew that the Pharisees (unlike the Sadducees) believed in resurrection in a vague sort of way, so why not set out a scenario which featured just that? They had fabricated so much already, why not fulfil Jesus's crazy prophecy by fabricating a little bit more? Admittedly at Mark 9.9 they had recorded the disciples' disbelief in resurrections, but they were writing long after the event and with luck there would be no one still around to contradict them.

This theory is bolstered by the accounts in all four gospels of Christ's post-resurrection appearances being contradictory and therefore probably imaginary. The only event on which all four agree is that early on the Sunday morning after his death Mary Magdalen goes to the sepulchre where he has been buried. Thereafter the accounts vary. In Mark she is accompanied by Mary, mother of James, and by Salome. They see that the stone guarding the entrance to the sepulchre has been rolled away. They enter it and see a young man sitting there in a white garment, which frightens them. He tells them not to be afraid: Jesus is risen and gone into Galilee where they will see him. They flee from the sepulchre, trembling and amazed.[3]

In Matthew Mary Magdalen is accompanied only by 'the other Mary', and when they reach the sepulchre, there is a great earthquake, and an angel of the Lord descends from heaven, rolls back the stone from the mouth of the sepulchre and sits on it. (All this is highly suspect: had there really been a great earthquake, we would have heard of it from elsewhere and angels are mythical figures.) The angel's face, we are told, was like lightning and his raiment white as snow. The angel tells the women that Jesus has risen and gone to Galilee where they will see him. On their way to tell the disciples what they have seen, Jesus appears. They hold him by the feet (to prevent him leaving?) and worship him. He tells them to tell his disciples to go to Galilee where they will see him. They do this and see Jesus on the mountain where he had first appointed them. They worship him 'but some doubted' (which I take to be an expression of Matthew's own doubts). He tells them to go and teach to all nations and says he will be with them until the end of the world.

In Luke Mary Magdalen is accompanied by Mary the mother of Jesus and by Joanna 'and other women'. They find the stone gone and enter the sepulchre. The body of Jesus has vanished. Two men in shining garments tell them that Jesus has risen as he said he would, but nothing is said about meeting him in Galilee. They go and tell what they have seen to the disciples who regard their words as idle tales.

The same day two of the disciples, one Cleopas the other possibly Jesus's brother James, walk to the village of Emmaus. Jesus appears but they do not recognise him. They tell him about Jesus, a great prophet, and of his death and the empty sepulchre. He chides them for not believing what the prophets said about him. In the evening they persuade Jesus to eat with them. Then he vanishes.

The two disciples return to Jerusalem and join the others at supper. Once again Jesus appears from nowhere. The disciples are terrified and think he is a spirit. He reassures them that it is really him. He eats a piece of broiled fish and some honey. He reminds them of what was written about him in the scriptures and tells them to preach the gospel of repentance and remission of sins.

Lastly John, the longest and most detailed account of all. Mary Magdalen comes alone to the sepulchre, finds the stone removed and Jesus's body no longer there. She goes to tell Simon Peter and the disciple whom Jesus loved. They run to the sepulchre and find Jesus's grave clothes lying on the floor. Then they go home.

Mary meanwhile looks into the sepulchre and sees two angels in white sitting on the place where Jesus's body lay. Suddenly Jesus himself appears. Mary doesn't recognise him and, mistaking him for the gardener, asks where the body of Jesus is, so that she can collect it. Then she recognises him and he tells her to tell the disciples what she has seen. That evening, when the disciples are behind locked doors, Jesus makes another surprise appearance, breathes on them and tells them to receive the Holy Ghost. Thomas, who was not present, doubts the story (John's doubt?) but later says he will believe only when he sees the print of the nails on Jesus's hands and thrusts his hands into Jesus's wounded side.

Eight days later the disciples assemble again. Again Jesus appears. Thomas is present and Jesus tells him to put his fingers on the nail prints on his hands and to thrust his hand into his side. He does so and believes. Jesus disappears.

The scene shifts to the Sea of Tiberias (Galilee). The disciples go fishing but catch nothing. Jesus makes an appearance on the shore but the disciples do not recognise him. He asks if they have any meat and they say no. He tells them to cast their nets to the right of the ship and when they do, they find they have caught 153 fish precisely. Having recognised Jesus, they land and see on the shore a fire of coals with fish and bread on them. In the Authorised Version Jesus says colloquially, 'Come and dine,' which they do. After dinner Jesus asks Simon Peter three times if he loves him, and when he says he does, tells him to feed his sheep and lambs. This is the nearest the fourth gospel gets to telling the disciples to preach to all the nations.

And finally we read of the dottiest miracle of all: Jesus's ascension into heaven. The Jews of that time saw heaven and hell in spatial terms, as we all used to as children and as some Christian adults still do today.[4] Hell was down below in an underworld and heaven up above the bright blue sky. Matthew doesn't mention the Ascension nor does John; Mark says briefly that he was received into heaven and sat on the right hand of God; Luke says he was parted from his disciples and carried up into heaven, but Acts gives it the full treatment:

> And when he had spoken these things, while they beheld, he was taken up; and a cloud received him out of their sight. And while they looked steadfastly at heaven as he went up, behold, two men stood by them in white apparel; Which also said, Ye men of Galilee, why stand ye gazing up into heaven? This same Jesus which is taken up from you into heaven, shall so come in like manner as ye have seen him go into heaven.

My reactions are the same as Thomas Paine's:

> The resurrection and ascension, supposing them to have taken place, admitted of public and ocular demonstration, like that of the ascension of a balloon or the sun at noon, to all Jerusalem at least.
>
> A thing which everybody is required to believe requires that the proof and evidence of it should be equal to all and universal . . . Instead of this a small number of persons, not more than eight or nine, are introduced as proxies for the whole world to say they saw it, and all the rest of the world are called upon to believe it.
>
> The story, so far as it relates to the supernatural part, has every mark of fraud and imposition stamped upon it. The best surviving evidence we now have respecting this affair is the Jews. They are regularly descended from the people who lived in the times that this resurrection and ascension is said to have happened, and they say, *it is not true.*

Is it any wonder that of the thirty-two bishops polled at the time that

Dr David Jenkins, Bishop of Durham, said that nothing in the New Testament could be taken as certain, between one-third and a half expressed doubts about the resurrection? The wonder to me is that the remaining half to two-thirds could still give it credence. Why?

If the stories of the resurrection and the Ascension are, as I believe, not credible, one might at least hope other events recorded in the gospels to be true. But many – too many – can be proved not to be. I have already referred to the dubiety of the Nativity story as recounted in Matthew and Luke. Nor do we know, or ever will know, the exact year, month and day of Jesus's birthday. December 25, the day of the winter solstice, was not decided on until four centuries later when Rome's Christians chose it to coincide with the date of the great pagan festival of Mithras. The actual year is equally uncertain, as Herod the Great was later discovered to have died in 4 BCE and the census of Judaea to have been held in 6 CE, so the claim that Jesus was four at the beginning of our era is doubly wrong.

4. Jesus the Guru

Turning to the events at the end of Jesus's life, we find similar falsehoods. To emphasise the significance and importance of the crucifixion, the synoptic authors fabricated a number of events that they say took place during the time that Jesus was on the cross. To fulfil the prophecy of Jesus at Mark 13:24–5 that the sun and the stars would fail, Mark says at 15:33 that there was darkness over the whole land until the ninth hour, Luke says much the same and that the veil of the Temple was rent, but Matthew goes even further:

> And behold the veil of the temple was rent in twain from the top to the bottom; and the earth did quake and the rocks rent; And the graves were opened; and many bodies of the saints which slept arose, And came out of the graves after his resurrection, and went into the holy city and appeared to many.

Again one has to say that if there was an earthquake when Christ was on the cross, and darkness over the land and the curtain of the Temple torn in two, there would surely have been some confirmation from other sources. There is none. As for the graves opening up and the saints spilling out of them and being seen in Jerusalem, one can only say that if people can believe that, they can believe anything. In addition each of the gospels contains contradictory statements about the same event. One good example is John telling us at 3:22 that Jesus baptised people and then at 4:1–2 saying that he didn't, but there are scores of others. In the end it becomes impossible to sort out what is true in the gospels and what isn't, what Jesus reliably said and the falsehoods the gospel writers put into his mouth.

And what can one say of the man himself? Descriptively, as with God, nothing; for the gospels represent him to us as an idealised, perfect human being, which was their authors' intention. Therefore we cannot envisage him pictorially: we do not know whether he was short or tall, lean or well built, beard fully grown or trimmed, hair luxuriant or balding; his preferences in food and clothing and sex, whether he was robust or prey to illness. He had to be seen to be human but not so human as to challenge his credibility as divine. Did his mother ever tell him he had been fathered by the Holy Ghost? I ask the question in all seriousness, because if she did, that could well have been the genesis of his subsequent fixation about being the messenger – if not the son (whatever that might mean) – of God.

Dr Anthony Storr has written a book on the subject of *gurus*, a Sanskrit word to describe those who believe they have a mission to bring spiritual enlightenment to their fellow beings. Among those he has chosen for study are Ignatius of Loyola, George Gurdjieff, Freud and Jung, Rudolf Steiner, the Bhagwan Shree Rajneesh and Jesus Christ:

> Gurus differ widely from each other in a variety of ways, but most claim the possession of special spiritual insight based on

personal revelation. Gurus promise their followers new ways of self-development, new paths to salvation. Since there are no schools for gurus and no recognised qualifications for becoming one, they are, like politicians, originally self-selected.

Although Jesus Christ was in many ways unique and in a different league to his fellow gurus, he does seem to share with them (past and present, good, bad and indifferent) certain characteristics, predominantly in holding a passionate belief of having been chosen, usually by 'God', to preach a new message of salvation. 'Such people,' says Storr, 'have the capacity of immediately impressing and influencing others and of attracting devoted followers.' Most gurus are charismatic, silver-tongued and uninterested in personal relationships or family ties ('Who is my mother? Who are my brothers?' Jesus once asked, when told they had come to see him). They need disciples, says Storr, as much as disciples need them, it being difficult to sustain a belief in the authenticity of a new revelation if no one else shares it. Some gurus are only ready to embark on their mission after a period of solitude and self-examination (as Jesus is said to have done during his forty days in the wilderness). There is of course one overriding difference between Jesus and Storr's other gurus: he, aided by the gospel writers, unknowingly begat a world religion. They did not.

Another characteristic of many gurus is that they are sexually active, especially with their own followers, both male and female. As regards any sexual inclinations Jesus might have had, this is a subject the gospel writers have avoided, wanting their readers to believe that he lived on a different plane, was above all that sort of thing. Yet in re-reading the gospel of John recently, I have begun to wonder. There are several references in this gospel to 'the disciple whom Jesus loved', and Robin Lane-Fox and other scholars think that this is the same John as John the son of Zebedee and brother of James and therefore an eye-witness and participant in Jesus's ministry. 'The disciple whom Jesus loved' is a curious phrase. Did he not love all his disciples, or did he love John in a special way?

I ask the question because it is the loved disciple that John at 13:25

finds lying on the breast of Jesus on conclusion of the Last Supper, which suggests not only that the traditional stylised paintings of Jesus and the twelve sitting like so many orderly monks on one side of a long refectory table are inaccurate – they must have been spread out on the floor on rugs and cushions – but that between Jesus and the loved disciple there was a close physical affinity. It will be recalled that after the supper (John 13:4–5) Jesus undressed, girded himself with a towel and after washing the disciples' feet took off the towel to dry them. It is not recorded whether, at the time the loved disciple lay on his breast, he still had the towel round him or not. I thought this was probably the source of a former Bishop of Birmingham, Hugh Sebag-Montefiore, suggesting that Jesus might have been homosexually inclined, but he assures me he came to this view on other grounds.[5]

If we read the New Testament gospels afresh and forget for a moment the status that Jesus enjoys in the western world, what is it about him that first strikes one? Surely his (or the gospel writers') oft-expressed delusions about who he is, who his father is and why he is there. Christians would say that as the Redeemer of the world, he is speaking no more than the truth, telling us as it was.

But not self-delusional? Consider:

I am the bread of life; he that cometh to me shall never hunger
and he that believeth in me shall never thirst;
No man cometh unto the Father but by me;
I am the light of the world;
Behold, a greater than Solomon is here;
Ye call me master and Lord; and ye say well; for so I am;
Verily, verily, I say unto you, Except ye eat the flesh of the
Son of man and drink his blood, ye have no life in you.

This last was too much for some of his followers, for in John 6:66 we read: 'From that time many of his disciples went back and walked no more with him.' Then Jesus, fearful of being deserted altogether, said to the twelve, 'Will ye also go away?' And Simon Peter reassured him. 'Lord, to whom shall we go? Thou hast the words of eternal life.'

Like all gurus, Jesus is presented as a fanatical believer in himself and his message, who at times becomes so over-excited he begins to contradict himself. At one moment he is saying, 'The Son of man is not come to destroy men's lives but to save them', at the next, 'Think not that I am come to send peace on earth. I came not to send peace but a sword' (Matt. 10:34), at another moment, 'Honour thy father and mother', and at the next, 'If any man come to me and hate not his father and mother and wife and children and brothers and sisters, yea and his own life also, he cannot be my disciple' (Luke 14:26). He instructs his disciples to 'Judge not, that ye be not judged', though later he tells them they will sit on twelve thrones to judge the twelve tribes of Israel, and he himself never stopped judging, for instance the much-maligned Pharisees ('ye serpents, ye generation of vipers' (Matt. 23:33)) and the rich, because he believes they cannot also be virtuous ('easier for a camel to pass through the eye of a needle than for a rich man to enter the kingdom of heaven' (Mark 10:25)). He also shows petulance and pettiness when, being hungry, he curses a fig tree for not bearing fruit and, by another alleged miracle, causes it to wither.

Much has also been made of two of Jesus's most famous sayings: 'Thou shalt love thy neighbour as thyself' and 'As ye would that men do unto you, do unto them likewise.' Both are thought to be original, but neither is. 'Love thy neighbour as thyself' is taken from Leviticus 19:18, while the other is as old as humanity. A hundred years before, the Jewish rabbi Hillel had said, 'Whatever is hateful to you, do not do to your fellow man.' And 400 years before that Confucius was saying the same: 'Do not do to others what you would not wish them to do to you.'[6]

More debatable is the doctrine of loving one's enemies which Tom Paine called a strange morality. 'Offering the other cheek is sinking to the level of a spaniel.' Carl Lofmark in his booklet *What is the Bible?* echoes him:

Turning the other cheek reduces a man to the moral status of a dog abused by his master: it destroys his self-respect. While it is generous to forgive your enemy, it is usually absurd and unrealistic to love him, and the effort to force yourself may lead you into the very real moral offence of hypocrisy; pretending to be something that you are not, sporting a false smile on your face that hides the real venom in your heart.

Of another saying of Jesus, *Resist not evil*, Lofmark says that it is the very opposite of morality: 'evil is precisely what we should resist.' And in answer both to turning the other cheek and in not resisting evil, he prefers the morality of Confucius: 'If you requite evil with good, with what will you reward good? No, I say, reward good with good and evil with justice.'

I do not wish to dispute everything that Christ is alleged to have done or said, nor to deny that for millions over hundreds of years his life and presence have been an inspiration and a comfort. With much of what he is said to have said, and said in memorable language, it would be hard to dissent: Blessed are the peacemakers and the meek and the pure in heart and the merciful; Forgive us our trespasses as we forgive them that trespass against us; Seek and ye shall find; the last shall be first; the humble shall be exalted; Bring in the poor and the maimed and the halt and the blind; Suffer the little children to come unto me; the Sabbath was made for man; the truth shall make you free. I acknowledge all that freely. My quarrel is with something more fundamental.

Throughout the gospels Jesus repeatedly tells us that his will is no more than that of the Father who sent him. His last two extraordinary prophecies were that within the lifetimes of those present he would come again with his angels in the glory of the clouds to establish the Kingdom of God on earth, and that for those who were believers there would be life everlasting. Although the prophecy about the second coming was, naturally enough, never fulfilled, the good news about life eternal was received with joy by his disciples and by both early and later Christians, even to this day.

To most people today the prophecy about the second coming seems deranged and the other about everlasting life highly questionable. A belief in life after death sprang originally from the fact that existence on earth was, and is, for most people at most times, a burden, for which they would be compensated by the promise that there will be love and laughter and peace ever after, as the popular song says, in a world to come. But how is this to be? Bodies decay and die, those that are buried rot, those that are cremated are reduced to a handful of yellow ashes. No signs of life there. But, I am told, the spirit, the soul, live on. I think I know as well as anyone what the word 'soul' conveys but what does it *mean*? Can the spirit or soul see, feel, communicate, comprehend, and if so, how? Bertrand Russell, the philosopher, said that he could not imagine an afterlife without a mind to be aware of it; and, as we shall see, the philosopher David Hume thought much the same.

What else is the afterlife but a belief among the insecure that at the last trump there will be cakes and ale, even caviar and trumpets for them too, that in some leafy Eden they will share happy hours with those who have gone before and others who may well come after? I have always found it strange that these glib prophets of a life after death have never expressed a belief in a life before birth (apart, of course, from the reincarnationists): the reason being, I suppose, that people are more interested in where they think they may be going rather than where they may have been. In my view they aren't going anywhere. This life is all we have, so we had better make the most if it.

One of the greatest barriers to criticising the life and mission of Jesus in any way is his death and the hideous manner of it; also the belief that he died as the Saviour of the world, the Redeemer of our sins. Those in history who have died heroic deaths, no matter for what cause, have usually been granted immunity from criticism. This belief in Christ as Saviour is very strong among Roman Catholics, even to this day. Paul Johnson is on record as saying that if there are other creatures living in outer space, Jesus must have died for them too. Against this I find the idea of Christ as Saviour makes little or no impression on today's younger generation. Many of them seem to regard him as they do the Queen or the Prince of Wales, as a person famous for being famous. Ask them what they think his significance is, and they are at a loss to tell you.

It would be no exaggeration to say that from the earliest days of their history the Jews were obsessed with a sense of sin, which came originally from Adam's fall and of their sense of guilt stemming from it. 'The awful reality and contagion of sin,' writes one scholar, 'affected both people and priests, and there was an intense realisation of the need for cleansing and propitiation, and of being on good terms with Yahweh.'

Hence the introduction of one of the most important events in the Jewish calendar, the Day of Atonement. This took place on the tenth day of the seventh month and involved a 'sin offering' as well as a burnt offering. As related of Aaron in Leviticus 16, the ritual was as follows. First, the high priest in the Temple laid aside his ornate vestments, bathed and put on a simple white linen tunic and girdle. Then he killed and bled a bullock for the first 'sin offering'. After throwing some incense on the live coals used for the burnt offering, he put the blood of the bullock in a basin and in the Most Holy Place sprinkled it once on the front of the mercy seat and seven times on the ground in front of the Ark of the Covenant. This act of atonement was on behalf of the high priest and the priesthood generally.

Next the high priest chose two he goats, one as a burnt offering for Yahweh, the other as a second sin offering for the spirit Azazel (literally 'scapegoat'). First he killed the goat for Yahweh, and sprinkled its blood in the Most Holy Place as with the blood of the bullock. Then, placing his hand on the head of the goat for Azazel, he made a solemn confession of the nation's sins which, by a process of transference, were believed to enter both symbolically and literally the goat's head. Loaded down with the nation's sins, the goat was then taken into the wilderness and left to die of thirst and starvation. In New Testament times, however, coincidental with the life of Jesus, the wretched creature was taken to a clifftop twelve miles east of Jerusalem where it was thrown over it backwards to meet its death on the rocks below, thus expunging the nation's sins.

No one was more conscious of the Jewish burden of a perennial sense of sin, induced by their fear of Yahweh, and the need to expiate it, than Jesus. There was hardly any area of life where this sense of sin did not play some part. It was a common belief in those days for instance that illness, disease and other infirmities were the result of sinning; which is why after many of the healing miracles, Jesus says to those he had healed, 'Thy sins are forgiven thee,' or 'Go thy way and sin no more.' According to Paul the wages of sin were death, and as all men and women had to die, all men and women were to some degree sinners. Sin and sinners loomed large in Jesus's consciousness – in that climate it would have seemed strange if they hadn't – 'I came not to call the righteous but sinners to repentance'; 'Let he who is without sin cast the first stone.' Yet, although Jesus might have been expected to condemn as sins such frailties as deceit, lasciviousness, envy, drunkenness, anger – he does not do so: what irks him most is blasphemy against the Holy Spirit and the pretentiousness and hypocrisy of the holier-than-thou Pharisees.

We now come to the first reference to Jesus claiming he will become the Redeemer of sins. It occurs in Matthew 20:28 and also in Mark 10:45 where he is quoted as saying, to his disciples, 'Even as the Son of Man came not to be ministered unto, but to minister, *and to give his life a ransom for many*' (my italics), once again foretelling his death. There are two things wrong with this. The first, according to the biblical scholar John Knox in his book *The Death of Christ*, is that Jesus had himself no reason to suppose that his death could or would redeem the sins of the world. Knox's argument is that it was the early Church (i.e. the gospel writers and Paul) and not Jesus who interpreted his death in the predestined role of Saviour. Jesus himself, he says, would have found 'the *choice* of such a death and the *purpose* to suffer it' both 'morbid and unnatural'. Furthermore, he says, there is evidence that in the garden of Gethsemane 'he hoped to the very end that the bitter cup might not need to be drunk'. Feeling as deeply as the early Church did about Jesus as Saviour, Knox concludes, was

77

enough for them to ascribe thoughts and words to Jesus which he never thought or said.

From so eminent a scholar I find this a mind-blowing statement, for if true, if Christ did not believe or say that his death would be a redemption for the sins of mankind, then that is a challenge to Christian belief as great if not greater than Swinburne's line that dead men rise up never and that accounts of the resurrection are a fraud. A.N. Wilson in his book *Paul: The Mind of the Apostle* agrees with Knox. 'There is nothing in the religious vocabulary of his [Jesus's] tradition which would have enabled him to see his death as an atoning sacrifice.'

Another reason for doubting them is what Jesus and the disciples were doing at the time – making their way from Jericho to Jerusalem for the feast of the Passover. On their entry into Jerusalem, Jesus was hailed as a hero: palm branches and garments were strewn in his path to the joyful cries of 'Hosanna in the highest. Blessed is he that cometh in the name of the Lord.' At this moment, therefore, Jesus could have had no reason at all to think that these same people would soon be demanding from the Roman governor his execution; and so once again one must conclude that the passage was put into his mouth by the gospel writers, and for the same reason – to fulfil the scriptures – as they also put into his mouth his prophecies about being scourged and mocked and spat upon, and being numbered among the transgressors. In that same passage (Isaiah 53:12) about the transgressors, we find this: *'and he bare the sins of many'*. Here for the gospel writers was another opportunity for establishing yet another bogus prophecy, that the person who bore the sins was none other than Jesus.

Again, when Jesus is said to have said to his disciples during the Last Supper, 'This is my blood of the new testament which is shed for many for the remission of sins', he cannot have known beyond doubt that he was about to die. In the event it would have required only a little more resolution by Pontius Pilate ('I find no fault in this man') to have prevented such an obvious injustice. But the gospel writers knew the end of the story, knew they were safe in ascribing to Jesus words he never said. In John, who, some believe, was present at the Last Supper, it is not mentioned.

In the matter of Jesus as a blood sacrifice, the gospel writers were aware of the long bloody history of all the Jewish temple sacrifices of bullocks and goats and sheep and pigeons, so that in their eyes Jesus's death as yet another sacrifice could be seen as a thrilling continuation of that tradition. Paul, or whoever else wrote the epistle to the Hebrews (9:12–14), saw it that way too.

> Neither by the blood of goats and calves, but by his own blood he entered in once into the holy place, having obtained eternal redemption for us. For if the blood of bulls and of goats and the ashes of a heifer sprinkling the unclean, sanctifieth to the purifying of the flesh: How much more shall the blood of Christ who through the eternal Spirit offered himself without spot to God, purge your conscience from dead works to serve the living God?

I find that hard to accept. Christ met his death because he had antagonised the Sadducee priests and elders who were guardians of the sacred Temple; first by the subversive nature of his teaching and preaching; and then by his violent conduct in the Temple, overthrowing the tables of the money-changers and of those who sold animals and birds for sacrifice to Yahweh (thus 'fulfilling' another alleged prophecy: 'I desired mercy not sacrifice; and the knowledge of God more than burnt offerings' (Hosea 6.6)), then antagonising them further by telling them that God had made the Temple a house of prayer for all nations but they had made it a den of thieves (Isaiah 56:7 and Jeremiah 7:11). And with hundreds of temple workmen and servants at their command, it was not difficult for the priests and elders to stir up the people who had welcomed Jesus so joyously a day or two before to clamour for his death. It is true that under Jewish law they could themselves have sanctioned his death by stoning, but in view of the following he had acquired they were unwilling to take the responsibility. Instead they persuaded Pilate that his continued subversive actions constituted a threat to the Roman civil order for which the supreme punishment was death by crucifixion; and he did not have the strength of character to resist them. The redemption of sins or sinners didn't enter into it.

Whatever the beliefs of the Church then and later about Christ dying for the sins of the world, it is a belief that cannot be sustained today. For the Church to continue to preach, as it does, that 2,000 years ago Christ died for our sins *then, now and for ever* makes no kind of sense at all. When sin was interpreted as being an offence against God, it was obviously meaningful to many; but the departure of God from most of our lives has also meant the departure of sin. Crime we know about and talk about and deplore, but sin as a subject for discussion has gone out of circulation; I suppose the nearest definition today would be an offence against one's conscience; and that is a private not a public matter.

As we have seen, the Jews under Yahweh were oppressed by sin. It was a legacy they handed on to the Christians and particularly to St Paul who was quite obsessed by the subject; for instance in Chapter 6 of his epistle to the Romans which consists of twenty-three verses, he uses the word no fewer than fifteen times. Here's how it opens:

> What shall we say, then? Shall we continue in sin, that grace may abound? God forbid. How shall we that are dead to sin, live any longer therein? Know ye not, that so many of us as were baptised into Jesus Christ were baptised into his death? Therefore we are buried with him by baptism into death; that like as Christ was raised up from the dead by the glory of the Father, even so we should also walk in newness of life. For if we have been planted together in the likeness of his death, we shall be also in the likeness of his resurrection. Knowing this, that our old man[7] is crucified with him, that the body of sin might be destroyed, that henceforth we should not serve sin. For he that is dead is freed from sin . . .

This sounds like gibberish and maybe is; difficult too to reconcile with the force and clarity of the memorable lines he wrote in

1 Corinthians 13 ('Though I speak with the tongues of men and of angels and have not charity, I am become as sounding brass or a tinkling cymbal . . . faith, hope and charity, and the greatest of these is charity'). But gibberish or not, in the Church's early days Paul was Christianity's creator and standard-bearer; without him and his missions to the Jews and Gentiles, it would never have been established. He, and later others, must be held responsible for the dominant and destructive role, a legacy from Judaism, that the obsession with sin played in the life and teachings of the Church to come; also for the sense of shame and guilt that often accompanied it, especially in matters of sex. 'Flee fornication,' he wrote in his disapproving way, but far from fleeing it, the human race has been vigorously pursuing it ever since. For centuries congregations were made to feel, and in church to declare publicly, that they were miserable sinners and this gave many a Calvinist preacher the opportunity to warn of the perils of hell-fire unless one chose to repent. The consequence of this negative, pernicious and allegedly Christian (though in fact Jewish) doctrine was that, for many, self-esteem — without which the medical profession tell us there can be no *mens sana in corpore sano* — was often at a low ebb, minds and emotions were troubled, and there were shackles on the joy of living. One way and another Paul and, as we shall see, other Church Fathers have to answer for a lot.

Chapter Five

THE SPREADING OF THE WORD

1. Gains and Losses

And so the apostles did as Jesus bade them, set out on their missionary journeys across the known world, of which Luke in the Acts of the Apostles and Paul in his epistles have given us vivid accounts. Their object was to convert the Gentiles while other apostles led by James, Jesus's brother, worked among the Jews. Stephen became the first casualty, having done (Acts 6:8) 'great wonders and miracles among the people'. Vexed by the success of his preaching and healing, the scribes and elders brought against him false witnesses who said he had spoken against Moses and God, and that Jesus had promised to destroy the Temple. But he was unabashed and 'with the face of an angel' gave as good as he got. 'Ye stiff-necked and uncircumcised in heart and ears,' he told them, 'ye do always resist the Holy Ghost; as your fathers do, so do ye'; and he called them Jesus's betrayers and murderers. Little wonder that they 'were cut to the heart and gnashed their teeth', and they took Stephen outside the city walls and killed him by stoning. Paul, then Saul and unconverted, was a witness to his death.

Another early casualty was James, the son of Zebedee whom Herod killed with a sword. Later James, the brother of Jesus, who after Peter became the accepted head of the Church in Jerusalem, was martyred by the scribes and Pharisees, who threw him off the roof of the Temple. Peter, the early Church's first leader, was imprisoned by Herod and beaten but managed to escape. Despite restrictions against him, he preached the gospel among the Samaritans, at Caesarea and Antioch and Corinth. Eventually he made his way to Rome where in about 64, it is believed, he became a martyr to the persecution of the Christians under Nero. Legend has it that at his own request he was crucified upside down as he did not think himself worthy to die in the same manner as his master; thus atoning, it might be said, for the betrayal of his master before the crowing of the cock in long-ago and faraway Gethsemane.

After the trauma of his conversion Paul, who had never been a disciple of Jesus and seemed to know little about him, set out on his three great missionary journeys across Asia Minor, on one or two of them accompanied by Luke. Paul has been described as 'a man of little stature, thin-haired, crooked in the legs, a good body, eyebrows joining and hooked nose, full of grace'. He had great vitality and stamina which stood him in good stead on his often arduous travels and on the occasions when he was beaten and imprisoned and had to flee hurriedly from place to place to avoid physical attack.

What was it that attracted people to the new faith? Not entirely, I think, the news of the coming of a god who was loving, just and merciful, not even the promise of life everlasting. Persuasive these may have been, yet more so in an age even more gullible than ours was the untrue but entirely convincing message that throughout the Jewish scriptures of the Old Testament God, in passage after passage, had proclaimed that he would send a Saviour to redeem his people Israel, and that he had fulfilled that promise in Jesus who by his life, death and resurrection had not only redeemed Israel but become a Saviour of the world. In those early days the apostles did not have the gospels to reinforce their message, for they had not yet been written or published, but they knew the scriptures like the backs of their hands and they had the example of Paul and their own missionary zeal to sustain them.

There are several instances in the missionary life of the apostles of how they persuaded their hearers of what they said was God's long-term purpose. At Acts 13:33 Paul cited Psalms 2:7, 'Thou art my son, this day have I begotten thee,' as proof that a hundred years later Jesus had been fathered by God, a meaningless concept today but perfectly plausible then (the Greek gods, it will be recalled, often had carnal relations with humans). Another rather charming example is related in Acts 8:27–39 when Philip, travelling from Jerusalem to Gaza, meets 'a man of Ethiopia, a eunuch of great authority under Candace queen of the Ethiopians, who had the charge of all her treasure and had come to Jerusalem to worship'. He was now on his way back to Ethiopia and sitting in his chariot by the roadside reading aloud the prophet Isaiah. Philip approached the chariot, heard the reading of Isaiah and asked the Ethiopian if he understood what he was reading.

> And he said, How can I, except some man should guide me? And he desired Philip that he would come up and sit with him.
>
> The place of the scripture which he read was this, He was led as a sheep to the slaughter; and like a lamb dumb before his shearer, so opened he not his mouth.

Of whom was Isaiah speaking, asked the eunuch, of himself or of some other man? Philip, incorrectly, said Jesus and preached to him the gospel.

> And as they went on their way, they came unto a certain water; and the eunuch said, See, here is water; what doth hinder me to be baptised?
>
> And Philip said, If thou believest with all thine heart, thou mayest. And he answered and said, I believe that Jesus Christ is the Son of God.
>
> And he commanded the chariot to stand still; and they went down both into the water, both Philip and the eunuch; and he baptised him.
>
> And when they were come up out of the water, the Spirit of

the Lord caught away Philip, that the eunuch saw him no more; and he went on his way rejoicing.

Surely one of the quickest conversions in history; but it paved the way to Ethiopia becoming one of the first and longest-lasting Christian countries in the world.

In Acts too there are accounts of disciples performing miraculous healings, some just credible, others not at all. At 9:37 for instance we find an account of Peter, like Jesus, raising a woman from the dead. Her name was Tabitha called Dorcas, the healer was Peter, the place Joppa. Tabitha had died and her body laid out in an upper chamber. Peter was at nearby Lydda and disciples at Joppa asked him to come quickly to do what he could to revive her.

When he was come, they brought him into the upper chamber, and all the widows stood by weeping and showing the coats and garments which Dorcas made . . .

But Peter put them all forth, and kneeled down and prayed; and turning to the body, said, Tabitha, arise. And she opened her eyes; and when she saw Peter, she sat up.

Hardly less credible to us are the two occasions (Acts 3:1 and 14:8–9) when Paul allegedly restores to full health those who had been *crippled from birth*; and not credible at all (Acts 13:11) is the story of how Paul, irritated by the sorcerer Bar-Jesus, struck him blind 'for a season'. Yet passed from mouth to mouth, these fictions were believed.

On some of his travels Paul was to experience verbal as well as physical abuse. In Athens, which he described as wholly given over to idolatry (Acts 17:19), the Stoic and Epicurean philosophers called him a babbler, an expositor of unknown gods, and asked him, 'May we know what this new doctrine is? For thou bringeth certain strange things to our ears; we would know what these things mean.' Paul stood on Mars Hill and in a moving speech told them; but when he came to the resurrection they, understandably, mocked. Even newly recruited disciples were sometimes perplexed. When Paul asked them at Ephesus whether they had received the Holy Ghost since they had come to believe, they replied, 'We have not so much as heard that there be any Holy Ghost.'

Towards the end of his ministry Paul, staying with Philip at Caesarea, made plans to join the brethren in Jerusalem and to preach there. His companions urged him not to, for although many Jews had come to believe, they bitterly resented Paul's strictures on Moses's insistence on the need for circumcision. Paul dismissed their fears and said that, if it came to it, he was ready to die for Jesus. However, they had not been long there when there was uproar, certain Asian Jews having seen Paul bring a Gentile into the Temple; and after a hostile reception from a crowd to whom he spoke, he was seized and taken to the castle. There his nephew, hearing of a plot to kill him, arranged for an escort to take him back to Caesarea and into the care of the Roman governor Felix.

A few days later the high priest Ananias together with elders and a public speaker named Tertulus came to Caesarea from Jerusalem to press charges against Paul for sedition. Paul denied the charges, believing the real reason why Ananias and the elders were angered was his preaching the resurrection of the dead which he as a Pharisee believed in and which Ananias and the elders denied.

The trial fizzled out and Paul was released on conditional liberty. He remained at Caesarea two years when Felix was replaced by Porcius Festus who, 'to please the Jews', kept Paul bound. The high priests and elders being still keen to press charges, Festus invited them to Caesarea to put their case. When they had done so, Festus asked Paul if he would be willing to go to Jerusalem to stand trial. Paul, knowing that that way lay certain death, refused and proclaimed his right as a Roman citizen (a legacy inherited from his father) to be tried before Caesar in Rome. And in a dramatic and memorable reply Festus answered, 'Hast thou appealed unto Caesar? Unto Caesar thou shalt go.'

And so Paul was handed over to a centurion and, after further adventures including a shipwreck in Malta, arrived in Rome. He was never called to trial but is said to have lived under guard in a rented house for two years, and then, like Peter, to have met his death in the persecution of the Christians under Nero. If that is so (and it is by no means certain) it seems entirely appropriate that Paul and Peter, the two great protagonists of Christian belief, should have ended their days in Rome, for it was from Rome in addition to Byzantium and despite many future setbacks, that Christianity would finally take root and spread.

Nero was the first though not the last of the Roman emperors to persecute Christians, and by all accounts one of the worst. He was a man who enjoyed inflicting cruelty for cruelty's sake. He first murdered his mother and then his wife Octavia. Later he murdered his second wife Poppaea by kicking her while she was pregnant. He then proposed to Antonia, daughter of Claudius, but as he had already had her brother Britannicus poisoned, she not unnaturally refused him, as a result of which he had her executed. Finally he murdered the husband of Statilia Messalina in order to marry her himself. At the age of thirty-one, when there was a movement to oust him, he fled the city and committed suicide.

He may also have been an arsonist, for on a July night in 64 two-thirds of Rome was destroyed by a fire which, many believed, he had started. Looking around for a convenient scapegoat, wrote the historian Tacitus:

> Nero fixed the guilt on a class of people hated for their abominations, who are commonly called Christians. Christ, from whom their name derives, was executed by the Governor, Pontius Pilate, in the reign of Tiberius . . . An immense number of Christians were arrested. And not only arrested but crucified, mutilated, tortured and sacrificed to wild beasts.

According to Tacitus, Nero had Christians dressed in animal skins which he then hunted with hounds in his gardens, while other Christians, having had some combustible material sprayed over them, were set alight as human torches to illuminate the scene.

The abominations referred to by Tacitus were inventions by Roman citizens who had come to resent the growing number of Christian converts and their secret ways. Rumours about them spread. At night when they met in each other's houses (for they had no churches then), it was said they indulged in sexual orgies and practised cannibalism on babies. (It is possible the origins of this lay in some passing Roman hearing a snatch of the Eucharist: 'This is my flesh, this is my blood, eat this, drink this, in remembrance of me.') Eighteen years after Nero's death, the great central amphitheatre of the Colosseum, still there today, was completed, and here 50,000 seated spectators, with thousands of others standing, watched Christians, including Bishop Ignatius of Antioch, being torn to pieces by lions and bears.

Some persecutions took place outside Rome. At Lyons in France, forty-eight Christians were massacred, among them their bishop aged ninety, a boy in his teens and a servant girl; while Pliny, the governor of Bithynia, wrote to the Emperor Trajan of his concern at 'the spread of the Christian contagion' and the Roman temples deserted. He could find no evidence of orgies or cannibalism, but 'a base and extravagant superstition'. He had had brought before him Christian slave girls 'whom they call deaconesses'.

> I asked the accused, 'Are you Christians?' If they said Yes, I warned them, and asked a second and third time. If they still said Yes, I condemned them to execution. I had no doubt that one must punish obstinacy and unbending perversity. Others I let go, because they recited after me a prayer to the gods . . . and what is more, cursed Christ which, it is said, real Christians cannot be made to do.

After this the persecutions wore off, largely because a succession of emperors' relations or staff had Christian connections; and it had always been the custom for the Romans not only to tolerate the various sects within their empire, but often to adopt their practices themselves. The Christians however seemed to be a quite different species, unlike any other foreign belief system they had yet encountered. And they looked on them with a cynical eye.

Celsus said: 'They worship to an extravagant degree this man who appeared recently. They are like frogs holding a symposium round a swamp, debating which of them is the most sinful.'

Lucian was equally scathing:

> The poor wretches have convinced themselves that they are going to be immortal and live for all time, by worshipping that crucified sophist and living under his laws. Therefore they despise the things of this world and consider them common property. They receive these doctrines by tradition, without any definite evidence.

Despite these strictures the numbers of converts continued to grow. Being impressionable, they were seduced, as the converts of Luke and Paul had been seduced, by coming to believe that the passages in the Old Testament prophesying Christ's coming were true. The Greek missionary Justin was convinced of it. He called the scriptures 'the best and truest evidence [*evidence?*] of the coming of the son of a virgin, the healing of the sick and raising of the dead, being crucified, rising again and ascending to heaven'. He told the Jews whom he hoped to convert, 'You Jews have the prophecies. We Christians have the fulfilment.' His pupil, the Syrian Tatian, believed the same, praising the scriptures for their foretelling of future events. Later, in about 250, the great Christian scholar Origen echoed him: 'By careful study of the Prophets, the Gospels and the words of the Apostles *we prove clearly* [my italics] that Christ was the one foretold.'

Tatian in his *Address to the Greeks* also expressed thankfulness, as a Christian, for being delivered from the innumerable gods and spirits of polytheism. This novel idea, the substitution of many gods by one, and a loving and forgiving one at that, also made its mark; for the slaves and dispossessed the good news was that heaven was not for the rich but the poor and humble, and that having once passed through its holy gates one would exist there blissfully for ever.

Yet to my mind the clinching argument for Christian belief, one so powerful that the gullible could not gainsay it, was the story of the resurrection. By this time all four gospels had seen the light of day and each contained its own graphic account of Jesus's dramatic reappearance which Paul's teachings had confirmed. To the critical mind of course these accounts were contradictory and therefore suspect, but in those days critical minds were at a premium. Taken together with the seemingly convincing proposition that Christ's arrival on earth as Messiah had been prophesied for hundreds of years, people were learning and believing that something had happened in history that was entirely new and original – a man or god-man had actually and uniquely *risen from the dead*. If there are people today who can accept that as fact (and there are still some) how much easier for those living in those far-off superstitious times.

People everywhere were ready for these delusional beliefs and didn't recognise, as we can today, that they were delusional. Yet by them, their lives gained a sense of spirituality, wholeness, contentment, which the older Greek and Roman gods had not been able to impart. Not only in Rome but in the eastern Mediterranean and Asia Minor where Paul had converted so many, people found themselves altered, and became, to use the Christian phrase for it, reborn. 'Many have been overcome,' wrote Justin, 'and changed from violence and bullying by having seen the faithful lives of Christian neighbours, the wonderful patience of Christian fellow-travellers when defrauded, the honesty of Christians with whom they do business.' While the Greek Aristides wrote:

> They try to do good to their enemies. Their wives are pure, their daughters modest. As for their slaves, they persuade them to become Christians, and then call them brothers without distinction. Falsehood is not found among them and they love one another. He who has, gives generously to him who has not . . .

What also impressed the Gentiles was Christian concern for works as well as faith. According to Tertullian, a Roman lawyer who became a Christian convert:

> We have our money-box contributed to by those who wish and

are able to, once a month. The money is used, not for feasting and drinking, but to help the poor, orphaned children, the old, the shipwrecked, Christians sent to forced labour in the mines or exiled to islands or shut up in prison. This is why people say of us, 'See how these Christians love one another.'

By this time there had been so many conversions within the Roman Empire – Christians called themselves *imperium in imperio* (a state within a state) – that the authorities felt threatened and compelled to act. From 250 on a succession of emperors instigated a new campaign of Christian persecution. First came Decius who issued a decree that every citizen should sign a document, countersigned by two witnesses, that in the presence of the Commissioner for Sacrifices he or she had sacrificed to the Roman gods, offered wine and eaten of the sacrificial food. If they refused, they were tortured until they falsely confessed (which many did) or continued to refuse which meant martyrdom. The policy of Decius's successor Valerian was to execute bishops and senior clergy so as to leave the Church leaderless. Finally came Diocletian, the eastern emperor who, persuaded that Christians constituted a real danger to the state, gave orders for all churches to be destroyed, all devotional books to be handed over to be burned, and all worship to cease. Eusebius of Caesarea, the great chronicler of early Christian history, was a witness to this and much else.

> He saw churches pulled down [say Foster and Frend], scriptures burned in the market place and bishops and presbyters hunted, jeered at when caught, and crowded into prisons to wait their turn to die. He tells of terrible mass murders. In Phrygia a church was surrounded and set on fire with its congregation inside it. In Nicodemia people were bundled into barges, taken out to sea and thrown overboard. In Egypt there were beheadings 'until the executioner grew weary'. He also spoke of men and women having one eye gouged out and burning the tendons of a leg to make escape impossible.

2. The Conversion of Constantine

After this things began to change, though Diocletian was succeeded as eastern emperor by Galerius, an even more notorious anti-Christian than his predecessor. Left in his care was Constantine, son of the western emperor Constantius who was then on a mission to France and England. Constantius, we are told, worshipped Sol Invictus, the Unconquered Sun, a cult adopted by the emperor Aurelian forty years earlier who had declared 25 December, the day of the winter solstice, to be the sun's 'birth' day and a national festival – and which in time Christians annexed as Christ's birthday too. But Constantius also had leanings towards Christianity and called one of his daughters Anastasia which means 'resurrection'. Under his rule there had been no massacre of Christians as had occurred in the east under Diocletian.

Unhappy in the company of Galerius, the young Constantine decided to join his father in the west which he did at Boulogne and then travelled with him to England for an expedition against the Picts. But at York Constantius fell ill, and before dying proposed Constantine as emperor of the west in his place, an appointment welcomed by the army. Having heard that the usurper Maxentius was now ruling in Rome in his place, he took the army south to do battle against him, crossing the Alps at Mont Cenis. On the outskirts of Rome, Constantine found Maxentius and his troops drawn up at the Milvian Bridge over the Tiber. On the night before the battle (he later told Eusebius), he turned to the Christian god half worshipped by his father and prayed for victory the next day. Later Eusebius wrote:

> He saw a cross of light in the sky and the words 'In this sign conquer'. Night came, and in his sleep he dreamed that Christ came with the same sign for him to copy, as a guard against his enemies. I have myself seen the copy which the goldsmiths made for the emperor next morning – a lance covered with gold,

turned into a cross with a bar going over it; on the end of the
lance a garland of gold and gems; and inside this the Greek letters
CHI-RHO, the first letters of the word of Christ.

Constantine also had the logo painted on his soldiers' shields and
with this to protect them, they went into battle. The result was
an outstanding victory for Constantine, and with Maxentius's head
mounted on a lance, Constantine led his conquering troops into
Rome. There the famous arch of Constantine was erected in his
honour and still stands today; on it is a frieze depicting Maxentius
and his troops falling into the Tiber, together with the words: 'At the
instigation of the Deity.' Constantine also had two medallions struck
in honour of his victory. One shows his head alongside that of the
sun god Sol Invictus worshipped by his father, the other his head
with a CHI-RHO sign on his helmet and beneath it a horse's head
to indicate the sun god's chariot.

Constantine was tall, heavily built and had a commanding presence.
It would seem that the *only* reason he became a Christian was the
vision of Christ that had appeared to him on the eve of Milvian
Bridge. In no respect did he follow his teachings: there was no
question of him loving or even tolerating his enemies or indeed
some of his relatives, or of obeying Christ's commandment not to kill.
He was, says Paul Johnson in his *History of Christianity*, 'overbearing,
egotistical, self-righteous and ruthless'. He sent prisoners of war into
combat with wild beasts with inevitable results; he fought against
Licinius the new emperor of the east, and when Licinius submitted,
had him executed, thus becoming sole emperor of the east and west.
Later in life he followed Nero's example by executing his eldest son,
Crispus, his second wife Flavia (by boiling her alive) and his favourite
sister's husband. He also, says Johnson, 'showed an increasing regard
for flattery, fancy uniforms, personal display and elaborate titles'; and
according to his nephew Julian made himself ridiculous by wearing
'weird, eastern garments, jewels on his arms, and a tiara on his head
perched crazily on top of a tinted wig'.

On the credit side Constantine decreed that Christianity should be tolerated throughout the empire, as well as Judaism, Mithraism and every other cult, and on the site of ancient Byzantium built a magnificent new city which he named Constantinople after himself and which acted as a springboard for the spread of the word to Russia, Armenia and the east in the shape of Greek Orthodoxy (in the west it would become and remain Roman Catholicism).

From Constantinople Constantine wrote this gratifying letter to Eusebius, now Bishop of Caesarea:

> Many people are joining the Church in this city which is called by my name. The number of churches must be increased. I ask you to order fifty copies of the Holy Scriptures, to be written legibly on parchment by skilful copyists . . . as quickly as may be. You have authority to use two government carriages to bring the books for me to see. Send one of your deacons within them, and I will pay for them generously. God keep you, dear Brother.

Within the Roman Empire, Christians had now become so numerous and strong that they felt free to splinter into a variety of sects such as Donatists, Docetists, Gnostics, Montanists, Marcionites and others. Another development was the abandonment of belief in the relevance of the Jewish scriptures. They had served their purpose in (wrongly) convincing converts that Jesus's ministry had long been foretold, but after that their usefulness was over: in itself the Jewish religion meant nothing to Greeks and Romans. Yet although Marcion and the Gnostics wanted to rid themselves of the Old Testament, the orthodox Church insisted on keeping it. And then over a period of time and after discussions among Church elders such as Eusebius and Athanasius, it was decided that the canon of the New Testament should consist of twenty-seven books; and these are the same twenty-seven that we have today. Thomas Paine, needless to say, took a dim view of the choice.

About three hundred and fifty years after the time that Christ is said to have lived, several writings of the kind I am speaking of were scattered in the hands of divers individuals; and as the Church had begun to form itself into a hierarchy or church government with temporal powers, it set itself about collecting them into a code, as we now see them, called *The New Testament*. They decided by vote which of those writings out of the collections they had made should be the word of God and which should not.

He was referring to the fact that some books referred to as the Apocrypha had been omitted; and concluded by saying, 'It is consistent to suppose that the most miraculous and wonderful writings stood the best chance of being voted. As to the authenticity of the books, the vote stands in the place of it, for it can be traced no higher.'

In the year 324 the Christian Churches in the Mediterranean were deeply divided on an abstruse piece of theology. In the gospels mention had been made of the Father, the Son and the Holy Ghost. So far, however, they had existed in isolation, and many felt that the time had come to co-ordinate them. But just how was this to be done? All sorts of wondrous proposals were put forward:

If the Father begat the Son, he that was begotten had a beginning of existence; hence it is clear that there was a time when the Son was not.

No. The Son has always been with the Father, not only since time began, but before all time. For the Father could not have been so named unless he had a Son; and there could be no Son without a Father.

If you say that the Holy Ghost proceeds from the Father as the Son does, why do you not say that he is the brother of the Son? If he proceeds from the Son, why do you not say he is the grandson of the Father?

In the Greek-speaking Churches the debate raged to and fro, becoming to the west European mind increasingly tortuous. Finally

Alexander, the Bishop of Alexandria, and his archdeacon and successor Athanasius held that Jesus was as much God as God, that he was 'One with God the Father'. But an ascetic-looking priest on Alexander's staff by the name of Arius disagreed. He believed that the Christian faith could be best understood if it was agreed that while God was One and Indivisible, Christ was neither wholly God nor wholly man, but somewhere between the two. According to a Roman historian his formula was, 'If it be true that there was a time when the Son was not, it follows of necessity that he had his existence from the non-existent.' This would seem to be partly true, partly nonsense and partly a contradiction in terms. No wonder that when St Bernard came to study the theory of the Trinity centuries later, he found the whole thing incomprehensible.

Alexander was shocked by Arius's views and accused him of heresy. But Arius had his supporters, among them Eusebius and the Bishop of Nicodemia where Constantine had his palace. At the time Constantine was preparing for a trip to the River Jordan to be baptised. When told about the dispute, he despatched a joint letter to Alexander and Arius, saying that having looked into the matter, 'I find the cause to be of a truly insignificant nature, quite unworthy of such bitter contention', a verdict with which most of us today would agree; and he asked the pair to restore for him his 'quiet days and untroubled nights' by resolving the dispute.

But by now it had grown so bitter and the gulf between the two camps so wide that a consensus was impossible; and Constantine saw no option but to cancel his trip to the Jordan and to summon a meeting at the lakeside town of Nicea (today Iznik in Turkey) of all the Church's bishops the following year.

It must have been an impressive gathering with more than 500 bishops attending, some from as far away as Spain, Scythia (the area north of the Black Sea) Libya and Persia. The Bishop of Rome said he was too old to travel but sent two priests as his representatives. And Constantine, 'dazzlingly robed and dripping with gold and jewels of a decadence earlier emperors would have abhorred, took his place on a low, wrought-gold chair'.

Eusebius put the Arian point of view forcibly and asked his fellow bishops to accept a formula on which the whole assembly could agree:

> We believe in one God the Father Almighty, maker of all that is seen and unseen, and in one Lord Jesus Christ, the word of God, God from God, light from light, life from life, only begotten son, first-born of all creation, before all ages begotten from the Father, who for our salvation was incarnate and lived among man.

This is the Nicene Creed, part of the liturgy read at Holy Communion today. But it was not strong enough for Athanasius and others because it made Jesus seem less important than God, and in their view he was equally important.

The time came for Constantine, seated on his golden chair, to decide. He was no theologian, but a capable administrator and for him there was no problem in the deification of a human being. After all it had been the custom for previous Roman emperors to be made gods; he had deified his father Constantius, and after his own death he would be deified. He therefore ruled in favour of Alexander and Athanasius. The agreed formula, which Constantine required all the delegates to sign, established the doctrine of the Trinity, Father, Son and Holy Ghost being equal, and Father and Son 'of one substance'; a doctrine subsequently confirmed at the Council of Chalcedon in 451. This clearly meant something important to Christians of that time and later, but to the twentieth-century secular mind it is reminiscent of Humpty Dumpty in *Alice Through the Looking Glass* saying that for him words mean just what he chooses them to mean, neither more nor less. The concept of the Holy Ghost or Spirit is one that has perplexed not only St Bernard but many other Christians through the ages and indeed it is difficult to know what is meant by it. If it is trying to say that the Trinity in all its aspects is divine, then it is worth remembering that 'divine' and 'holy' and 'sacred' are not descriptions in the way that 'blue' and 'fat' and 'lame' are descriptions and provable, but attributes bestowed on gods or places by some humans and with which other humans may or may not agree.

All the bishops signed as ordered, even Eusebius, Arius and their followers, but some came to regret it. 'We committed an impious act, O Prince,' the Bishop of Nicodemia told Constantine, 'by subscribing to a blasphemy for fear of you.' Nor was there a word in the Nicene declaration about the ethos of Jesus's teaching.

In declaring Jesus one with the Father, Very God of Very God, the Nicene declaration had two important consequences. Firstly it meant that the Jews had killed God, a belief which became the genesis of the anti-Semitic sanctions and pogroms that were to disfigure European history during the next 1,500 years and find their hideous culmination in the Holocaust. Secondly, if Christ was God, where did that leave his mother? Was she not divine too? The matter had not merited discussion before, but now it increasingly came to be debated and finally in 431 at the Council of Ephesus (a few miles down the coast from Nicea) it was agreed that Mary should be deemed *theotokos*, literally God-bearing and therefore Mother of God. The mind-boggling cult of the virgin mother was now official, and 1,400 years later, in 1854, Pope Pius IX made it an article of faith for all Catholics that Mary should be considered to have been immaculately conceived, i.e. from the moment of her conception incapable of sin. Mindless romanticism could hardly go further.

And the word spread and spread: eastwards to Persia and down the Red Sea to Malabar and Socotra, to Ceylon and India and even on to parts of China; southwards to North Africa, westwards to Spain and Portugal; northwards to France and Germany and beyond. Long before Constantine had made the empire Christian, Origen was writing with foresight: 'By the coming of Christ, the land of Britain accepts belief in the one God.[1] So do the Moors of Africa. So does the whole globe. There are churches now on the frontiers of the world, and all the earth shouts for joy to the God of Israel.'

In Rome and Constantinople, however, great changes were taking place in the life of the Church and its senior clergy. What had earlier begun as a small victimised group of believers had now grown into an autocracy, dedicated to pageantry, power and riches. Bishops, many of whom were entitled to a quarter of Church revenues of their see, dressed extravagantly, some in the manner of wealthy noblemen. Jerome complained of them and lesser clergy who set out to flatter and deceive silly, rich women. 'They think of nothing but their clothes, use scent and smooth out the creases in their boots. They curl their hair with tongs, their fingers glitter with rings.' In vain did Jerome and John Chrysostom, who led frugal lives themselves, protest that this was not Christ's teaching.

Church services too became more elaborate and ornamental with the lavish use of incense and ever richer vestments. Music was introduced with antiphonal singing of psalms and later Gregorian chanting. The churches themselves which had begun as private houses for prayer meetings became under Pope Damasus basilicas, cathedrals with room for several hundred worshippers, and with furnishings inlaid with coloured mosaics and gold.

In the matter of the acquisition of Church power at this time two men were outstanding. One was Bishop Ambrose of Milan, a patrician whose father had been prefect of half of Gaul, and described as 'a small, frail man with a high forehead, long melancholy face and huge eyes'.

Elevated from unbaptised layman to bishop in the space of eight days, his appointment was seen as a boost for Trinitarianism against the increasingly Arian east. He was a superb administrator, a scourge of the pagans, a believer in all senior clergy being drawn from the educated upper classes, and with his patrician's natural authority became the first of the Roman bishops to insist on the secular power conforming to the spiritual; not so much *imperium in imperio* as equal partners, with the Church the slightly more equal of the two. In 388 when a Jewish synagogue at Callinicum on the Euphrates was burned down on the orders of the local bishop, the emperor Theodosius, in line with the long-established imperial policy of live and let live, ordered it to be rebuilt at the Church's expense. Ambrose challenged this ruling, seeing it as a humiliation of the local bishop and his congregation and, echoing the gospel, wrote to Theodosius in terms of the Church rendering unto Caesar the things that were his but unto God the things that were God's. 'What is more important,' he wrote, 'the parade of discipline or the cause of religion? The civil law is secondary to religious interest.' And Theodosius was obliged to give way.

On a second and more famous occasion Ambrose humiliated Theodosius publicly. In 390 there was a riot in the city of Thessalonica in Greece because a popular charioteer had been put in prison. In the course of the riot the governor of the city was lynched. Theodosius gave orders for the rioters, some 5,000 in all, to be invited to the local amphitheatre to see a special performance. When they were inside, the gates were locked by Roman soldiers and in the course of the next three hours the 5,000 were massacred. When Ambrose heard of this he excommunicated Theodosius and refused to give him the sacraments until he had done public penance. For a long time Theodosius held out against the threat but in the end he discarded his imperial robes and asked public pardon. Not until he had repeated the penance on several further occasions did Ambrose sufficiently relent to give him the sacraments on Christmas Day. This was not just the triumph of one man's will over another's but of that of the spiritual over the temporal.

The other great churchman of his age, and even more authoritarian than Ambrose, was Augustine whose two books, *Confessions* and *On the City of God*, have become classics of their kind. He was born in what is now Tunisia of a pagan father and Christian mother. While studying at Carthage he enjoyed the services of a concubine who bore him a son; and it may have been the memory of this relationship that led to his famously endearing prayer: 'Oh, God, please make me chaste, but not just yet.' In time he went with his son to Milan where he was personally baptised by Ambrose who pushed him under the pool three times before clothing him in a white robe and giving him a candle. Later he returned to North Africa and in 396 became Bishop of Hippo, now Bone.

Powerful as the western Church now was, Augustine like Ambrose, knew that it could only retain its power with unity, and that therefore

the various semi-Christian splinter groups which still flourished had
to be crushed. With Augustine's approval Church and state pursued
heretics and dissidents vigorously. Jerome, author of the Vulgate,
the first Latin translation of the Bible from the Hebrew, spoke of
hideous tortures inflicted on those who refused to recant, red-hot
plates applied to the genitals, laceration with whips tipped with lead.
Augustine approved of violence to encourage discipline and ensure
conformity. 'If discipline were removed,' he said, 'there would be
chaos. Take away the barriers created by the laws and men's brazen
capacity to do harm, their urge to self-indulgence would rage to the
full.' Ambrose took a broadly similar view. Dissenters were traitors
to the state and those guilty of error enemies of society to be forcibly
exiled. And who were to be the judges of error? The Church, of
course, prosecutor too. Here was a living example of the dictum
first uttered by Lord Acton 1,500 years later, that power tends to
corrupt but absolute power corrupts absolutely. Here lay the road to
the Inquisition.

Yet as Ranke-Heinemann shows, what exercised the minds of the
Church leaders more than almost anything else at this time was
the matter of sex and sin, of the difficulties of reconciling in our
natures the idealistic and the animal. It was a subject to which the
Ancients had given much thought too. Plato, Aristotle, Hippocrates
and others all came to regard sexual indulgence as corrosive of
male energy, and some Greek doctors advocated celibacy instead
of satisfying lust. In the centuries before and immediately after
Christ the gloomy Stoics were to the fore in opposing sex for
pleasure and regarded marriage as a refuge for those who found
lust irresistible.

'Do nothing for the sake of enjoyment,' wrote Seneca, and
gradually the idea took root, both in Rome and among the early
Christians, that sexual indulgence that was not for procreation was
immoral. In many early books the elephant was held up as a model
of correct behaviour. 'Out of modesty,' declared Pliny the Elder,
'elephants never mate except in secret. They do it only every two

years and then, it is said, never for more than five days. On the sixth day they bathe in the river . . . They are unacquainted with adultery.'

The Stoics were followed by the Gnostics, an even gloomier sect, though at one time a challenge to early Christianity. The Jewish historian Josephus recorded some of the Jewish Essenes turning away from sex as though it were evil and embracing continence as a virtue; and the Hellenic Jew Philo of Alexandria was one of the first to propagate the notion, taken up so enthusiastically by the Catholic Church, of banning contraception. 'Those who during intercourse,' he said, 'bring about the destruction of the seed are enemies of nature.' Yet it had rarely occurred to the sages of the classical world morally to equate sperm with its consequences.

Because of the fall of Adam in the garden, and unlike the leaders of the Eastern Orthodox Church, both Ambrose and Augustine believed in original sin and that the responsibility for it lay with the genitals. Men should be ashamed of the lusts they felt stirring there; and it was wrong for married couples to make love whenever they felt like it instead of waiting until bedtime.

For women Ambrose believed the ideal state to be virginity, a choice which would redeem the sin of her parents in conceiving her – an antiquarian fancy which today's generation, to whom fornication and adultery are commonplace, would be at a loss to understand. Virgins should remain silent and avoid temptations where temptations might lurk. If a virgin was suspected of having had intercourse, she should be medically examined on the orders of the bishop. If found guilty, her head would be shaved and she would be required to do penance for life. Yet although suicide was then considered a crime against God and suicides were denied Christian burial, a virgin who committed suicide rather than submit to rape or forced prostitution would be forgiven.

The unpleasant Jerome on the other hand found virgins danger-ous and dirty – for the crafty ways in which they could ensnare men. He was tortured by carnal longings but believed it would be wicked to indulge them, thus giving Renaissance artists an excuse to include naked women in their portrayal of Jerome's temptation. Like Ambrose he tolerated marriage but thought it only one degree less sinful than fornication

But of all the early Church Fathers, it was Augustine who was the most obsessive about sex and sexual morality, fusing Christianity and a hatred of sexual pleasure into a systematic unity. Although a passionate lover in his youth, after his baptism by Ambrose he became a champion of asceticism. Like many celibates, he was terrified of women and of their power to attract.

The solution for Augustine was to avoid their company altogether. His friend Possidius records: 'No woman ever set foot inside his house. He never spoke with a woman except in the presence of a third party or outside the parlour. He made no exceptions, not even for his own elder sister and nieces, all three of them nuns.' Ranke-Heinemann says that like many neurotics he regarded love and sexuality as things apart and because of it generated a 1,500-year-long anxiety about sex and an enduring hostility to it. 'He dramatises the fear of sexual pleasure, equating it with perdition in such a way that anyone who tries to follow his train of thought will have the sense of being trapped in a nightmare.' For any man to gain pleasure from having sex with his wife and to arouse her sufficiently to gain pleasure from it too, said Augustine, was like treating her as a whore and for himself to become an adulterer.[2]

Like Ambrose, Augustine saw virginity as a moral ideal and marriage without sex as the next best thing. 'The husband and wife reach greater heights of moral development by jointly renouncing intercourse . . . anyone who has arrived at perfect love of God surely has no more than spiritual desire for children.' And because to him sex was unclean as well as sinful, he recommended that at certain times such as Sundays, during Lent, before communion and after prayers, people should not indulge in it. Prayer pleased God more, he said, when a supplicant was free of carnal desires.

Another matter to exercise the minds of the early Christian prelates and about which they knew little was menstruation. It will be recalled that in the Old Testament (Leviticus) a menstruating woman was considered unclean for seven days after her period and that anyone who touched her during her period was also unclean. Menstrual blood was thought to be poisonous and in the seventh century CE one Isidore of Seville blandly declared that when whoever or whatever came into contact with it, 'fruits do not sprout, blossoms fade, grasses wither, iron rusts, brass turns black, dogs that taste it get rabies'. In the thirteenth century the Church regarded intercourse during menstruation as a mortal sin because of the damage it might inflict on any offspring (itself a virtual impossibility). A famous preacher of the time, Berthold of Regensburg, told a gullible congregation on no evidence at all that children born from intercourse during menstruation could become lepers, epileptics, hump-backed, blind, idiots, have heads the shape of mallets.

Sperm, on the other hand, was life and the early Church laid down penances for those who wasted it. Apart from the sin of masturbation there were three ways of wasting it: anal intercourse, oral intercourse and *coitus interruptus* (withdrawing the penis just before ejaculation). *Coitus reservatus* was considered sinless because it meant withdrawing the penis but not ejaculating – a frustrating experience as anyone who has practised it knows. The Anglo-Saxon penitential of around 800 CE laid down seven years or a lifelong penance for oral intercourse, ten years for anal intercourse and seven to ten years for the taking of an abortifacient to destroy the foetus. Penances of other penitentials were similar, though taking an abortifacient often incurred lesser penalties than other offences.

The Church also laid down penances for methods of intercourse which did not have its blessing. The so-called missionary position (the husband on top of the wife) was approved of, but the woman sitting astride the man was thought to be particularly lustful as well as an obstacle to conception (presumably because of the law of gravity): the penitential of Egbert, Archbishop of York, required three years' penance for this. From the eighth century confessors were instructed to ask such questions as, 'Have you coupled with your wife or any other woman from behind, like dogs?' it being thought that this method was also unfriendly to conception: the penance was ten days on bread and water, the same for copulating with a woman in menstruation. For a husband to couple with a wife during pregnancy it was twenty days of bread and water, during Lent forty days, when drunk twenty days.[3]

So obsessed were the Church Fathers with the belief that sexual pleasure of any kind was a sin that they even debated whether involuntary nocturnal emissions (what we call wet dreams) of priests and monks were sinful or not. The general opinion was that those who were aware of the pleasure sinned venially, but those who surrendered to it wholeheartedly, savouring every delicious moment, sinned mortally.

In the midst of all these strictures there spoke one voice of sanity, that of the pagan emperor Julian, son of Constantius and half-brother of Constantine. This was his view of the doctrine of original sin:

> You ask me why I would not consent to the idea that there is a sin that is part of human nature. I answer, it is improbable; it is untrue; it is unjust and impious. It makes it seem as if the devil were the maker of men. It violates and destroys the freedom of the will . . . by saying that men are so incapable of virtue that in the very womb of their mothers they are filled with bygone sins . . .

But in the new, prevailing Christian climate, these words were carried away on the wind. In its authoritarianism and the homage paid to it by the state, in its intolerance and extreme puritanism, the Roman Catholic Church had now given itself an identity, a *persona* that for better or worse was to remain its hallmark for the next 1,400 years; and only then begin its slow decline.

Chapter Six

CHRISTIANITY'S KILLING FIELDS

1. Murders of Infidels and Heretics

Leaving aside the allegedly supernatural aspects of the life of Jesus which, as I have already indicated, I believe to be fantasies, his story was essentially one of service to his fellow men and women. In his preaching of love, mercy, forgiveness, unselfishness, he represented human altruism at its best. These are qualities approved and encouraged by people of most religions and of none, but which the Christian Churches have hijacked as their own and called Christian values. Jesus left a set of rules to live by, largely attributed to Moses and which are mostly as valid today as when the scriptures and gospels first recorded them. Do not kill, do not steal, do not lie, do not covet, do not commit adultery; be humble, aim for righteousness, give to the poor. Asked what were the greatest of the commandments Jesus said, firstly to love God with all thy heart and soul and mind and secondly to love thy neighbour as thyself: 'there is none other commandment greater than these.' Follow them and you will obtain everlasting life and be received into heaven by God the Father. But, if you fail to follow them and have not faith, you will be damned for ever and consigned to the flames of hell. The Jews were the first to preach the doctrine of rewards and punishments. Jesus followed them. Paul, in even greater intensity, followed Jesus.

You would have thought that those who ran the Christian Churches in the years ahead would have subscribed to these precepts, indeed that it was because they subscribed to them that they had become clerics. Yet in all the millions of words that have been written about the history of the Christian Churches between, say, 500 and 1800, there is very little recorded about love and mercy and forgiveness – I do not mean of God to humans but of humans to humans. There are on the other hand many accounts of Christian barbarities, some unspeakable, perpetrated by the Churches on those who disagreed with them; and I should warn the reader, as television companies sometimes warn the viewer, that some of what follows may be found distressing. For the next thousand years and more, heresy was regarded as a threat to the established order, to the whole fabric of society; and when it came to maintaining that fabric, Christian charity and compassion were ignored or forgotten. After all, Jesus himself had said that he had come, not to send peace but a sword, and he had also promised a hard time for unbelievers. St Augustine too had preached the just war, that violence in support of the faith could be justified so long as it was expressing the will of God; so that in its suppression of heresy the Church managed to convince itself that might was right and God firmly on its side.

Any criticism of the Papacy was regarded as heresy and therefore worthy of punishment. In 710, for instance, the Archbishop of Ravenna disobeyed a command of Pope Constantine for which the Pope ordered his eyes to be gouged out. This seems to have been a standard punishment at the time. When Pope Paul I died fifty years later, a local duke named Toto engineered a coup with three brothers in which one, another Constantine, was proclaimed Pope in Paul's place. A second claimant, one Christopher, resisted the coup, had his eyes gouged out, suffered other mutilations and died of his injuries a few days later. The same fate was meted out to another of the brothers and to his chief clerical supporter who in addition had his tongue cut out, thus being rendered dumb as well as blind. Constantine himself was dragged from his palace, locked up in a monastery where he too was blinded before being thrown at the feet of a further claimant who became Pope Stephen III.

Six years later Charlemagne, the Christian King of the Franks, came to Rome and under his protection Pope Hadrian I enjoyed a settled pontificate for the next twenty years. However, by 782, when the non-Christian Saxons rebelled against the Franks, Charlemagne went north to defeat them. Four and a half thousand Saxon soldiers were captured and for worshipping a non-Christian god Charlemagne ordered them all to be beheaded. It must have taken quite a time. But he was back in Rome in 799, having taken pity on the new Pope Leo III who had come begging for help after being set upon by the thugs of a rival claimant and narrowly escaped blinding and excision of the tongue; in return for which, while the two were celebrating Mass on Christmas Day 800, and Charlemagne was kneeling, Leo without warning placed a crown on Charlemagne's head to make him Holy Roman Emperor.

Christian barbarities abounded elsewhere. In England, which had become a Christian country in the seventh century, the Abbot of Glastonbury refused to say Mass until justice had been done to some counterfeiters by amputation of their hands. Later, when the Count of Champagne ordered that a man who had taken part in a duel was to be blinded and his goods confiscated St Bernard of Clairvaux sent him a reproof – not for the blinding but for the confiscation of goods which, he said, would unjustly harm his family.

Yet it was with the infidels rather than the heretics, with the enemy without rather than within, that the first major clashes with the Christian Church came. In the early years of the seventh century, around 610, an Arab merchant living in Mecca claimed that the angel Gabriel had spoken to him in a dream: 'Allah has made plain to you the religion which he enjoined upon Noah and Abraham and Moses and Jesus' (Koran 42:13).

Mohammed saw the last three and himself as messengers of Allah and the new religion which Allah had enjoined on them as Islam (literally 'submission to Allah'); and that its holy book, the Koran, dictated to Mohammed by the angel Gabriel (or so he said) would

109

become the Moslem equivalent of the Jewish Torah (the first five books of the Old Testament). Islam gave the Arabs of that time and place an identity, a cohesion which they had hitherto lacked and with it a restlessness, spurred by hunger, to expand. Three years after Mohammed's death Arab forces captured Damascus and the rest of Syria, Jerusalem and the rest of Palestine, then Alexandria and the rest of Egypt. In 652 they overran Persia and set up their own capital in Baghdad. Then they turned westwards, traversed the North African littoral until they reached and captured Carthage. Thence they crossed to Spain which they overran in six months and pressed on northwards; and it wasn't until they reached Tours near Poitiers in the middle of France that they were finally checked by Charles Martel, ruler of the Franks and grandfather of Charlemagne.

It is a wry thought that had the Arab forces overrun the rest of France and then England, as they might have done, then the newly established Christianity of both countries might have succumbed, and instead of our becoming Roman Catholics and Huguenots and Anglicans and Methodists as we did, we might all by now be devout Mussulmen, supplicating Allah on our prayer mats five times a day. As things turned out, most of the peoples of the Christianised countries which the Arabs had conquered were happy to convert to Islam. Apart from a sense of racial fraternity stretching from Alexandria to Carthage and beyond, the message of Islam was so simple: 'There is no God but Allah and Mohammed is his messenger.' No abstruse convolutions about Three-in-One and One-in-Three which was as far beyond Arab understanding as that of St Bernard and others. In the days of Augustine of Hippo, who had died in 430, the North African littoral, according to John Foster, supported 700 bishoprics: by the beginning of the eighth century, these had shrunk to between thirty and forty and would soon disappear altogether; while in Spain the Arabs had established so firm a hold that it would be another 800 years before Spain's Christians were able to expel them.

One notable aspect of the Arab conquests in the Middle East and North Africa is that they were for the most part bloodless. Furthermore, and because it was written in the Koran, Moslems were content to let Christians and Jews worship God in their own way, in Jerusalem, Alexandria and elsewhere, even though they believed the Christian claim that Jesus was the son of God to be blasphemy. As a result the three communities lived in relative harmony; and Christian craftsmen in Islamic-controlled cities who had designed mosaics and other ornamentation for Christian churches were happy to exercise their skills in doing whatever was required by way of adornment in Arab mosques. Other Christians learned the Arab tongue and came to appreciate Arab poems and romances. All this greatly shocked Christian pilgrims from the west. Yet, says one writer, 'there never was a demand from the Christians under Moslem rule to be liberated'.

Demand or not, liberated they were about to be. Under Pope Urban II, there grew in the course of the eleventh century the first stirrings of the movement that would culminate in the Crusades. Its motives were mixed, partly adventure, partly idealism – to regain for Christianity the holy places of Jerusalem – partly greed and partly to satisfy the powerful Christian propensity for violence. Addressing the crowd at a council held at Clermont, Pope Urban is said to have quoted Matthew in support of the First Crusade: 'And everyone that hath forsaken houses or brethren or sisters, or father or mother, or wife or children or lands, for my name's sake, shall receive an hundredfold and shall inherit everlasting life.' And in one mighty roar the Frankish crowd shouted back, 'God wills it.' The peasantry, for whom the main attraction of the adventure was the prospect of loot, were offered an additional bait. In an age when people were terrified of the punishments for their sins that awaited them in the afterlife and did penances (such as fasting, walking barefoot, wearing hair shirts) to absolve them, Urban decreed that no further penances to achieve salvation would be required of those who took part in the Crusade or even had contributed financially to it. As preparations went ahead, a variety of excuses was put forward to justify the coming slaughter. One popular slogan went, 'We shall slay for God's love', while St Bernard preached, 'A Christian glories in the death of a Moslem because Christ is glorified. The liberality of God is revealed in the death of a Christian, because he is led to his reward.' It was no part of Urban's plan for the Crusaders to try to convert the Moslems: in the light of the Moslem conversions that had occurred along the North African coast, he knew it would be futile to try.

And so in the year 1096 a body of French knights, their tunics embroidered with red crosses and led by two dukes, one of Normandy (son of William the Conqueror) the other of Lower Lorraine, and the Counts of Toulouse and Flanders and accompanied by a multitude of followers, set out for the Holy Land. They were joined by a body of German Crusaders who saw as their first task the terrorisation of rich Jews to hand over money to finance the campaign and then, because they hated the Jews even more than the Moslems (for killing Christ) began a pogrom against them; and, in a foretaste of the Holocaust, in cities like Mainz and Worms and Spier, butchered hundreds.[1]

By the autumn of 1097 the Crusaders had reached Antioch which, after a long siege, they succeeded in entering. Buried in its cathedral they found a piece of iron, encrusted in gold and jewels, which was said to be part of the lance that had pierced Christ's side – the Holy Lance. To Christians of the Dark Ages and later, relics of the Christian story possessed magical powers, and inspired by the sight and possession of this piece of iron, the Crusaders attacked the Moslem forces which had come to raise the siege and routed them.

On the plateau before Jerusalem the Crusaders were met by a body of eastern Christians. They also had cherished relics, a piece of wood which they claimed had been part of Noah's ark and another which they said was part of the crib in which Christ had lain as a baby – assertions that bore about as much relation to reality as the alleged portion of the Holy Lance.

If the presence of these objects instilled in the minds of the Crusaders a timely reminder of what had brought them here – to avenge the death of Christ on the despoilers of his holy places – the sight of what confronted them above the walls of Jerusalem – the golden-capped Dome of the Rock and beside it an imam calling the faithful to prayer from the minaret of the al-Aqsa mosque – provoked them to fury.

Yet for forty days during which the Moslem forces resisted the siege, their fury had to be restrained; and the Crusaders spent the time circumambulating the city walls, singing psalms and praising God in those places outside the walls – Mount Zion, the Garden of Gethsemane, the Mount of Olives and Calvary – where, they believed, his only son had suffered and died a thousand years before.

The attackers had two siege towers. The defenders set one alight with all the people inside it, but while this was *en train* the Crusaders in the other succeeded in breaching the defences near Herod's Gate, and poured in. Apart from the commander of the garrison and his guard who were given safe conduct to Ascalon they spared none. The Moslems who had sought refuge in the al-Aqsa mosque were all slaughtered, while the Jews who had thought to find sanctuary in their synagogues were burned alive inside them. It is estimated that between 30,000 and 40,000 Jews and Moslems were killed in two days. A Christian knight, Count Raymond of Aguilers, wrote:

> Wonderful sights were to be seen. Some of our men cut off the heads of our enemies, others shot them with arrows so that they fell from the towers; others tortured them longer by casting them into the flames. Piles of heads, hands and feet were to be seen in the streets of the city.
>
> What more shall I tell? Not one of them was allowed to live. They did not spare the women or children. The horses waded in blood up to their knees, nay up to the bridle. It was a just and wonderful judgement of God.

And that was not all. The Greek priests who guarded the shrine of the Holy Sepulchre were tortured until they revealed the where-abouts of what they claimed to be the True Cross on which Christ had died. Later Caesarea and Beirut suffered the same fate as Jerusalem: other Crusaders massacred the Moslems in their mosques. The Moslem memory is a long one, and the mindless barbarism of the Crusaders against people who had done them no harm and who had practised a policy of live and let live, exacerbated by British and

113

French interference in the Middle East in the first part of the twentieth century, led to a deep distrust of and hostility to the Christian west which is still with us today.

In the Second Crusade ships in the Red Sea carrying pilgrims on their haj to Mecca were sunk by Crusaders with huge loss of life. In 1187 Saladin recaptured Jerusalem peace-ably. The Third Crusade in which King Richard of England took part failed to retake the city, but did succeed in establishing the right of Christian pilgrims to visit the holy sites. The Fourth Crusade was launched from Venice whose doge provided the ships and money for the campaign which would be repaid by booty acquired in the course of it. But the expedition never travelled further than Constantinople where the Crusaders, dazzled by the riches of the then richest city in the world, and hating Greek Orthodox Christians even more than the Moslems, went on the rampage. The great church of St Sophia was ransacked, its hangings torn down and silver icons stolen. Soldiers drank the sacramental wine out of the chalices, a prostitute sat on the patriarch's throne and sang a bawdy song, nuns were indiscriminately raped. Treasures and works of art of all kinds were shipped back to Venice in the doge's ships to the city's great enrichment. But the Pope was outraged. Massacring Moslem women and children and burning Jews was God's will and a way of achieving salvation, but despoiling Christians was another matter; and he described their actions as the works of the devil.

The Fifth Crusade went to Egypt and was a humiliating failure. The Sixth Crusade was not the inspiration of the Pope but of the new, young Holy Roman Emperor, Frederick II, who had been brought up in cosmopolitan Sicily, was an admirer of Islam, spoke Arabic fluently, and at his Sicilian court where lived many Moslems, ignored papal commands forbidding the muezzin to call the faithful to prayer. The Papacy reviled him, accused him of calling Christ and Moses impostors, of denying the virgin birth and dismissing the Eucharist as mumbo-jumbo. Pope Gregory IX excommunicated him, and his successor Innocent IV was party to a plot to have him assassinated. It misfired and as was the way with bungled plots in those days, the conspirators were blinded, mutilated and burned alive.

Because of his partiality to Islam, Frederick's Crusade was unlike any other. He also felt he had a claim on the kingship of Jerusalem by his recent marriage to Yolanda, daughter of John of Beirut. Furthermore he persuaded his friend the Egyptian sultan to agree that rather than indulge in a war that would benefit nobody, some form of compromise would be preferable. And so it came about that the two dominant religions of the Middle East would share the Holy City. The Temple area along with the Dome of the Rock and the al-Aqsa mosque would remain in Moslem hands while the rest of the city along with Bethlehem, a corridor leading to the sea at Jaffa as well as western Galilee and Nazareth would go to Christianity. This arrangement would be guaranteed for ten years. To cap it all, the ruler of Nablus took Frederick to Jerusalem to be crowned. Because of his excommunication, no Christian priest would perform the ceremony, so in the church of the Holy Sepulchre he took a crown and put it on his head, just as Napoleon Bonaparte was to do in Notre-Dame 600 years later. Without any military action or the approval of the Pope, he had regained for the faith he had been barred from practising the right of access of Christians to its holy places, the *fons et origo* of where it all began.

Back in Europe Frederick kept up a tirade against papal corruption and the monstrous growth of papal power, warning other European monarchs of the stranglehold the Pope had or wanted to have on them. 'Has not the King of England seen his father King John held in excommunication until both he and his kingdom were made tributary?' he asked. Ravenous wolves, he called the Pope and his hierarchy, 'who sent legates hither and thither to excommunicate, to suspend, to punish, not as sowers of seed, which is the word of God, but to extort money, to harvest and reap that which they did not sow'.

After the ten-year truce between the Egyptian sultan and Frederick II had expired, there followed two more Crusades, the Seventh and Eighth. Both were fiascos. Any hopes the Seventh Crusaders might have had of occupying Jerusalem were thwarted by a bunch of brigands known as the Khwarismian Turks who, fleeing from the

Mongols in 1244, reached it before them, and exhibited a savagery to rival that of the First Crusaders. The monks and nuns in the Armenian convent were slaughtered as were the priests of the Holy Sepulchre. The bones of the previous kings were dug up from their tombs and scattered, and much of the city put to the torch. Of 6,000 citizens who had been promised safe conduct along the strip of land to Jaffa and the sea, only 300 arrived. Little wonder that a few years later the German monk Burchard was writing: 'Today there are very few inhabitants in so great a city, for the people in it live in continual terror.'

Contemporaneous with its wars against the Moslems, which left nothing but a legacy of bitterness, the Papacy turned to heretics nearer home. These were the people of Languedoc and Provence, known sometimes as the Albigenses because many of them lived around Albi, and sometimes as Cathari, 'the perfect ones', because of the purity of their beliefs. What made them heretical and enraged Pope Innocent III was that they felt no need for a Catholic priesthood; they believed in approaching God directly through a life of abstinence and prayer, and they had rejected the dogmas of damnation and hell.

The trigger for the Crusade against them was the assassination in 1208 in Toulouse of the papal legate by a servant of Raymond, Count of Toulouse. Innocent declared the murdered legate a martyr and called the Cathari children of Satan, 'heretics worse even than the Saracens'.[2] The Abbot of Citeaux took the bloodstained habit of the murdered legate north with him and persuaded the King of France, Philip II, and his barons to mount an expedition against the Cathars under Simon de Montfort. As with the Jerusalem Crusades, those who took part in this one were promised remission of sins as well as a moratorium on their debts and the prospect of plunder in a country far richer and more fertile than that of the Holy Land. In 1209 the force under de Montfort marched south and attacked the pretty town of Béziers. Not only was the town ransacked and its buildings set alight, but the slaughter of the inhabitants was on the scale of that of the First Crusade: Abbot Arnald Almaric estimated that between 15,000 and 20,000 had been killed. Asked beforehand how de Montfort's men would be able to distinguish between the town's practising Catholics and the Pope's children of Satan, he said, 'Kill them all. God will look after his own.' God however was powerless to do so, and no mercy was shown on account of order, age or sex. Prisoners taken were blinded, mutilated, dragged behind the hooves of horses and used as target practice by archers. Carcassonne and its spoils surrendered soon after, and in his zeal to execute faithfully the Pope's commands to stamp out all heresy in the south of France, de Montfort blinded and cut off the noses of the defenders of Bram and organised three mass burnings of Cathars who refused to recant. Then he invested Toulouse, where Catholics and Cathars fought and killed each other in the streets, until it too surrendered and was returned to Catholic orthodoxy.

It was the papal obsession with heresy that led Pope Gregory IX in 1231 to set up the most dreaded institution of medieval Christendom: the Papal Inquisition. The Inquisitors were the Dominican Black Friars (their robes were black) and the courts over which they presided ignored all recognised rules of court procedure. Prosecution witnesses and informers did not have to give their names, the accused were given no right of defence and there was no appeal against the verdict. Those who refused to confess were kept in prison and summoned again and again until they yielded, for convictions were what was required. Because many remained stubborn, torture was gradually introduced, though forbidden for pregnant women until they had been delivered; and only 'mild' torture was permitted for children and old people.

Punishments varied, from the wearing of yellow crosses, which made future employment hazardous, to terms of imprisonment, often chained to the walls of a dungeon and sometimes for life, and from 1252 to being strangled or burned (beheading was ruled out because of the Church's distaste for the shedding of blood). Some heretics were pursued not only to the grave but beyond. The corpses of those posthumously convicted (a not uncommon occurrence) were dug up from the consecrated ground where they were buried, dragged through the streets and burned on the common rubbish tip. Their houses were knocked down to make room for latrines and their children and grandchildren forbidden any office.

For the twentieth-century mind to understand the papal view of heresy it is necessary to understand the medieval mind. Belief in, and fear of, God was universal and undisputed and any dissent from it was considered the greatest of all sins; it was greater than treason against a king because it was an offence against the greatest of all kings. Also, as Professor Bainton put it, 'to burn a heretic was an act of love towards the community, deterring by fear others who were inclined to the same sin. It was an act of love towards the heretic, for he might recant by fear of the fire and save his soul.' To avoid heresy everyone from the age of fourteen was required to promise publicly every two years to remain a good Catholic, take communion at least three times a year and to denounce heresy whenever and wherever it might be found.

If in external affairs the Catholic Church continued to be preoccupied with the exercise of violence, internally in the matter of the conduct and image of the priesthood, it was still obsessed by sex. It will be recalled that during the time of St Augustine and Ambrose bishops and priests had been permitted to marry, though Church leaders had advocated celibacy, both in the Church and without, as a marital ideal.

But with the passing of the first millennium there came a change. Celibacy in the priesthood was to be obligatory for all. In 1139 Pope Innocent II declared that priests could no longer marry, and later at the Council of Trent married men were barred from joining the priesthood. This was no sudden decision, for the idea that those in close proximity to the gods should observe sexual abstinence derived from pagan times and was always, as it were, hanging in the air. From now on, and to the consternation of many long-and-happily-married women, married priests were not allowed to sleep in the same bedrooms as their wives and married bishops were urged to regard their wives as sisters; on travels they were expected to share their bedrooms with a cleric so as to pre-empt intercourse. Thus were many good marriages needlessly destroyed.

In Germany, after priestly celibacy had become canon law, St Boniface persecuted many lascivious priests, monks and nuns. A priest found guilty of intercourse was to be imprisoned for two years, then publicly flogged. Monks and nuns were to be beaten three times, then imprisoned for a year during which the nuns, like French female fraternisers with the Nazis in the Second World War, had their hair shaved off. When the Eastern Orthodox Church split with Rome over enforced priestly celibacy, a Roman cardinal who attended a Mass at Byzantium could write: 'Young husbands, exhausted from carnal lust, serve at the altar. And immediately after, they again embrace their wives with hands that have been hallowed by the immaculate body of Christ [i.e. the sacramental bread]. This is not the mark of a true faith, but an invention of Satan.' Later a pious zealot named Peter Damiani declared that only virginal hands should be allowed to touch the bread that was the body of Christ: when reminded that St Peter, the first Pope, was married, he commented, 'Peter was able to wash away the filth of marriage with the blood of his martyrdom.'

As is well known, Jesus was on open friendly terms with women and happy to be in their company. But with his disciples of the first millennium it was a different matter. The long tradition of women being treated as second-class citizens in a bachelor-dominated society persisted, much to their detriment and to that of society as a whole. Senior churchmen did not understand or want to understand them, treating them with a mixture of repressed fear, arrogance and distrust. The fear was largely because of their power to attract. St Chrysostom, speaking untruthfully of 'their ready inclination to sin', said: 'The eye of woman touches and disturbs our souls, and not only the eyes of the unbridled woman but that of the decent one as well.'

To prevent temptation, synods in the sixth and seventh centuries followed Augustine's example of not allowing women to enter his house. That of Tours in 567 decreed that the only women permitted in a cleric's house were his mother, sisters and daughters. Nuns, widows, maidservants were barred; while the synod at Toledo directed that clerics found harbouring strange women in their houses were to be punished and the women to be sold by the bishop into slavery.

But these synods had not reckoned on the force of the sexual drive (the greatest human imperative after the satisfaction of hunger and thirst) on young men ordered to be celibate. In 604 Pope Gregory I warned bishops not to live together even with mothers and sisters; and in 658 the synod of Nantes reported priests having wicked relationships with their mothers and other relatives. 'Horrible acts of incest,' it reported, 'have already taken place'; while in 888 the synod of Metz recorded that some clerics had gone astray, 'even with their own sisters'.

Further indignities were inflicted on women during the first millennium. One decree said they could take communion only if their hands as well as faces were veiled; another that they could not write or receive letters in their own name; a third that in church they should silently pray the Psalms: 'they should speak only with their lips so that nothing can be heard.' They were also forbidden to touch the priestly vestments or to serve at the altar (a decree confirmed by Pope John Paul II in 1980); nor were they permitted to sing in church, which led to boy sopranos having their testicles removed so as to sing castrati to the greater glory of God. All in all, says Ranke-Heinemann, in the repression, defamation and demonisation of women, the whole of Church history added up to one long, arbitrary, narrow-minded masculine despotism over the female sex. 'The male Church has never understood that the reality of the Church is based on the shared humanity of man and woman.'

Two more arch puritans were Thomas Aquinas and Albert the Great who both lived in the thirteenth century. Albert said a number of wonderfully dotty things such as, 'Woman is less qualified [than man] for moral behaviour. For the woman contains more liquid than the man and it is a property of liquid to take things up easily and to hold on to them poorly.' Also, 'Frequent intercourse makes one bald sooner because sex dries you out and cools you off.' Albert claimed that those who over-indulge in sex are followed around by dogs. 'Dogs love strong smells and run after cadavers, and the body of a person who has a great deal of intercourse approaches the condition of a cadaver because of all the rotten semen.'

In hatred of sexual pleasure, Ranke-Heinemann sees St Thomas Aquinas as inheriting the mantle of Augustine. 'Perpetual continence,' he declared, 'is necessary for perfect piety.' Virgins of either sex will receive 100 per cent heavenly reward, widows and widowers 60 per cent and married people only 30 per cent. *Any* kind of contraception was 'quasi-murder'; and all sexual acts not intended for procreation[3] were described by Thomas as 'filthiness', 'disgustingness', 'staining', and the like. Deviation from the missionary position, he said, was an unnatural vice *and worse than intercourse with one's own mother* (my italics) which, if incestuous, was at least natural in that it opened the way to procreation; while a later cleric, Bernardine of Siena, thought it better for a woman to have relations 'in the natural manner' with her father rather than with her husband in an unnatural manner.

There was some easement among Catholics with the coming of the Reformation when scores of Catholic priests, including Luther himself, abandoned the burden of celibacy by marrying. But for the Catholics left behind, the doctrines of continence and decrees against *coitus interruptus* and contraception continued.

Throughout Europe, for the next hundred years, the power and influence of the Papacy was paramount. Pope Boniface VIII spelled it out in *Unam Sanctum*, his pronouncement of 1302 when he said, 'It is altogether necessary to salvation of every human creature to be subject to the Roman pontiff.' There was almost no aspect of life that did not concern the Holy See and did not require papal approval. Was a certain monastery to be permitted three cows or only two? Was sex permitted on Sundays? How often should one fast? As time went by there was growing antagonism between the European kings and princes over which a succession of Popes thought they should have dominion, the temporal power, as Boniface put it, being subject to the spiritual. The clergy, said Boniface, wherever they lived, were not to pay taxes; those who did and the officials to whom they paid it would be excommunicated, a hollow threat today (as the IRA have recognised) but promising hell-fire then. Edward I of England responded by withdrawing the protection of the courts from clergy who refused to pay tax and by ordering his sheriffs to seize Church lands. In France King Philip put an end to subsidising the Papacy by gifts of bullion to Rome. Boniface threatened excommunication. Philip's response was to charge the Pope at the court of the Louvre with illegal election, simony, immorality and heresy and to obtain the authority of the court to have Boniface arrested. He duly was, though he died soon after; but future Popes were to find that *vis à vis* nation states their power had been gravely weakened.

In matters of heresy however there was little change. Philip of France had long wanted to disband the Knights Templar who had led the Crusades to Jerusalem because he coveted their wealth. Fortuitously for him, a renegade knight brought charges of heresy against his fellow Templars, claiming that they worshipped the head of a cat, blasphemed the Mass, practised sodomy and had betrayed the holy places to the infidels. No evidence was brought in support of the charges but they were enough in themselves for the entire order to be arrested overnight. Torture was used to extract confessions, whereupon the Pope, Clement V, took over. Most of the knights then retracted their confessions but in 1314 they were sentenced to death and fifty-nine of them including their grand master were burned in Paris at the stake.

2. Fake Relics. Papal Sodomy. The Spanish Inquisition

As with all religions, magic and superstition formed an integral part of Christian faith in the Church's early history, as they still do today, and nowhere was this more evident than in the collections of relics:

animal, vegetable and mineral artefacts allegedly from the days of the scriptures and gospels which, to those who saw or touched them, would ward off evil spirits and give protection and comfort to believers just as crucifixes, St Christopher medallions, rosaries and worry beads perform a similar service today. To us, on the eve of the third millennium after Christ, it is plain that most if not all of the relics collected were fakes and laughable fakes at that: but, as I mentioned earlier when assessing the veracity of the gospels, people were even more gullible then than they are now, and proof of an allegation in order to confirm it was not a factor that entered their consciousnesses.[4] When the portion of the lance – the so-called Holy Lance that was said to have pierced Christ's side – was dug up in Antioch Cathedral and shown to the First Crusaders, it never occurred to them, as it would to most of us, to question whether it was what it claimed to be. Similarly with the alleged True Cross (so called because of the numbers of fakes in circulation) kept by the Greek priests who guarded the Holy Sepulchre. All believed implicitly and without question that the nailed hands and legs of Christ had been spread-eagled upon it; and they felt a sense of awe and wonder at being given the privilege of observing and handling an object which brought them into direct contact with their Saviour.

The lists of contents of some of the grander collections have come down to us. Among the 242 items housed at Reading Abbey in England during the twelfth century for instance were the magical rods of Moses and Aaron which had struck water from the rocks in the wilderness, various bits of John the Baptist, Jesus's swaddling clothes and a shoe, blood and water from his side, his mother's hair, bed and belt, and leftovers from the feeding of the 5,000 and the Last Supper.

During the thirteenth century there are records of relics being kept in the Lateran Basilica in Rome, among them the heads of St Peter and St Paul encased in resplendent reliquaries, the Ark of the Covenant, the tablets on which God had written the Ten Commandments for Moses, another rod of Aaron, an urn full of manna which God had dropped from heaven to feed the children of Israel in the wilderness, the shirt of John the Baptist, a garment worn by Jesus's mother, remains of the five loaves and two fishes from the feeding of the 5,000 and the dining-table on which Christ and his disciples had eaten the Last Supper. In the nearby chapel of St Lawrence were housed Christ's umbilical cord and foreskin whose reliquary was a crucifix filled with oil.

Other thirteenth-century relics included the bodies of saints, in whole or part, but mostly bones. Shown a bone said to have been that of Mary Magdalene, a Bishop of Lincoln bit off one end when no one was looking and carried the fragment back home to be admired in Lincoln Cathedral. Chartres Cathedral had a collection which must have tested the beliefs of all but the most devout: Christ's milk teeth, tears and drops of blood he had shed, and Le Saint Prépuce, his foreskin (at one time no fewer than fifteen churches or cathedrals in Europe claimed to possess it), though whether it was removed before or after the resurrection is not recorded.[5]

The biggest and most imposing of all the reliquaries was the Sainte Chapelle in Paris which in 1248 King Louis IX had built to house a Crown of Thorns for which he had paid the staggering sum of the equivalent of £135,000 to Baudoin II in Constantinople (where there was a lucrative trade in relics) on his way back from the Seventh Crusade. Today Sainte Chapelle, adjacent to the Law Courts in the Ile de la Cité, is one of the city's great tourist attractions. The lower chapel is dedicated to Christ's mother, the upper is where Louis housed his relics. Here the beauty of the refracted light coming from the 6,500 square feet of the huge stained-glass windows on every side, red and green, blue and white, is breathtaking. High up at the far end and under a canopy of blue with gold stars is a raised dais on which stands a golden casket, and it was on top of this that the Crown of Thorns was displayed to the faithful every Good Friday. Louis IX hated Jews and Moslems equally, yet it is said that his carrying what he believed to be the original Crown of Thorns barefoot through the streets of Paris to its final resting place was an impressive and moving sight. Other relics he kept in the Sainte Chapelle were a portion of the True Cross, Christ's swaddling clothes, the lance, the sponge, the rod of Moses and the skull of John the Baptist.

In the coming centuries collections of relics continued to accumulate, mostly in the hands of kings and prelates. In the early part of the sixteenth century there were two outstanding collections: that of Archbishop Albert of Mainz whose 9,000 items included whole bodies of saints, a bone of Isaac, manna from heaven, a branch of Moses's burning bush, a wine jar (complete with wine) from the wedding feast of Cana, a single thorn from the Crown of Thorns and one of the stones that had killed St Stephen. In competition with this were the 19,000 items amassed by Germany's Prince Frederick the Wise which included no fewer than 204 bits of the Bethlehem babies said to have been massacred by Herod, six bits of St Bernard, four of St Augustine, the thorn from the Crown of Thorns which had pierced Christ's brow and a crumb from the Last Supper. 'Anyone who saw all these on the correct day of the year,' says one writer, 'could be excused nearly two million years of purgatory.'[6]

The reader may well ask whether, in the fearful mix of violence, cruelty, bloodshed, superstition and magic that characterised the Roman Catholic Church between the eleventh and sixteenth centuries, there were any redeeming features, ones that reflected and endorsed the altruism of the gospel message. That there were was due mainly to the monastic orders and particularly those of the Franciscans and Dominicans who believed that the rich trappings and lifestyles of the contemporary Church were blurring the image of the very different sort of life led by Christ and his disciples in faraway Galilee.

Francis, or Francesco ('the little Frenchman') was born in Assisi in 1181, the son of a rich cloth merchant and Provençal mother. In his early years he seems to have led a comfortable and carefree existence but after a serious illness and a vivid dream, he made a conscious decision to give up all his personal possessions, become a hermit and devote his life to those at the bottom of the social ladder, looking after lepers and other sick people, helping the poor and preaching and praying. Poverty, chastity and obedience were the rules of his order which he founded with eleven like-minded companions when he was twenty-nine. They refused to accept large donations to further their work and instead became mendicants, begging publicly for their daily needs. The Pope of that time, Innocent III, gave the new order his blessing but stipulated that because of their lack of learning (its friars were mostly working class) they were not to preach theology about which they knew little but rather the importance of penitence. St Francis also preached against luxury, sodomy (which seems to have been rife in medieval Europe), usury, vanity and vengeance.

An early recruit to the order was a girl of noble family called Clare, and this led to the setting up of a separate order for women who came to be known as the Poor Clares, their commitment to poverty being as basic as that of the men. In 1223 when Francis was forty-two he went to the Holy Land, hoping but failing to convert Moslems to Christianity, but he did persuade the Sultan of Egypt to give more consideration to Christian prisoners. By this time the order had grown to some 5,000 members with another 500 awaiting entry.

Francis died in 1226 aged forty-five in the church of San Damiano which he once helped to build. Two years after his death Pope Gregory IX canonised him. The most attractive thing about him was that, unlike many Christian mystics whose devotions became almost too much of a burden for them, he was essentially a happy man: 'Humble,' as one writer said, 'but without any sense of self-mortification' and exhibiting 'a sunny sort of saintliness'. By having nothing, he said, he had everything. In his famous Canticle of the Sun, he praised God for bringing to his creatures Brothers Sun and Wind, Sister Water and Mother Earth with all her fruits and coloured flowers and then, when he knew he was about to die, another Sister, that of Death, 'from whom no man may escape'. He also sang to the birds.

Throughout the thirteenth century the movement continued to grow until, a hundred years after Francis's death, the order consisted of 1,400 houses with 28,000 friars. These were good men and women, leading and practising good Christlike lives, yet in the life of the

Church in the Middle Ages violence and bloodshed were never far away. Early in the fourteenth century there was a breakaway movement of Franciscans who refused to recognise clerical property and who stressed, as their founder had done, the extreme poverty of Christ. In 1318 four of them were burned as heretics because of their views, and in 1322, and no doubt to ease a guilty conscience, the Pope declared as heretical the assertion of the poverty of Christ. One writer says that these rebel Franciscans, the *fraticelli* as they were called, were hunted and burned all over Europe, especially in their native Umbria. 'The victims of the flames,' he adds, 'usually died screaming in pain and terror, thus appearing to confirm the justice of the proceedings.'

The other great monastic order of that time were the Dominicans, founded by a Spanish priest in Toulouse at the time of the campaign against the Cathari. Dominic was a contemporary of Francis and like him imposed on his followers a rule of absolute poverty; also like him he instituted an order of nuns. But their functions were quite different. Whereas the Franciscans saw their work as succouring the sick and the poor, the Dominicans, who were mostly middle class and better educated, concentrated on preaching, both to the clergy and the laity, so that they might know how to avoid heresy. Indeed, some of them were among the chief persecutors of heresy and became known as *domini canes*, the hounds of the Lord. Dominic died five years before Francis at the age of fifty-one; but six years after Francis's canonisation in 1228, he too was canonised by the same Pope, Gregory IX. Later Thomas Aquinas and the German mystic Meister Eckhart were two of the better known Dominicans.

Another order which came about in the Netherlands towards the end of the fourteenth century called itself the Brethren of the Common Life. Like the Franciscans they were extremely pious, believed in following the way of life of Jesus rather than indulging in theological assertions but took the Dominicans as their role model in educating the ignorant, placing their members as teachers in Church-endowed schools and universities throughout Europe. They embraced laymen as well as clerics and practised a very personal religion, their bible being *The Imitation of Christ* by Thomas à Kempis. They also supported a female branch, the Beguines, who worked in hospitals and among the poor – at one time in Cologne there were 2,000 of them; and some of the tranquil *beguinages* where they lived can still be seen in Holland today. The Beguines were paragons of piety but Rome and its bishops kept a sharp eye on them, lest their very personal relationships with God be seen to degenerate into heterodoxy.

To return to where we were. In 1348, or thirty years after the burning of the four Franciscan friars for heresy, Europe was struck by a natural disaster in scale and scope greater than any other before or since. It was a plague which originated in China, quickly spread westwards and was known as the Black Death. It killed one in four of the population of Europe, in some places like Siena three out of five. The Church declared that the plague had been ordained by God as a punishment for sins. On another level a more accessible scapegoat was needed and once again it was the Jews whom Christians blamed and then massacred in their thousands.

After that diversion the Church resumed its old obsessional ways of rooting out heretics and killing them where they could not be persuaded to recant. But with this difference: whereas in the past most heretics were seen as independent-minded people like the Cathars, believers going their own way, the burning motivation of the new breed of heretics was Church renewal, a desire to take the first tentative steps on the long road that would lead to the Reformation still a hundred years away. Two of the first of this new breed were the Czech dissident cleric John Huss and his friend Jerome of Prague. In England Jerome had been much influenced by the teachings of the English reformer John Wycliffe at Oxford, some of whose writings he brought back to Prague; and these in turn influenced Huss. Wycliffe was living and preaching at the time when the Popes were all Frenchmen, resident at Avignon in princely, decadent splendour. Of one, John XXIII (1410–15), the historian Gibbon wrote: 'The most scandalous charges were suppressed. The Vicar of Christ was only accused of piracy, murder, rape, sodomy and incest.' Sodomy and fornication, it would seem, were not unknown to other Vicars of Christ. Wycliffe attacked their abuses, called them Antichrist and said the Church would be better without them. He also denied the priestly power of absolution and the system of confessions, penances and indulgences, and declared that instead of the Latin Bible being filtered to the people through clerics, every man should have the right to read the Bible in his own language; and he utterly refuted the doctrine of transubstantiation whereby the body and blood of the long-dead Christ were transformed by magic into the bread and wine of the Eucharist. The Pope, Gregory XI, tried to persuade the King of England, Richard II, and the Archbishop of Canterbury to have Wycliffe imprisoned, but was unsuccessful.

Huss and Jerome took up Wycliffe's cudgels and preached in Prague's Bethlehem Chapel along much the same lines as he had. One of their prime targets was the degeneration and loss of authority of the Papacy; for most of Huss's life there had been two rival Popes and then in 1409 they were joined by a third. The ridicule afforded by this situation was reflected in the murals painted on the walls of the Bethlehem Chapel: Christ walking barefoot, the Pope mounted on a charger, Christ washing the feet of the disciples, the Pope having admirers kiss his feet, Christ ascending into heaven, the Pope in full gear descending to the other place. For the Papacy this was too offensive. First Huss was excommunicated, then having been promised safe conduct to attend a general council of the Church at Constance to sort out the business of the three Popes, he was betrayed, arrested, tried and condemned to death. At the stake a crown was put on his head decorated with three devils and the words 'This is a heretic', and when he had been burned, his ashes were scattered in the Rhine to prevent bits of him being converted into relics. Ten months later Jerome was burned on the same spot, while in England, so greatly had Church authority been offended that the body of Wycliffe was dug up from his grave at Lutterworth and thrown into the local river.

The last of the fifteenth-century clerics to fall foul of charges of heresy was the fiery Girolamo Savonarola. He lived during the birth of the Italian Renaissance, a time which heralded the liberation of the human spirit and saw its manifestations in literature, art, architecture and commerce, particularly in the city of Florence. Throughout the century there were more than seventy banks in Florence, which was also the birthplace of the florin, the first stable European currency as some hope that the euro will be in our own day. It was a time when the ancient classic texts of Plato and Aristotle, Pliny and Livy were being rediscovered and revalued, when artists such as Botticelli, Piero della Francesca and Mantegna first gave the fruits of their genius to the world, forerunners of Michelangelo and Leonardo, Titian and Tintoretto. It was also a time of increased moral laxity among the clergy, not excluding the Popes. Pope Alexander VI, born Rodrigo Borgia, had four children before he became Pope and at least three after. His illegitimate son Cesare had difficulty in being accepted for the priesthood until granted dispensation. His sister Lucrezia, also illegitimate, was married three times to satisfy her father's ambitions and left behind her, some say unfairly, a legend of vice and wickedness. Things reached such a pass that a Church council of 1512 decreed that priests should not attend the marriages of their sons and daughters.

It was this sort of backsliding, understandable enough to us but the Achilles' heel of the Roman Catholic priesthood throughout its long history, that Savonarola fulminated against; that and the general free-loving, free-spending climate of the times. 'Oh Florence, the time of singing and dancing is over,' he wrote; 'Now is the time to weep for your sins with torrents of tears'; while of the clergy he said: 'With courtiers and grooms, horses and dogs, with mansions full of tapestries and silks, perfumes and lackeys, would you hold them to be pillars of the Church or temporal lords?' And he urged his Florentine flock to make bonfires of their vanities – gaudy clothes, musical instruments and playing cards. This vivid and memorable phrase the American author Tom Wolfe borrowed for the title of his novel about the vanities of twentieth-century Manhattan.

But as with Huss and Jerome, Savonarola had gone too far; and in 1495 he was summoned to Rome to answer a charge of heresy, which he ignored. Two years later he received an order of excommunication and ignored that too in that he continued to preach. In the end he was brought to trial for claiming to have seen visions and uttered prophecies, and was found guilty of sedition and religious error. Under torture he admitted to some of the charges, vague though they were, but later withdrew. In May 1498 he and two other Dominican friars were hanged and their bodies burned. Today in the main square in Florence a plaque marks the spot.

Although the Reformation was now just over the horizon, two mass persecutions of alleged heretics came into being in the last quarter of the fifteenth century, as savage and cruel as anything in the Church's history, including the massacre of the Cathars and the First Crusade.

The first mass persecution took place in Spain and continued on and off for 300 years. Its progenitor was a Dominican monk by the name of Thomas de Torquemada who in 1474 became chaplain to King Ferdinand and Queen Isabella. Because southern Spain had been under Moslem rule from the eighth to the end of the fifteenth centuries, Christianity did not become Spain's official religion until later than other European countries: consequently there were thousands of Moors living peacefully in Spain at this time, many of whom had left their mark on Spanish culture (e.g. the Alhambra); and many Jews too, some of whom had settled in the country as refugees from persecution in central Europe. These were divided into two groups: the orthodox who practised their faith and the *conversos* who had gone over to Roman Catholicism to avoid persecution but (as was well known) continued to exercise their Jewish rites and practices in secret. Both the pure Jews and the *conversos* contributed greatly to the administrative, financial, commercial and artistic life of the country, but their numbers were now so great that Torquemada, who himself was partly Jewish, proposed to the king and queen that they seek the approval of the Pope to set up an Inquisition similar to the Roman one to examine the *conversos* for signs of heresy. The Pope, Sixtus IV, gave his blessing and in 1484 the much-feared Spanish Inquisition was established.

Between then and his death thirteen years later Torquemada as Inquisitor-General presided over an organisation ruthless in its pursuit of heretics and rigorous in the punishments it meted out. As with Rome, torture was routinely employed, even if the accused were old people and children of twelve and thirteen because it was vital to get confessions; and no attention was paid to recantations afterwards; the proceedings were held in secret, the accused were not permitted defence lawyers and were forbidden from questioning hostile witnesses. The executions were the traditional ones of burning and took place in public, in a grand ceremonial *auto da fé* with the victims hoisted as far above the stake as possible so that their agonies might be prolonged. Because of the secrecy of the proceedings, nobody knows the exact numbers of those executed. Dr Joachim Kahl in his book *The Misery of Christianity* suggests a figure in Torquemada's period of office of more than 10,000 with another 90,000 sent into slavery but he does not give the source and it is probably an exaggeration. Some were not burned but kept chained in dungeons for the rest of their lives: the Archbishop of Toledo was kept in prison for seven years and released only two weeks before his death. In 1492, the year that Columbus (who may have been a Jewish *converso*) set sail for America, and as a final solution to the Jewish problem in Spain, 170,000 Jews were expelled from the country. Ten years later the remaining Moors followed them.

The last execution in Spain for heresy was as late as 1826 when a schoolmaster was hanged for substituting the *Ave Maria* in school prayers with *Praise be to God*.

3. The Burning of Witches

The other great mass persecution of new enemies of the Church began in Germany and over a period of some two centuries spread throughout Europe. In the same year that the Spanish Inquisition was set up, two German Dominican friars, Heinrich Kramer and Jakob

Sprenger, having compiled a dossier of confessions by so-called witches made under torture, later distilled into a book called *Malleus Maleficarum* (*The Witches' Hammer*), persuaded Pope Innocent VIII to issue a bull authorising them to extirpate witchcraft in Germany.

The myth of witches and witchcraft had had a long history, having been first mentioned in the Bible, 'Thou shalt not suffer a witch to live' (Exodus 22:18), and later Charlemagne and others condemned their practices as evil and brought in laws and penalties against them, including the death sentence. Witches and their male counterparts warlocks were believed to be agents of Satan who throughout medieval history was as vivid and powerful a figure as, to many people, God still is today. Witches preached that Satan in the feminine form of succubus or masculine form of incubus had sexual relations with men and women while they slept.

The early Church had rightly regarded witchcraft as a relic of pagan superstition, but to Innocent VIII the dossier compiled by the two Dominicans indicated a grave danger to the established Church. And so, all over Germany and elsewhere in Europe wholly innocent women were hunted relentlessly, tortured until they falsely confessed, and then burned. The newly formed society of Jesuits were fanatical witch-hunters but even the great reformers were not far behind. Luther, for instance, arranged for the burning of four witches at Wittenberg and Calvin quoted Exodus to authorise that witches should be killed: and they were in their hundreds of thousands. Archbishop Johann von Schoneburg burned 368 witches in twenty-two villages, so that in two of them there was only one female left. The Bishop of Würzburg burned more than 900, including his nephew, nineteen priests and a child of seven, while at Bamberg the bishop had 600 burned in a period of ten years. Witch-hunters who became lax in their duties were themselves held to account. At Trier, von Schoneburg had the chief judge of the electoral court, Dietrich Flade, arrested for undue leniency, tortured, strangled and burned. At Bamberg the bishop's chancellor was also accused of leniency and tortured, implicating five innocent burgomasters, one of whom sent a letter to his daughter saying their confessions were lies. 'They never cease to torture until one says something.' And a Jesuit priest who had acted as confessor to some alleged witches went to the heart of the matter: 'If all of us have not confessed ourselves witches, that is because we have not all been tortured.' The witch-hunting bishops knew in their hearts that this was true, but it was not in their interests to admit to it.

For proof of the efficacy of torture, one need not look further than England where torture was forbidden and where fewer than 1,000 witches were hanged in a hundred-year period, and compare it with the much smaller population of Calvinistic Scotland where torture was permitted and in roughly the same period some 4,500 witches were hanged, strangled or burned.

And it is to Scotland one must turn to appreciate the full horror of what the persecution and killing of alleged witches truly meant. That the Bishop of Würzburg burned more than 900 and the Bishop of Bamberg 600 are chilling enough statistics yet veil the human agony. But agony was there in plenty in the case of the persecution, trial and execution of the innocent Paisley Seven in 1697.

It began in the house of John Shaw, laird of Bargarran, situated near Paisley in Renfrewshire, a few miles west of Glasgow. One day his daughter Christian caught one of the maids, Katherine Campbell, a comely young Highland girl with a mass of black hair and flashing green eyes, stealing some of the household milk and drinking it. She told her mother what she had seen, and the quick-tempered Katherine, taxed with the offence, heaped curses on the child, among them that the devil would drag her soul through hell. Now in sermon after sermon in her local church Christian had heard the minister warn of the dangers of letting Satan into one's life, and coming after that, Katherine Campbell's curses that the devil would drag Christian's soul through hell seem to have triggered off in Christian, an impressionable child, a kind of hysterical fit. That night in bed, she woke in terror, crying, 'Help, help,' and then to the astonishment of her parents and others she suddenly flew across the room until arrested in flight (or so the story goes) by one of the women present.

For a considerable time afterwards she showed all the manifestations of the true hysteric, being at times rendered blind, deaf and dumb, suffered violent fits which afterwards rendered her body rigid and seemingly lifeless, screamed when touched, drew out of her mouth straw, balls of hair, coal cinders, small bones which, either consciously or unconsciously, she had put there herself, and shouted out that she was being attacked by the devil's crew whom she identified by name as male and female neighbours.

Gossip about the case spread to Edinburgh and commissioners from the Scottish Privy Council were despatched to Paisley to make enquiries. Among those they interviewed was one Elizabeth Anderson, the unkempt daughter of a well-known local blasphemer and said to know every witch in the county. She told the commissioners that on several occasions she and her father had met the devil's crew in the Bargarran orchard and named them; as well as Katherine Campbell, three respected and respectable local farmers, two old women, one whose mind had almost gone, and the local midwife, described as a comely woman with bright pink cheeks and kind blue eyes who had practised her profession in the parish for thirty years and was known as a good woman and true Christian. Elizabeth described the devil as a black man wearing a bonnet and cravat, and said they had all danced with him.

Asked the object of these meetings, she said for the crew to discuss the best way to kill Christians. What induced Elizabeth to spin such fantasies, money or a desire for notoriety, is not known, but incredible as it might seem, her story was believed, as perhaps she knew it would be. All seven were arrested, imprisoned and brought to trial before a High Court judge at Renfrew.

Mr Grant for the prosecution said that this was not a case of hearsay evidence. Witnesses had testified at being present at meetings of witches and had seen the accused there, plotting their evil deeds. 'Satan carried them there in his hurricanes,' he solemnly declared. All the best authorities, he concluded, were agreed that the apparition of witches was common and most real.

For the defence Mr Robertson called in aid common sense. Stories of meeting with the devil were incapable of proof; the indictment had not specified the times and dates of the meetings in the orchard, thus depriving the accused of the defence of alibi; and the law had laid down that witches were never to be condemned until they had confessed and even then their confessions must be confirmed by other evidence. But none had confessed.

All very true but it did the defendants no good. The jury brought in a verdict of guilty against all seven, and then the judge ordered them

> to be taken to the gallows green at Paisley upon the second Thursday of June next being the tenth day of the month betwixt two and four in the afternoon and there to be strangled at a stake till they be dead, and their bodies immediately to be burned to ashes upon the said place, and all their moveable goods and gear to be escheat and inbrought to his Majesty's use which is pronounced for doom.

June 10th dawned bright and sunny and hundreds of people from Glasgow and the west of Scotland began arriving early at the green. Many were making it a family occasion, bringing children and picnics to while away the hours until the time appointed for the executions. In a good position for watching the proceedings were the carriages of three or four noblemen who were entertaining their friends.

Soon after one o'clock the prison gates were opened, and the innocent seven, preceded by a drummer beating the dead march, guarded by a posse of soldiers and with their hands tied behind their backs, filed slowly out. The three men, determined, though guiltless, to die well, had all put on their Sunday suits. When they reached the gallows green they saw that beside the scaffold a peat fire was burning and knew it was there to consume their bodies after they had been hanged.

The hangman, who was the local chimney-sweep, despatched them one after the other. The one who made the most impression on the crowd was the Highland girl Katherine Campbell whose curses on Christian had set the whole affair in motion.

Katherine, once a healthy, buxom girl was now, after months in prison, a pitiful sight, her hair all matted, her face a deathly white. But she still had fight in her, on the scaffold throwing herself against the hangman and screaming insults. As the noose was about to be tied round her neck, there was a murmur from the crowd, 'Let her speak.'

She did, and many of the spectators, distressed that one so young and far from home should have to die, would remember for years what she said and how she said it. 'O, sirs,' she cried, 'would you stand by and see a young lass hanged?' What had they taken from the two old women who had gone before but a year or two of pain and misery? But from her they were taking her youth and the husband and children she might have had.

In a high, wailing voice, she showed her grief to all. 'Now I must sing my ain coronach [funeral lament] alane amang strangers. Woe on the day I left my hame and my kin and sought the cruel Lowlands where a chance word in anger to a lady's child could bring trouble and death to the poor and friendless. Oh, that I could be a bird, to fly away and never tire till I perched on my ain rooftree.' To those in the crowd who were weeping openly she cried, 'Keep your tears. They'll do no good for you or me. Let me go free, and I promise you you'll never see hint or hair of me again.'

One of the bailiffs signalled the hangman to go ahead, and seeing him approach, Katherine let out a fearful scream. And then a shocking thing happened. As she was thrown over the ladder, the scream dying in her mouth, she caught hold of its side in a last desperate attempt to save herself, and her head became wedged between two of the rungs. There was gasp of horror from the crowd before the hangman threw her clear. For many of the spectators Katherine's ordeal had been altogether too much: several fainted and had to be laid out on the grass.

The last to go was the saintly midwife, Margaret Lang, and then it was time for the final enactment of the day. The seven bodies were coated in tar to make them burn the quicker, then laid on the peat fire; and soon there came to the nostrils of the already departing crowd the sweet, sickly smell of roasting human flesh.

As the spectators began to wend their way home, the emotions of some were mixed. They had come to the gallows green not only to see the wicked punished but to hear them confess, hear from their own lips of the evil they had practised but would no more, thus enabling the living to sleep easier in their beds at night. In court their guilt had been proved beyond doubt, so why hadn't they confessed? Why choose hell-fire when a confession and repentance could bring them to heaven, and the means of grace? It seemed so unnatural.

But these could have only been passing thoughts. On the whole they felt that they had seen a good job done. Witches were evil creatures, the devil's own, and these had been given their just deserts.[7] So it was in scores of cities all over Europe (and briefly at Salem in Massachusetts). The names of the inquisitors and their victims and the manner of the victims' deaths were different, but in essence the proceedings and what motivated them were the same: because of their links with Satan, the Prince of Darkness, witches posed a threat to Christianity and therefore, as the Bible commanded, had to be destroyed.

In time, indeed not before time, people would come to see that Satan himself, like God and all devils and all gods, were projections of the imagination and could be discarded as readily as they had been adopted. The last witchcraft trial in Scotland took place thirty years later, in 1727, when the Sheriff Depute of Dornoch in Sutherland sentenced an old woman to be strangled for turning her daughter into a pony; while in mainland Europe the last recorded execution of a witch took place in Switzerland in 1787.

4. Rebellion against Rome. Hell. Massacres of Huguenots

The Reformation had many causes, some of long standing, one pressingly new. This, as Karen Armstrong says, was the fundamental change of consciousness that had come about with the birth of, or at least the stirrings of the foetus that heralded the scientific revolution. From now on logic and reason were to assume an importance in human affairs they had not done before. Propositions that had been previously accepted unthinkingly, like the authenticity of relics, were about to cry out for proof. The belief too that the bread and wine of the Eucharist had literally been transformed into the flesh and blood of Christ could no longer be sustained. If this was intellectual progress, which it was, it also contributed to the Christian Church's ultimate decline in that it led to the growth of literalism in the interpretation of the scriptures and gospels, currently deplored by so many scholars who hanker after the pre-Reformation days when interpretation rested on the Cloud of Unknowing, allegory, metaphor, mysticism.

On a more practical level, Luther's nailing his theses against indulgences to the Wittemberg church door was for many like the lancing of a boil. Among the most long-standing complaints of the poor against the Catholic clergy was that when the head of the household died, it was incumbent on the family to present to the local priest a beast or the deceased's bedding or a piece of cloth. Even the poorest were obliged to follow this custom on pain of being denied the sacraments, just as even the poorest were obliged to pay tithes. For their part the priests declared that without such obligatory gifts they would not be able to survive.

There was widespread dissatisfaction too for the degenerate lifestyle into which many of the clergy had fallen. At a council of Scottish bishops which met in 1549 and again in 1552 to discuss measures to put their house in order, it was agreed that the rejection of the faith by so many was due to 'the corruption of morals and profane lewdness of life in churchmen of almost all ranks', together with crass ignorance of literature and of all the liberal arts. Foremost among them was David Beaton, the Cardinal Archbishop of St Andrews, who led a life of great sexual promiscuity and his successor, Archbishop Hamilton, who submitted (one imagines willingly) to medical advice that he should undergo a ten-week course of 'carefully regulated' sexual incontinence. The Scottish crown accepted all this and indeed contributed to it. James IV created one of his illegitimate sons

139

Archbishop of St Andrews at the age of eleven; while in 1532 James V persuaded Pope Clement VII to agree to three of his illegitimate sons, all of them babies, becoming titular abbots of the monasteries of Kelso, Melrose and Holyrood, thus providing the little bastards with an income at the Church's expense. Contemporary Scottish abbots were said to be lewd and dull and nuns to be 'unchaste and too illiterate to write their names'.

The ordinary clergy were, if anything, worse. Of every bastard legitimised in the early sixteenth century two out of every seven were the offspring of priests. There were tales of priests arriving at the altar drunk while others 'hardly knew the letters of the alphabet'. The Latin liturgies which almost no one understood were virtually solo performances: the priest mumbled through the rites of office, the congregation gawped or slept: there were no communal prayers, no responses, no singing. The incomes of many parishes were being siphoned off to pay for the upkeep of cathedrals and abbeys, so that the underpaid priests refused to bury the poor until they had received the customary cow or sackful of wool. It was much the same in England. In the town of Salisbury in Wiltshire, at the time of the dissolution of the monasteries, it was found that of seventeen diocesan priests only five could translate from Latin into English the first sentence of the collect for the day; the remaining twelve and most of their congregation had no idea at all what the priest was attempting to say. The time for reform was overripe.

Yet there were other causes, equally pressing, that precipitated the Reformation and the starting point of which rested on the universal view that people held about the afterlife. Of all the matters on which Christ preached, the one that up to this time (and for some time after) undoubtedly had the most and longest-lasting influence was his promise that there *would be* an afterlife with rewards and punishments, that after you had died and were buried, you would in some magic way manage to continue living, a fantasy which many intelligent men and women believe in to this day.

What really terrified people was the prospect that if you were a sinner – and most believed they were – and had not repented, you were bound for hell. Hell was a real place in the medieval mind, even more real than heaven; and in sermon after sermon and book after book churchmen painted the horrors of hell in the most lurid terms. Great emphasis was laid on the physical agonies to be suffered there, the advocates of this seemingly forgetful that if you had left your physical body behind and had become a spirit, physical pain was no longer an option – but this sort of reasoning was too subtle for the simple mind. St Augustine of Hippo preached that hell was inhabited by ferocious animals which tore sinners to pieces, slowly and painfully. Another cleric said that the pains of hell were so unspeakable that if anyone so much as conceived of them, he would die of terror. Adam Scotus said that those who practised usury would be boiled in molten gold, while a colleague wrote of sinners being beaten with red-hot hammers. Richard Rolle envisaged a place where people would cut up and eat their own flesh, drink the gall of dragons and venom of asps, and vermin would contaminate their clothes and bedding. St Thomas Aquinas believed in *Schadenfreude*, that observing the torments of those in hell was one of the pleasures of being in heaven.

As late as 1758 St Alphonse di Liguori, founder of the Order of Redemptorists, wrote of the intensity and all-embracing presence of fire in hell: 'The unhappy wretch will find an abyss of fire . . . His body will become all fire, so that the bowels within him will burn, each reprobate will become a furnace of fire.'

Later Pusey thought that hell was central to Christianity. 'Is it more probable that eternal punishment should be true or that there should be no God? For if there is a god, there is eternal punishment.' Other Victorian clerics thought that hell, while certain, was only for the lower classes. But that there would be no end to it for those who had been consigned there was confirmed in *The New Catholic Encyclopaedia* of 1967 which quoted a papal pronouncement of 543 of hell being for eternity as still binding. A few still believe in the traditional view of hell today, no doubt fearful of the old Catholic adage that those who doubt hell are destined for it. Paul Johnson is one such. Conditioned by the teachings of the Holy Sisters at infants school, of the Holy Brothers at preparatory school and of the Jesuit

Fathers at Stonyhurst, he tells us that there has never been a time in his life when he has not believed in it. He also believes in the Catholic invention of the halfway house of purgatory and wonders how long he will have to stay there atoning for his sins before being allowed into heaven. 'I have prayed all my life for a premonition of death,' he writes, 'so that I have a chance to repent of my sins, to confess them and receive absolution.' Such worthy, if old-fashioned longings these days must be rare.

There were times in the Church's history when fear of hell-fire diminished. The post-Enlightenment period of the eighteenth century was one, and led the Rev. Williams Dodwell to preach in 1741: 'It is but all too visible that since men have learned to wear off apprehension of eternal punishment, the progress of impiety and immorality among us has been very considerable.' There was little evidence for this, but it is a battle-cry which churchmen have been fond of trumpeting to every generation, and parliament was persuaded to increase the number of offences punishable by death from some fifty to more than 300, among them the stealing of a sheep or a piece of yarn. Young boys were not immune from the gallows and several were in due course hanged: a minister who attended one hanging said before it, as well he might, 'I never saw boys cry so.' But, like his fellow clerics, he thought the death penalty a unique deterrent; and the commandment by God via Moses not to kill, reiterated by Jesus, could be forgotten.

Fear of hell-fire being what it was, ways and means had to be devised to avoid it. First among these was the introduction of penances which, it was hoped, would wipe the slate clean. In sixth-century Ireland the Church produced a tariff for specific offences.

> A boy who communicated in the sacrament although he sinned with a beast shall do penance for a hundred days on bread and water.
>
> He who vomits the host because of greediness, forty days of penance. If he ejects it into the fire, he shall sing one hundred psalms.

Cicero: 'There are no miracles. What was incapable of happening never happened, and what was capable of happening is not a miracle.'

Pierre Charron: 'We are circumcised or baptised – Jews or Moslems or Christians – before we know we are human beings.'

Denis Diderot: 'People who believe it is a god and not laws that make men honest are but little advanced.'

Baron D'Holbach: 'To speak of "soul" or "immaterial" or "supernatural" is to create an imaginary world beyond experience, conceptually incoherent and unproductive of future knowledge.'

David Hume: 'It is an absurdity to believe that the Deity has human passions and one of the lowest of human passions, a restless appetite for applause.'

P.B. Shelley: 'Reasonable people do not require religious belief. Christianity is unreasonable and incredible.'

Charles Darwin:
'Disbelief crept over me
... I have never since
doubted even for a single
second that my
conclusion was correct.'

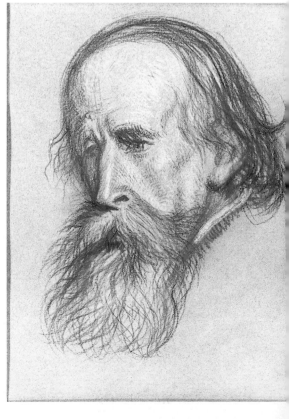

The Rev Sir Leslie Stephen (father of
Virginia Woolf) after reading Darwin:
'I now believe in nothing, but I do not
the less believe in morality. I mean to
live and die like a gentleman, if
possible.'

Charles Bradlaugh, M.P. being expelled from the House of Commons for attempting to take his seat (and not, as legend has it, for refusing to take the oath): 'I do not deny God because that word conveys to me no idea. I cannot war with a Non-entity.'

Sigmund Freud: 'God is an illusion that mature men and women should lay aside.'

William Winwood Reade: 'It is as foolish to pray for the healing of a disease or for daily bread as for help in sickness or adversity ... A day will come when the European God of the nineteenth century will be classed with the gods of Olympus and the Nile. Poetry and the fine arts will take that place in the heart that religion now holds.'

Bertrand Russell, on being asked what he would say to God if he ever met him: 'God,' I would say, 'why have you made the evidence for your existence so insufficient?'

Dr Margaret Knight (left), author of two BBC 1955 radio broadcasts, entitled *Morals without Religion*, about to debate the subject with Mrs Jenny Norton, wife of a clergyman, who told her that her anti-religious views were rubbish: 'She looks, doesn't she, like the typical housewife? But make no mistake about it, Mrs Knight is a menace. The misguided BBC have allowed a fanatic to rampage along the air lines, beating up Christianity with a razor and bicycle chain.' (*Daily Sketch*)

Sir Julian Huxley: 'Operationally God is beginning to resemble not a ruler but the last fading smile of a cosmic Cheshire cat.'

The Rt Rev David Jenkins: 'Nothing in the New Testament can be regarded as certain.'

The Rev Don Cupitt, former Dean of Emmanuel College, Cambridge: 'We cannot save God, for God is dead.'

He whose sperm flows while he is sleeping shall do penance for three days.

Among penances approved by the Church were wearing a hair shirt which was prickly and uncomfortable, walking barefoot, and fasting. More ambitious penances were going on a Crusade or making a pilgrimage to holy places like Rome or Jerusalem, as the wife of Bath did in Chaucer's *Canterbury Tales*, thus earning for the penitent full remission of sins. One reason for the invention of purgatory was to provide a stopping-off place for the penitent who had died before completing his penance. In the days of the early Church we find instances of penitents paying others to perform penances for them, and in the tenth, eleventh and twelfth centuries rich sinners expiating guilt for their sins by paying for the founding of cathedrals, abbeys, monasteries. Papal indulgences which required payment and which greatly increased papal revenues served the same purpose. Sinners were permitted to buy indulgences on their death-beds which after full confession allowed them to enter heaven immediately in what Roman Catholics call a state of grace. Soon indulgences were granted so frequently and for such deflated sums of money that they lost their value; and it was the abuse of indulgences that led Martin Luther in 1517 to nail to the church door at Wittenberg his ninety-five theses on indulgences questioning the right of the Pope to grant absolution for the remission of sins.

The German Luther and the French Calvin are the two names which most people today associate with the Church's Reformation, largely because they changed the course of Church history in begetting the Protestant ethic with its opposition to papal authority and long-overdue social reforms such as allowing priests to marry. Yet neither man could rid himself entirely of the killing-fields mentality which had disfigured papal rule for so long. Luther's tract *Against the Murdering, Thieving Hordes of Peasants* who were then in rebellion against their rulers contains some strong, unchristian language. He urges the rulers to brandish their swords and 'smite, stab and slay all that you can'. He also called for the deaths of the members of a new sect, the Anabaptists. They had come into being because of an increasing belief that the baptism of a tiny baby who was quite unconscious of the event was meaningless, and baptism should be delayed until the person to be baptised fully understood what it meant. But renouncing one's baptism for whatever reason was one of the greatest sins in the Roman Catholic canon and punishable by death. A crude saying among the Lutherans and Calvinists was that if the Anabaptists wanted water, they should have it, and they executed them by drowning while the Catholics stuck to their traditional method of burning. Both men denied that consciences should be free, and in addition Calvin arranged for the execution of one Michael Servetus, prior of an abbey in Vienna, who had declared in a tract, sensibly enough, that Christ was man only, not God.

The real spirit behind the Reformation was a quite different sort of person, a Dutch scholar by the name of Desiderius Erasmus. Son of a union between a Catholic priest and his washerwoman, he studied at most of the cultural centres of Europe including Florence, Paris, Oxford, Cambridge and London where he became a friend of Henry VIII's Lord Chancellor Sir Thomas More, and during his life wrote a number of books including a Greek version of the New Testament which were reprinted numerous times. His most famous book was *In Praise of Folly* in which he satirised the frailties of mankind, not excluding those of monks and popes. He was particularly severe on the cult of relics, complaining of 'the folly of those who revere a bone of the apostle Paul encased in glass and feel not the glow of his spirit enshrined in his epistles'. In religious matters he eschewed theology and doctrine, believing in piety and charity and that no one needed a third person to mediate between him and his God. He was equally scornful of indulgences, pilgrimages, masses for the dead and whatever else penitents paid money for: 'Perhaps thou believest that all thy sins are washed away with a little paper, a sealed parchment with the gift of a little money or some wax image, with a little pilgrimage. Thou art utterly deceived.' As a boy he had seen 200 prisoners of war broken on the wheel at Utrecht, and was against violence of any kind.

He condemned those who wanted to burn others for heresy, adding that if he were the judge he would not dare deprive a man of his life, and was greatly shocked when he heard that Henry VIII had ordered the beheading of Sir Thomas More for refusing to recognise him as the new head of the English reformed Church. His translation of a passage arising from the Arian controversy by the French Humanist theologian Sebastian Castellio sums up his own general philosophy: 'You will not be damned if you do not know whether the Spirit proceeding from the Father and the Son has one or two beginnings, but you will not escape damnation if you do not cultivate the fruits of the Spirit which are love, joy, peace, patience, kindness, goodness, mercy, faith, modesty, continence, and chastity.'

Here was a wind of change indeed and he persisted in it; the minds of others too were moving in the same direction. Castellio again: 'I have carefully examined what a heretic means, and I cannot make it mean more than this: a heretic is a man with whom you disagree. To kill a man is not to defend a doctrine. It is to kill a man. Who would not think Christ a Moloch[8] if he wanted men to be immolated to him and burned alive?' And this, on the forcing of consciences by torture, written near the end of his life: 'Either the victim resists and you murder his body, or he yields and speaks against his conscience and you murder his soul.' In 1588, the year in which Philip of Spain sent his armada against England to restore the country to Catholicism, the Bishop of Le Mans spoke to the States Assembly at Blois. 'Heretics,' he told them, 'should be loved and brought back by instruction and good example.' At this, we are told, the assembly shouted with indignation and stamped its feet and would not allow the bishop to continue, thus confirming Montaigne's dictum that there was no hostility that exceeded Christian hostility. 'Our religion is made to extirpate vices; in fact it protects them, fosters them, incites them.'

And so the ground was cleared for the Protestant ethic, as defined by Luther and Calvin and the Swiss Zwingli, to put down roots in Germany and Switzerland, Holland and Denmark, Norway and Sweden, England and Scotland. Common to all the new Churches in these countries was a denial of papal authority, the abolition of the Mass, the abrogation of the doctrine of transubstantiation, and an end to priestly celibacy. This last, for centuries more honoured in the breach than the observance, was particularly welcome; though it posed a dilemma for some reformist priests who, while enjoying the favours of their concubines, had no wish to marry them.

Rome was outraged by this contempt for papal power, but because of the increasing power of the secular authorities was unable to burn the reformers or otherwise bring them to book. Juan Mariani, adviser to the King of Spain, wrote disparagingly of Protestant princes: 'It is a glorious thing to exterminate the whole of this pestilential and pernicious race from the community of mankind.' Mary Tudor made a start when she brought back Catholicism to England on ascending the throne in 1553 and within three years two of her bishops, Latimer and Ridley, and the Archbishop of Canterbury, Thomas Cranmer, were burned at the stake; subsequently there was a massacre of 300 Protestants. In 1548 the Roman Inquisition was re-established and two reformers who saw no difference between Christian and secular knowledge, Francesco Pucci and Giordano Bruno, were arrested, judged and burned. Nine years later the *Papal Index of Prohibited Books* was published and remained in force until, incredibly, *1966*. It included the works of Copernicus and Galileo, to which were later added those of Bacon, Montaigne, Locke, Mill, Hobbes, Berkeley and Darwin (but not Hitler's *Mein Kampf*).

The killing fields *par excellence* however were those of France, where from 1562 for ten years French Roman Catholics and Protestant Huguenots fought each other with increasing ferocity. Huguenot soldiers went on the rampage, smashing church ornaments and killing priests: a Huguenot captain wore a necklace of priests' ears. The Roman Catholics replied in kind, taking Huguenot prisoners up to battlements and pushing them over the side; there were also pitched battles. The culmination of all this occurred on 24 August 1572 when hundreds of Huguenot guests invited to the wedding of Princess Margaret, daughter of Catherine de Medici, to Henri of Navarre, himself a Huguenot, were pulled from their beds and murdered: the massacre included other Huguenots elsewhere in France, lasted two full days and resulted in the deaths of thousands. In time Henri became heir to the French throne but because Paris would not accept a Protestant monarch, converted to Roman Catholicism just before his coronation. In 1598 he established the Edict of Nantes whereby Huguenots were granted freedom of worship; but thirty years later Cardinal Richelieu, seeing the Huguenots developing into a state within a state, invested the Huguenot fortified town of La Rochelle. It surrendered after a heroic siege of a year when many of the inhabitants sailed for America where they established the town of New Rochelle. Richelieu allowed the remaining Huguenots freedom of worship but in 1685 Louis XIV revoked the Edict of Nantes and once again Huguenots were savagely attacked. Some converted to Catholicism but a great mass of others – estimated at between a quarter and half a million – went into exile in America, Prussia, England, Holland, Switzerland, South Africa. Catholic obduracy had insisted on a unitary state with one king, one faith, one law, but at the cost of losing many of France's most industrious and talented citizens.

Thus the dream held by some that after the Reformation the Roman Catholic and Protestant faiths might somehow merge into one was shattered, and more killing fields came into play as and when opportunity offered. The first and longest lasting was the Thirty Years War which began as a religious conflict in Bohemia in 1618 and ended in 1648 as a power struggle between France and Spain for control of the Rhineland. In the 1630s William Laud, Archbishop of Canterbury under King Charles I, reintroduced the dreaded Star Chamber and Court of High Commission to try to punish Calvinists and Puritans. In this he authorised the employment of the sort of mutilations that had not been seen since the early Middle Ages. Alexander Leighton, for instance, was first defrocked by the Court of High Commission and then sentenced by the Star Chamber to be whipped, have his ears cropped, his nose slit and his forehead branded, in addition to being fined and imprisoned; William Prynne and John Bastwick suffered the same fate. But Laud had not reckoned with parliament which in 1644 impeached him for treason and, after a trial at which he was found guilty of attempting to overthrow the Protestant religion, he was beheaded on Tower Hill.

Charles himself was beheaded in 1649 and his son Charles II, before his coronation at Scone Palace in Scotland, swore an oath to respect the Solemn League and Covenant whereby it was agreed that the Scottish Presbyterian Church would not have bishops foisted on it. However, on his accession to the English throne in 1660 he reneged on the promise and appointed bishops. This was anathema to the democratic Scots who fled into the countryside and held Presbyterian field services in farms and glens. However, they were ruthlessly hunted down and in the period 1660–88 some 18,000 Covenanters were killed.

They were not the only Celts to be massacred at this time. In 1649 Oliver Cromwell, later Lord Protector of England, crossed over to Ireland to end the civil war there and massacred the garrisons of Wexford and Drogheda, in retaliation 'for the most unprovoked and most barbarous massacre done by the Irish to the English', and he ordered the deportation of priests, the confiscation of estates, the establishment of English Protestant landlords and the prohibition of Roman Catholic services. Fifty years later the Protestant King William of Orange defeated his father-in-law, the Catholic King James II, at the Battle of the Boyne, guaranteeing that Ulster would remain Protestant, a victory whose consequences are with us to this day.

If, with the dawn of the eighteenth century, religious killings began to tail off, as they did, this was because European societies were approaching the age of Enlightenment. The grip that Roman Catholicism and Protestantism had previously held on men's minds and the intolerance and bigotry that had resulted from it were in the process of crumbling. Freedom of conscience was beginning to creep in and with it the freedom to try out other forms of Christian belief; thus came into being Congregationalists, Independents, Unitarians, Methodists, Quakers, the last of whom believed in direct communion with God and solved the bitter controversies concerning ministers, liturgy, sacraments, music, episcopacy and presbyteries by abolishing the lot. What had united Christians in the past was their fierce belief in God and Jesus Christ, two of the three persons of the Trinity: what divided them and made heresy possible was the different interpretations they placed on that relationship. Now a generation was coming into bloom which was thinking the previously unthinkable: not about such refinements as the Arian controversy and whether the Holy Ghost proceeded from the Father or the Son, but whether God existed and what reasons were there for thinking so? These were questions which in the coming century would be addressed by Voltaire and the French *philosophes*, Thomas Paine, Diderot, d'Holbach, David Hume and others.

But before embarking on them, let me record a last example of killing-field practices which, because it occurred as late as 1766, was truly shocking. In that year in northern France the young Chevalier de la Barre was walking along a street in Abbeville. A Capuchin religious procession passed by. Because it was raining the chevalier did not doff his hat as was then the custom. This was observed and reported on, and the chevalier was arrested. The charge against him was blasphemy. He was found guilty. The sentence of the court was amputation of the hands, the tongue to be torn out with pincers and then for him to be burned alive. Yet this was the age of Haydn and Mozart, of Gainsborough and Fragonard, of Boswell and Johnson. Voltaire said he was haunted by the story for the rest of his life. So am I.

PART TWO – DISBELIEF

Chapter Seven

THE COMING OF THE ENLIGHTENMENT: COPERNICUS, GALILEO AND NEWTON

For more than a millennium of history it was widely believed that the Church was incapable of error; that it had a monopoly of wisdom not only in matters of religion but in learning generally. God, so the Pope and all Christians believed, had created the earth as the centre of the universe and the nourishing sun to make its daily orbit over it. Other celestial bodies might also make their way across the heavens, but the earth was anchored in a fixed position in space, immobile, static.

Some 250 years before the birth of Christ, however, a Greek astronomer by the name of Aristarchus of Samos took a different view. He believed that all the planets including the earth revolved round the sun which was itself static and that the earth rotated on its own axis once every twenty-four hours. The writer Plutarch recorded that Aristarchus had proposed this theory as a hypothesis but that his successor Seleucus had confirmed it as a fact. We do not know whether, nearly 2,000 years later, the Polish astronomer Copernicus was aware of the findings of Aristarchus and Seleucus but, whether or not, he came to the same conclusions in a book which he published just before his death in 1543. He might have published his conclusions earlier but was inhibited by knowing that what Bertrand Russell called his dethronement of the earth (and of man) from its

153

geometrical pre-eminence was contrary to the Church's teachings and therefore might land him in trouble. By the time the Catholic Church came to consider the matter Copernicus was dead but even so the breakaway Protestants were outraged. 'People give ear,' wrote Luther, 'to an upstart astrologer [*sic*] who strove to show that the earth revolves but not the heavens and firmament, sun and moon . . . This fool wishes to reverse the entire science of astronomy; but Sacred Scripture tells us that Joshua commanded the sun to stand still, not the earth.'[1] Calvin too quoted scripture – Psalm 93:1: 'The earth is established, it cannot be moved,' and added, 'Who will venture to place the authority of Copernicus above that of the Holy Spirit?' Here were the first stirrings of the irreconcilable differences between religion and science which would lead ultimately to the Church's decline, for churchmen at this time, Protestants no less than Catholics, believed the words of the Bible to be historical fact. Before he died Copernicus protested vigorously against the strictures on his findings, for it had not seemed to him that he was violating anything written in the Bible.

Unlike Copernicus, Galileo had to live with the consequences of what he had written. A brilliant mathematician and astronomer, he was born at Pisa in 1564 or some twenty years after Copernicus's death, later becoming Professor of Mathematics there and at the University of Padua. He discovered the value of a pendulum for measuring time and proved that falling bodies descend with equal velocity, whatever their weight. He invented a thermometer and perfected a refracting telescope through which he became the first to observe that the moon supported mountains and valleys, a claim to which his detractors gave little credence.

However, it wasn't until he was over fifty that Galileo came to believe in Copernicus's theory and then in a somewhat roundabout way. He wanted to write a book on the rise and fall of earthly tides, phenomena which he claimed would be impossible were the earth stationary; and in 1616 he approached the Pope through an intermediary to enquire whether he might use Copernicus's findings on an entirely hypothetical basis to support what he intended to say.

154

The Pope referred the matter to the newly re-established Inquisition whose rulings were as follows:

Proposition
That the sun is in the centre of the world and totally immovable as to locomotion.
Ruling
All say that the said proposition is foolish and absurd and . . . heretical inasmuch as it contradicts the express opinion of Holy Scriptures in many places, according to the words themselves and to the common expositions and meanings of the church Fathers and Doctors of Theology.
Proposition
That the earth is neither in the centre of the world nor immovable, but moves as a whole and in daily motion.
Ruling
All say this proposition receives the same censure in Philosophy; with regard to Theological Verity it is at least erroneous in the Faith.

As a result of these rulings Galileo was informed that he could no longer hold, defend or teach the propositions stated and that if he did the Inquisition might proceed against him. Eight years later, in 1624, he visited Rome to pay his respects to a new Pope, Urban VIII, and in the course of six audiences was given permission, or thought he had been given permission, to refer to the Copernican theory as a hypothesis in support of his treatise on tides. In 1632, when Galileo was sixty-eight, his treatise on tides was at last published, and no one was more astonished than he to be summoned to Rome to stand trial before the Inquisition on a charge of suspicion of heresy. He was told that by bringing the Copernican theory in aid to support his views on the tides, he had broken the promise he had made after the 1616 edict not to do so: as sixteen years had passed since making the promise, he may well have forgotten it. Galileo was therefore obliged to recant a little, admit there were passages in his treatise where in supporting the

Copernican theory he had gone too far, but he assured the cardinals he had intended no offence. Three of the cardinals dissented from the majority verdict that he was guilty of heresy: the sentence, which Galileo had not expected, was indefinite imprisonment.

Thanks to the intercession of his friend and admirer the Archbishop of Siena, Galileo was spared the public prison, though had to suffer house confinement, with officers from the Inquisition keeping an eye on him. During the ten years of life that remained to him, he stayed first at a villa next to a convent at Arcetri where his elder daughter Virginia was a nun ('There are two pigeons in the dovecote waiting for you to eat,' she had written to him, 'and beans in the garden waiting for you to pick') and later, after Virginia had died and he was growing blind, with his son in Florence.

In his old age and before blindness prevented it, Galileo wrote in his own hand in a copy of one of his books:

> Take note, theologians, that in your desire to make matters of faith out of propositions relating to the fixity of sun and earth, you run the risk of eventually having to condemn as heretics those who would declare the earth to stand still and the sun to change position when, at such a time, it might be physically or logically proved that the earth moves and the sun stands still.

While to a distinguished French scientist who had once heard him lecture at Padua and who had written to the Pope beseeching a pardon for him, he replied:

> . . . when a man is wrongly condemned to punishment, it becomes necessary for his judges to use greater severity in order to cover up their own misapplication of the law. This afflicts me less than people may think possible, for I have two sources of perpetual comfort: first that in my writings there cannot be found the faintest shadow of irreverence towards the Holy Church; and second the testimony of my own conscience which only I and God in Heaven thoroughly know.

156

He died on 9 January 1642, and a few days later a member of the staff of Francesco Barberini, one of the three cardinals who had refused to condemn him, wrote to tell a friend the sad news. 'Now,' he concluded, 'envy ceasing, the sublimity of that intellect will begin to be known, and will serve all posterity as guide in the search for truth.'

It was well said. For Galileo had struck the first of many blows in the cause of science against religion. Others would follow, whose resonances are with us still.

After Galileo the brightest star in the firmament of European science and mathematics was Isaac Newton, born on Christmas Day in the year that Galileo died. His own father died before he was born and he was brought up by his widowed mother at Woolsthorpe Manor near Grantham in Lincolnshire. He was educated at Grantham Grammar School and Trinity College, Cambridge, where he eventually became a Fellow and at the age of twenty-six Lucasian Professor of Mathematics (a post held in our own time by the brilliant Stephen Hawking). In 1696 Newton became Master of the Royal Mint, was later President of the Royal Society and was knighted by Queen Anne. He died in 1727.

> Nature and Nature's laws lay hid in night,
> God said *Let Newton be!* and all was light.

So wrote his near contemporary Alexander Pope, and the light that Newton shone on the workings of the universe immeasurably improved human understanding of it. Having left Cambridge in 1665 when the plague was rampant, Newton joined his mother at Woolsthorpe, and for the next two years applied his mind to mathematics, in which time he discovered what he called the direct method of fluxions or, in modern speech, the differential and integral calculus. He also developed a theory on the composite nature of light, as well as discovering the binomial theorem (i.e. one consisting of two terms such as *a* plus *b*).

Next, and as every schoolchild is led to believe and whether true or not, he saw an apple falling to the ground which directed his mind to the theory of gravitation. Was it possible, he asked himself, and in the light of the German astronomer Johann Kepler's laws governing planetary orbits, to fashion a theory of universal gravitation? He tested it, says Jacob Bronowski, by calculating the motion of the moon round the earth.

The moon was a powerful symbol for him. If she follows her orbit because the earth attracts her, he reasoned, then the moon is like a ball (or apple) that has been thrown very hard; she is falling towards the earth, but is going so fast that she constantly misses it – she keeps on going round because the earth is going round. How great must the force of attraction be? Newton himself gave the answer.

> I deduced that the forces which keep the planets in their orb[it]s must be reciprocally as the squares of their distances from the centres about which they revolve; and thereby compared the force requisite to keep the moon in her orb[it] with the force of gravity at the centre of the earth; and found them answer pretty nearly.

This, says Bronowski, is characteristic of Newtonian understatement. 'His first rough calculation had in fact given the period of the moon close to its true value, about 27¼ days.'

With his theory of universal gravitation Newton could be said to have completed the work begun by Aristarchus, Copernicus, Galileo and Kepler, and proved that the hitherto unmapped universe worked to a set of precise and regular laws. But if it did, where did that leave God? Contemporary theologians were worried, fearing that the dent that Galileo had made in the armour of their beliefs was about to be repeated. Bertrand Russell:

> The solar system [it was now agreed] was kept going by its own momentum and its own laws: no outside interference was needed. There might still be need of God to set the mechanism working; the planets, according to Newton, were originally hurled by the

hand of God. But when he had done this and decreed the law of gravitation, everything went on by itself without further need of divine intervention . . . [God] might remain as Creator but even that was doubtful, since it was not clear that the world had a beginning in time. Although most of the men of science were models of piety, the outlook suggested by their work was disturbing to orthodoxy, and the theologians were quite justified in feeling uneasy.

He went on:

Another thing that resulted from science was a profound change in the conception of man's place in the universe. In the mediaeval world the earth was the centre of the heavens, and everything had a purpose concerned with man. In the Newtonian world the earth was a minor planet of a not specially distinguished star; astronomical distances were so vast that the earth in comparison was a mere pinpoint. It seemed unlikely that this immense apparatus was all designed for the good of certain small creatures on this pinpoint . . . The world might have a purpose, but purposes could no longer enter into scientific explanations.

'As for damnation,' he concluded, 'surely the creator of so vast a universe had something better to think about than sending men to hell for minute theological errors.'

Newton himself, however, though denying both the Trinity and the Incarnation, believed that religious truths and scientific truths were compatible not contradictory. But the board of the Royal Society which had originally been founded along religio-scientific lines saw in the light of Newton's discoveries a dichotomy. 'They were coming to accept,' says Johnson, 'that institutional Christianity, with its feuds and intolerances, was an embarrassment and a barrier to scientific endeavour. Hence they decided to concentrate purely on science and ruled that religious matters were not to be discussed at the Society's meetings.'

In 1714 when Newton was seventy-two and President of the Royal Society, he was consulted by the parliamentary committee appointed to look into the best ways of discovering longitude, a solution which was desperately needed if ships were not to suffer continuing losses on ocean voyages. The best method, he thought, was a watch to keep time exactly (one degree of longitude equalling four minutes of time) 'but by reason of the motion of the ship, the variations of heat and cold, wet and dry, and the difference of gravity in different latitudes, such a watch hath not yet been made'. To encourage the making of one, the government offered a prize of £20,000 for whoever first determined longitude to within half a degree of accuracy.

Seven years later, while waiting for Flamsteed, the Astronomer Royal, to complete his map of the heavens and thus pave the way to astronomical observations, Newton wrote to the secretary of the Board of Longitude:

> A good watch may serve to keep a reckoning at sea for some days and to know the time of a celestial observation, and for this end a good jewel watch may suffice till a better sort of watch can be found out. But when the longitude at sea is once lost, it cannot be found again by any watch.

Thirty-two years after Newton's death and after a number of failed attempts, a self-taught watchmaker by the name of John Harrison completed a large and exquisite pocket watch which after submission to the Board of Longitude won him part of the £20,000 prize. Tested on board HMS *Deptford* on a voyage from Madeira to Jamaica, it was found to have lost only five seconds during a passage of eighty-one days. Today, with its 753 separate parts which include diamonds and rubies, it rests in London's National Maritime Museum and is viewed by thousands with admiration and curiosity every year.

When did atheism, by which I mean in broad terms a denial of the existence of an external god, first manifest itself? Many in Britain today believe it to be a comparatively recent development, a product of the last hundred years. In fact, as the researches of such scholars as Ginzburg, Lefebvre, Berman, Gregory and Kors have revealed, its European origins go back to the late sixteenth or early seventeenth centuries. It was, they are agreed, the Renaissance that first encouraged non-Christian learning and non-Christian moral values, and the Reformation which by defending the right of freedom of thought encouraged people to think rationally; both of which, in conjunction with the scientific revolution, were corrosive of religious belief. A further weakening of religious thinking was provided by the works of such philosophers as Hobbes, Spinoza and especially Locke who, while accepting the gospel narratives and the resurrection, balked at the doctrine of original sin and of the Trinity. 'His uncompromising subordination of revelation to reason,' say Hunter and Wootton, 'had revolutionary implications. He identified the good with the pleasurable, and morality with the pursuit of happiness; he gave the critique of the hold of religion on men's minds a solid philosophical foundation.'

On the other hand the great mass of people in western Europe had been conditioned to believe or at least passively accept Christian doctrine for so long, and the Church was so fierce in its persecution of dissenters, that those who deviated from orthodoxy did so at their peril. The long list of martyrs who had gone to the stake for denying God or the Trinity or the immortality of the soul was a stark reminder of the risks they ran. As a result, say Hunter and Wootton, the history of unbelief became and for a long time remained disreputable. Such was the power of orthodoxy that there was a time, as I remember from my youth, when polite society regarded a self-proclaimed atheist with the same sort of distaste and suspicion as they did a Communist or Fascist, and it is only now, when many of us have freed ourselves from Christianity's shackles, that attitudes have begun to change.

Chapter Eight

THE FIRST ATHEISTS 1540–1840

1. Italy and France: From Sozzini to d'Holbach

It was the rediscovery of the works of the ancient Greeks and Romans at the time of the Renaissance that led to the first beginnings of dissent from Christian orthodoxy. George T. Buckley in his *Atheism in the English Renaissance* says it brought about a shift of interest to the affairs of this world as opposed to the next, and to the individual as opposed to the Church or state: 'Men began to be aware that Plato and Aristotle were not forerunners of Christ but representatives of a culture in which Christ and his church had no part.' Although there were few specifically religious works in ancient classical texts, 'there was a considerable body of works of a sceptical, enquiring nature – works which clearly had an agnostic if not atheistical import and which could not be reconciled to the tenets of Christianity'.

One of the most popular of Renaissance books was Pliny the Younger's *Natural History* which went into thirty-eight editions in western Europe between 1469 and 1532. If there was a god, said Pliny, he had no providence over the lives of men nor was he concerned with their mundane affairs. The soul was not immortal, though he agreed with Aristotle that the world was, thus offending Christian sensibilities on three counts, for they looked backwards to a divine Creation and forward to the last judgement. Others whom the Roman Catholic Church did its best to ignore were Lucian who held no belief in the supernatural nor, like Cicero, in miracles. The poet Lucretius did believe in gods, but saw them as concerned only with their own welfare and not the least interested in man; he too denied the immortality of the soul, and his great anti-religious poem *De rerum natura* was first published in Brescia in 1473. Most pleasing of all, however, to Humanists of the time were the works of Plutarch and Seneca who preached a morality based on reason and conscience rather than on one dictated by a god; which led Erasmus to say, 'Remain good Christians but profit by ancient wisdom.'

Yet it was not until the middle of the sixteenth century that atheism or a disbelief in gods first began to be publicly voiced. It occurred in Italy where (despite or because of papal proximity?) there had always been a strong anti-clerical tradition. In 1551 the English Humanist Roger Ascham reported the country to be rife with atheists. Here, he said, 'a man may freely discourse against what he will ... against any Prince, any government, yea against God himself and his whole religion'; and two years earlier one of them, Lelio Sozzini, told Calvin that he doubted the divinity of Christ, the resurrection of the body and the reliability of scripture. Resurrection was a subject that perplexed many, particularly Commodo Canuove who was denounced to the Venetian Inquisition for having declared: 'We have never seen any dead man who has returned from the other side to tell us that Paradise exists or purgatory or hell. All these things are the fantasies of friars and priests.' A fellow traveller was the Venetian ambassador to Paris and later London, Antonio Foscarini, who, in addition to questioning the existence of paradise, mocked the doctrine of the Trinity and spoke disrespectfully of Christ and the sacraments.

In 1542 Francisco Vimercati, King's Reader in Greek and Latin philosophy at the University of Padua, declared that matter was eternal without beginning or end, that everything that exists had a natural cause and there was no personal immortality. Cesare Cremoni, Professor of Philosophy at Padua University, and Simone Simoni, professor at Heidelberg University, also disbelieved personal immortality, but for denying that God created the world and for declaring miracles to be absurd, Simoni's university expelled him. In 1577 Alvise Capuano was denounced to the Venetian Inquisition whose judgement, after he had recanted to save his life, was unequivocal in its condemnation:

> You believed that the world was created by chance and that when the body dies, the soul dies also. You believed that Christ was the adopted son of the Madonna, born as other men are, and that angels and demons do not exist, that there are no true witches and that belief in witchcraft arises from melancholic humour. When you were an atheist, you did not believe that God existed or indeed any supernatural beings . . . and that the entire Old Testament is a superstition.

Giulio Cesare Vanini, one of the most outspoken atheists of his time but who did not recant, was less fortunate. For declaring in his two books *Amphitheatrum* and *De Admirandis* that an immaterial god could not create a material world nor a spiritual being communicate with a corporeal one, for saying that Christianity was a fiction for rulers and priests to secure power, and various other blasphemies, he was condemned to death by the Inquisition and burned to ashes at the age of thirty-four. A similar sentence was passed in 1550 on an apostate Franciscan, Francesco Calcagno, for denying the existence of God or the soul, affirming that Christ was only human and the Bible an untrustworthy invention designed to frighten the laity.

Others criticised the faith in more general terms. In 1606 Paolo Sarpi was theological consultant to the Venetian government; but he must have experienced a conversion from belief to disbelief as dramatic and intense as that of Paul in the opposite direction, for the following year he was excommunicated for saying that in his picture of the universe there was no place for God at all. The human sense of God, he said, articulated a human need; but the wise could lead a moral life without fear of God or the afterlife. Vimercati thought the same. Religion, he said, was the product of fear, an invention of rulers.

In the archives of the Venetian Inquisition and elsewhere there are many other similar recorded expressions of apostasy; yet most, and especially those willing to recant, were spared from death, the charges against them being considered to be impious rather than blasphemous. Most were able to prove to the Inquisition's satisfaction that whatever views they may have expressed, they had continued for every week of their lives to attend Mass, the celebration of the sacrament of the Lord's supper; and the Inquisition must have reasoned that any man who could subscribe to that could not, *ipso facto*, be an unbeliever. Whether the apostates continued to attend Mass as a kind of insurance against death at the hands of the Inquisition or fear of what the Lord they didn't believe in might do to them on judgement day, we shall never know. Yet in the face of such unreserved and explicit atheism, the leniency of the Inquisition does seem surprising: perhaps they feared that the burning at the stake of so many professors, ambassadors, theologians and other distinguished personages might cause a public outcry. Not for the first or last time in history the establishment looked after its own.

In 1541, at around the time the Italian atheists were beginning to make known their views, Pierre Charron was born in France. When he grew up he at first studied law but later went into the Church. He also became a friend of the famous essayist Montaigne whose sceptical religious views undoubtedly influenced him; from having written one book in defence of Catholicism, *Les Trois Vérités*, he then, at the age of sixty and within two years of his death, published a minor masterpiece and runaway bestseller, *De la Sagesse* (*Concerning Wisdom*) in which he recanted his former beliefs. It was a bold thing to do, for the Inquisition was still active and in 1574 a nobleman from Orléans, Geoffroy Vallée, was burned at the stake in Paris for denying God. Although something of an oddball, Vallée said some wise things, such as, 'There are two types of belief: one, the evidence of our senses which is imposed upon us by nature and is natural; the other, belief in the Creed, for instance, which is imposed upon us by society and is irrational.' Charron was astute enough to avoid the attentions of the Catholic hierarchy by attacking not Christianity but religion generally; and during the first seventy years of the seventeenth century *Sagesse* was reprinted many times. First he prepared the reader for what was to come:

> I do not intend to oblige anyone to agree with me, nor do I aim to persuade them. I do not argue dogmatically. I simply lay out my views as a stallholder displays his wares in a market . . . If anyone puts forward a better argument than mine, I will listen to it with pleasures and delight.

Then:

> All religions have this in common, that they are an outrage to common sense, for they are pieced together out of a variety of elements some of which seem so unworthy, sordid and at odds with man's reason that any strong and vigorous intelligence laughs at them; but others are so noble, illustrious, miraculous and mysterious that the intellect can make no sense of them and finds them unpalatable.

> All religions, without exception, share the same characteristics. All discover and publicise miracles, prodigies, oracles, sacred mysteries, saints, prophets, festivals, articles of faith and beliefs necessary for salvation; each pretends to be better and truer than the others . . . In religion one finds the most extraordinary claims and the most transparent impostures, but these only serve to inspire greater reverence and more unquestioning admiration.

> One's nation, one's country, one's home determines one's religion. One is of the religion of the place where one was born and brought up. We are circumcised or baptised – Jews or Moslems or Christians – before we know we are human beings.

> Because he shapes his own behaviour in the light of his fear of

167

punishment in the next world, the superstitious man does not allow either God or his fellow man to live in peace . . . He trembles with fear . . . anxious that God may not be pleased with him, he tries to please him and conquer him with adulation, importuning him with prayers, vows, offerings, inventing miracles of his own and easily giving credence to those invented by others.

Charron waxed particularly fiercely against what he called custom or universal assent, the belief that if something had been accepted by a large number of people over a long period of time it must therefore be true. 'Universal assent,' says Professor Tullio Gregory, 'had been regarded in the Stoic tradition as a criterion of truth and, having been taken up by Christian theology, was used in the seventeenth century as a proof of natural theology, a reflection of divine inspiration.' Charron disagreed. The strongest argument for truth, he said, was the assent of the whole world and because of the diversity of religions that was not forthcoming.

Despite his strictures, and by way of a nod to the Catholic elders, Charron agreed that religion was the bond and cement of human society, and that the customs and laws of any country should be observed simply because they were established. But as a guide to right conduct and living, he was in no doubt where his own loyalties lay: 'I want men to be good and to be solidly and firmly dedicated to what is right . . . motivated by love of themselves and by the desire to live up to their nature as men. Any other commitment is a betrayal of one's self and leads to the destruction of oneself.'

This insistence on the autonomy of ethical choice, says Gregory, 'marks the secularisation of morality, its separation from the sphere of the sacred'. It led also, he says, to the emphasis on conscience as the principle of moral behaviour: 'The abandonment of the ethics of the sacred marked the birth of that theology of man which . . . freed reason from the heavens.' No wonder that in the course of the seventeenth century *Sagesse* went into edition after edition, touching a chord to which literally hundreds of thousands responded. But so great was the fear of their destiny among ordinary mortals and so tight was the stranglehold the Church had on them that it would be another 400 years before the universal assent of dissent began to come into its own.

In the course of the seventeenth century other anti-Christian groups formed, among them Christianised Jews from Spain and Portugal who had fled to Holland to avoid the Inquisition: Spinoza was one of them. Here, as it were, they regained their faith and identity as Jews, among them Saul Levi Mortera, chief rabbi of Amsterdam's Portuguese synagogue (still standing) and Isaac Orobio, a Spanish *converso* and court physician who, after torture by the Spanish Inquisition, fled first to France and then to Amsterdam where he had himself circumcised. These two and others denied the doctrine of the Trinity and Christ's divinity and resurrection, and claimed that the law of Moses as set out in the Old Testament sufficed for Jewish faith. Asked why, if Christ as a Jew was as perfect and heroic as Christians maintained, the Jews had not also claimed him for their own, they replied that the Christian belief that the Old Testament prophecies were fulfilled in the New Testament and on which the Christian faith was founded was false (as I have already sought to show) and that therefore Christianity was groundless.

A book which attacked not only Christianity but all three of the great Middle Eastern religions was first published in The Hague early in the eighteenth century under the title of *La Vie et L'Esprit de Spinosa* [sic] (*The Life and Spirit of Spinoza*), and in the latter part of the century came to be reprinted several times as *Le Traité des trois imposteurs* (*Treatise on Three Impostors*). The impostors in question were Moses, Christ and Mohammed, and Silvia Berti, who has studied the book and its origins in detail, has this to say about the *L'Esprit* section (*La Vie* was a portrait of Spinoza), believed to have been written by a young Dutch diplomat named Jan Vroesen:

> The argument of *L'Esprit* is bold and uncompromising. The author maintains that blind prejudice preserves the ridiculous conceptions of God that men are brought up to believe and that they never pause to examine. Ignorance and fear have given birth to

169

superstition, have created the gods and, assisted by the impostures of rulers, have transformed laws that are actually human into inviolable divine decrees. Thus the ideas that men form regarding the nature of the world are the products of imagination, not of reason.

Religion, Professor Berti continues,

is the term for this subordination of reason to imagination, a subordination motivated by fear. Building on this foundation, Moses, the descendant of a magician, legitimises his role as a regulator by laying claim to a divine investiture, which he confirmed by carrying out fraudulent miracles. Later Jesus Christ drew men to him by offering them the illusory expectation of a life after death. The Christians believed him to be God, although they recognised him as a man; which is equivalent to believing that a circle is a square. Finally the imposture was perfected by Muhammad, whose authority derived from force of arms and who claimed to be a prophet for all nations, sent to give witness to the true law of God, which had been corrupted by the Jews and Christians. Other beliefs that men have acquired over time, such as the belief in the immortality of the soul or in the existence of immaterial beings, are equally groundless.

In the cafés of the university towns of France (and other countries of western Europe) students and others were beginning to question publicly, some for the first time, the debatable doctrine that 'God' had made the world in seven days and later on had sent his only son to earth to preach the redemption of sinners and by his sacrificial death had saved us from ourselves. Some exchanged their views by word of mouth, others circulated them in pamphlets. In 1729, Alan Charles Kors tells us, a police memo warned of the dangers of the 'self-proclaimed wits' of the Paris cafés who were speaking against religion. 'If order is not restored,' the police inspector urged, 'the number of atheists or deists will grow, and many people will make a religion of their own design for themselves.' Reference was made to the Paris bookseller Morléon who was selling to abbeys and others, 'works filled with impieties and maxims contrary to the existence of God'. The police were quite right, the number of atheists did grow – Marin Mersenne in the previous century claimed there were 50,000 living in Paris alone – and for the Church the question arose as to how best to deal with them.

Some thought it prudent to take a leaf from the atheists' book and deny their existence just as they denied the existence of God. One such was La Bruyère who spoke of depraved, immoral men who *might wish* that God did not exist and added, 'I would like to see a moderate, sober, chaste, equitable man utter the phrase that there is no god . . . This man cannot be found.' To the pure all things were impure, especially atheists who, if they did exist, were necessarily libertines. 'An atheist is a lewd person,' one saying went, 'and a lewd person is an atheist.' François Pouget, with the approval of the Archbishop of Paris, wrote in a book published in 1707:

> The ungodly person wishes there were no God in order to be able to smother all remorse and gratify his passions with more liberty. The depravity of his heart impels him later to say to himself that there is no God. But he tries in vain to numb himself to this truth; it is so strongly imprinted in the mind of man, that it is virtually impossible for it to be entirely effaced.

The Jesuit Rapin agreed: 'Of all the natural truths the most deeply engraved in the heart of man is the existence of God. All times, all nations, all schools agree on it. There is nothing more monstrous in nature than atheism [which is] only found among those with disordered minds and whose hearts are the most corrupt.' And from the Church came this warning: 'To live as if there were no god is to place oneself in peril if there is.'

Others of the orthodoxy took a different tack. Jacques Basnage declared, and in our own time Paul Johnson has echoed him, that just before their deaths and out of fear of what might come after, atheists return to Christian beliefs – a piece of wishful thinking as false then as it is today; while the Huguenot theologian Jacques Abbadie wrote: 'To reject as a speculation what one does not see or touch forms one of the prejudices of the atheists who do not believe there is a God because they cannot see him.' He naturally did not add the corollary that it was no less speculative to believe there was a god as to disbelieve it.

And Rapin's bland and ignorant assertion that all times, all nations, all schools, agree that God exists suffered a setback after Locke's statement in 1689 that the Ancients had had no belief in a personal god and that there were whole nations existing which had no notion of a god nor of any religion. For this was the time of the seafaring peoples of Europe exploring and mapping the world and, in the process, of meeting people of other lands of friendly disposition but no religious beliefs and of whose previous existence they had been barely aware. The missionary priest Chrétien Le Clerq found that the Indians of the Gaspe peninsula had never formed a conception of any divinity but, he noted in 1691, 'they were charitable beyond anything imaginable in Europe'; while the Jesuit La Jeune described the natives of Cap Breton who also lacked a knowledge of God as 'exceptionally clever, honest and decent, very generous and with a cheerful disposition'. In Siam, now Thailand, Louis XIV's envoy de la Loubère reported the inhabitants as having no belief in a god or in the immortality of the soul, though some added that they did have a god once but he had since disappeared, they didn't know where. There were countless other examples, of which one of the most touching concerned black atheists living in the Antilles, as related by the Dominican missionary Jean-Baptiste du Tertre, whose Church had taught him to expect the most depraved and corrupted of men. But he found otherwise. 'The love that they have for one another is extremely tender, and those on the same land have connections among themselves that are so close and so intimate that they assist each other in all their illnesses, and cannot see their companions mistreated without feeling their pain.'

Charles de Rochefort found the same among the Caribs whom he described as censorious of theft of any kind and wonderfully respectful towards their elders. Even more surprising to Rochefort was their attitude of moral superiority over Europeans. 'They reproach us for our greed,' he wrote, 'and are amazed by our love of gold. They themselves live in harmony and love one another very much.' Other missionaries and voyagers brought back similar stories from China and Japan.

Strangely enough, it was from Christianity's theologians that France's atheists found unexpected support. In proposing his famous five reasons for declaring that God exists, St Thomas Aquinas felt bound by logic also to argue the opposite:

> (1) If God existed, nobody would ever encounter evil. But evil is encountered in the world. God therefore does not exist. (2) It seems that everything we observe in this world can be fully accounted for by other causes without assuming a God. Thus natural effects are explained by natural causes, and contrived effects by human reasoning and will. There is therefore no need to suppose that a God exists.

Jacques Abbadie also argued against himself. If God existed, why did he allow rain to fall on uninhabited deserts, introduce flies and other noxious insects and permit the lack of wisdom and order that existed elsewhere in the world? And secondly, *pace* Aquinas, if the mysteries of nature in regard to motion and matter were truly understood, 'we would find nothing in them that constrained us to recognise a First Cause'.

Nor, atheists noted with interest, were the mass of the French people, the peasants and workers, shining examples of Christian belief. They went to church because church was obligatory and they feared the consequences of non-attendance. Their children would follow them in ignorance. When the Grand Archdeacon of Evreux, Henri-Marie Bourdon, was making pastoral visits to Church schools at the end of the seventeenth century, he found nothing but bafflement.

> We question the children, sometimes quite advanced in age, some

173

of them thirteen or fourteen years old; they answer perfectly all the questions that are found in the catechism . . . But if you ask them about their thoughts and sentiments with regard to God, you will see that they have not the least knowledge of him. They do not understand in any manner what they are talking about; they are without comprehension.

Boudon must have sympathised with an earlier priest, Jean d'Aubry, who had written of what he had preached being laughed at. 'I was plunged into a profound melancholy, seeing that our Religion . . . could not be usefully communicated.'

And every now and then, after all the huffing and puffing against the atheists by the orthodox, came some braver and brighter than the rest. The author of a book called *Histoire des Ouvrages des Savans*, reviewing some work of Basnage, said this:

The atheist avers that his attachment to his opinions is disinterested; no passion attaches itself of it . . . Atheists do not dive into debauchery nor abandon themselves to the *voluptés* of the world . . . they ordinarily seek seclusion and are little concerned for applause; their most sensual pleasure consists of meditation and contentment of mind.

In addition to Charron there were two other outstanding atheistic thinkers in eighteenth-century France. The first was Pierre Bayle, a Protestant philosopher from the Languedoc. Not only was he among the foremost to deny the doctrine of universal assent, citing the experiences and observations of missionaries and other travellers mentioned above, but he also challenged in his books the deeply held Christian belief that you could not have morals without religion, a theme, as we shall see, that an English philosopher, Margaret Knight, propagated in two broadcasts in 1955 to the great consternation of many. Another commonly held belief of Bayle's time, and even subscribed to by many disbelievers including David Hume, was that, whether true or not, religion was the cement that held society together and without it there might be anarchy. Almost alone, Bayle disputed it. He believed, said Kors, that while it was true that the corruption of morals could lead to lack of faith, it in no way followed that lack of faith led to corruption of morals. There was no evidence at all, he said, that atheism was subversive of the existing social order. 'There could be wicked believers and virtuous unbelievers', as indeed there always have been and still are today.

Yet it was not until the second half of the eighteenth century that avowed atheism in France reached its apogee with the coming of the little group that became known as the *philosophes*, who were said to be the fathers of the French Revolution. They had already seen the birth of the scientific revolution which in turn would lead to the Industrial Revolution – roads and railways, the growth of capitalism to finance new manufacturing, internal and international trade. It was a time of major political and social change, a time when European minds first experienced the heady joys of enlightenment, freed from the shibboleths and restrictions of the past; a time of intellectual freedom when almost anything went, and taboos on subject matter were out.

Such a climate made it possible for *les philosophes* to come together and flourish. Its founder was Paul Thiry, Baron d'Holbach, an aristocrat by acquisition not birth. He was immensely rich and owned two grand houses: No. 2 Rue Royal in the heart of Paris where what Jean-Jacques Rousseau called the *coterie Holbachique* met for dinner on Thursday and Sunday evenings; and a country estate called Grandval where, according to one chronicler, d'Holbach had 'an excellent chef, many servants, abundant and memorable foods, a remarkable collection of vintage wines and a library of more than 3,000 volumes'. Despite these conveniences and the company of an attractive wife, he was said to have often felt lonely at Grandval and it was to enjoy the company of other like-minded freethinkers that in 1750 he first formed the *coterie Holbachique*; and for the same reason supported at Grandval a variety of poor artists, writers and composers. Some of the *coterie* also came to stay at Grandval, sometimes for weeks on end so that there were times when d'Holbach was himself unsure who was living in the house and who had come to visit.

The numbers of those attending the regular *coterie* dinners varied but would seem to have been between twelve and twenty with up to half a dozen guests. Most of the *coterie* were connected with literature in some form or other such as Denis Diderot, editor of the famous *Encyclopédie* and d'Holbach's closest friend. Others included Friedrich Grimm, born a German, Suard and Marmontel, the Abbé Raynal, an apostate priest, Le Roy, the royal Lieutenant of the Hunt, Roux, a doctor and chemist, and St Lambert, soldier and philosopher.

It was in the period 1770–80 that the group reached its peak of fame. The clerical establishment called it a den of virulent atheists, and there's no doubt that three members, Jacques-André Naigeon, d'Holbach and Diderot were unequivocal in their atheistic beliefs. D'Holbach once said that he doubted if Christianity in Europe would last beyond the end of the eighteenth century and Diderot that a people who believed that it was a god and not laws that made men honest were but little advanced. Yet what characterised the group as a whole was their readiness to discuss any subject under the sun, to take one side of a debate or the other irrespective of personal belief and at times both sides simultaneously. It was their love of genuine free thought, untrammelled by religion or the law, that led one writer to call them 'the most intellectually stimulating and widely known private discussion group in Europe'.

Among the guests in 1763 was David Hume, the Scottish philosopher known as 'The Great Infidel' because of his anti-Christian views; and Diderot left this account of his visit:

> The first time that M. Hume found himself at the table of the Baron, he was seated beside him. I do not know for what purpose the English [*sic*] philosopher took it into his head to remark to the Baron that he did not believe in atheists, that he had never seen any. The Baron said to him: 'Count how many we are here. We are eighteen. It is not too bad a showing to be able to point out

to you fifteen atheists at once: the three others have not made up their minds.'

Here Hume's memory was letting him down, for according to Boswell he had once met an avowed atheist in the shape of Lord Marischal who, after Hume had declared that there *might* be a god, 'would not speak to me for a week'. It is also likely that d'Holbach was exaggerating when he told Hume there were fifteen atheists at his table. My feeling is that he said it to provoke Hume into a reaction of surprise and perhaps approval; for in this same year Sir James Macdonald of Sleat, then living in Paris, wrote to a friend in England: 'Poor Hume who on your side of the water was thought to have too little religion is here thought to have too much.'

Another guest *chez* d'Holbach was Rousseau who suffered from an acute inferiority complex and convinced himself that people were conspiring against him. In the year 1753 he wrote in his *Confessions*: 'The moment I appeared at the Baron's, general conversation ceased, people gathered in little knots, whispering into each other's ears, and I was left alone, at a loss for anyone to speak to.' The final straw came on a later occasion when he took offence at something the baron said to him and, consumed by self-pity, 'was finally driven from his house . . . and decided never to return'. The English writer Horace Walpole had rather more mature misgivings, saying of d'Holbach and the *coterie*: 'There was no bearing the authors, *philosophes*, *savants* of which he had a pigeon-house full. They soon turned my head with a new system of antediluvian deluge.' He much preferred, he said, the Jesuits to the *philosophes*.

In 1770 (or twelve years before publication of the first avowedly atheistic book in England) d'Holbach published anonymously (to avoid prosecution) his avowedly atheistic *Système de la Nature* with an introduction by Jacques-André Naigeon, whose views have recently been analysed and commented on by Alan Charles Kors. If the French establishment had been shocked by rumours of the goings-on at the *coterie* dinners, they were outraged by what they now read in cold print in *Système de la Nature*. Belief in God, wrote Naigeon in his introduction, was the barrier to all essential human progress. The natural impulses of mankind were for happiness, and we were predisposed to love one another and love peace. Religion was against those natural tendencies and its claim to authority was that it spoke on behalf of a fierce god whom it presented as the tyrant of the human race. Religion was the product of fear, melancholy, ignorance and a disordered imagination, and its agenda was irrational or unthinking resignation, detachment of reason and hatred of pleasure, coerced by the illusory fear of eternal punishment.

On this theme d'Holbach expanded. Man was a product of nature and wholly subjected to its laws.

> Ignorant of the real cause of our happiness or pain, we create gods, superstitions and myths as paths to wellbeing, increasing our misery in the process. Helpless and fearful, we trust to an authority that can justify itself neither by evidence nor by reason nor by moral consequence, but bases its claims of legitimate rule upon occult knowledge of, and our relationship to, realms beyond our experience.

Was the universe cause or effect? asked d'Holbach. Christian theology had taught that it was effect and this raised questions about a First Cause and the origins of Motion (i.e. God); or, as he put it, in order to explain what you hardly understand, you have need of a cause that you do not understand at all. But the universe seen as a cause of all effect made more sense. We experienced not the creation or destruction of matter, but the inextinguishability and recombination of matter – a body that decomposed became the stuff of a new combination. Why hypothesise beyond that?

The world, said d'Holbach, cannot be other than what it is. Let us not speak of its perfection nor its wisdom nor its goodness. All such attributes of moral qualities to a reality of blind matter acting according to its nature are expressions devoid of meaning. The universe as a whole and in its details offers nothing that can be praised or condemned. The assumption that matter exists eternally as Aristotle believed, makes more sense than the incomprehensible hypothesis of its creation, as in Genesis, out of nothing. To speak of 'soul' or 'immaterial' or 'supernatural' was to create an imaginary world that was beyond experience, conceptually incoherent and unproductive of future knowledge.

Naigeon agreed with Hobbes (and Paine) that theology was literally and figuratively nonsense (*le non sens*) and the words that referred to 'Beings' unperceived by the senses to be sounds without significance. Substance without dimension, i.e. spirit, was a contradiction in terms and the word 'incorporeal' was without meaning.

If not from theology, then, they asked themselves, where did we gain our knowledge of the world? From our senses, they answered, and only from the senses, as Locke and Aristotle had averred. 'Whatever knowledge the senses furnish us with is the only knowledge we have. We find ourselves forced to be content with it and we see that it is sufficient to our needs.' Words were names agreed upon to allow us to communicate about the objects of our sensory experience.

Materialistic atheism, concluded d'Holbach, put human beings in a relationship with natural phenomena and the quest for wellbeing that offered our only hope of amelioration. There was no reason to be resigned to suffering and we (humanity) were our only source of moral concern. How absurd to prostrate ourselves before the amoral! D'Holbach also made the point in defence of his beliefs that 'Man's thoughts, his reflections, his manner of viewing things, of feeling, of judging, are neither voluntary nor free'. In other words, beliefs that arise spontaneously, being passive, are beyond the believer's control; a view which in the next century the poet Shelley would propagate with much passion.

Finally d'Holbach asked himself, What if I am wrong and God punishes me for having followed my compassion and my reason? His answer was typical and what one might have expected. 'I should congratulate myself,' he replied, 'for having been free for a time from his tyrannical yoke.'

But despite d'Holbach's earlier hopes that Christianity was on the wane and would soon disappear for ever, neither he nor Naigeon held out any hope that their published views would weaken orthodox beliefs. Man, admitted d'Holbach, was a weak being filled with needs that he could not give to himself. 'He who combats religion resembles one who uses a sword to kill fruit flies: as soon as the blow is struck, the fruit flies ... return ... and take again in people's minds the place from which one believed to have banished them.' Naigeon was equally despondent, seeing the need for religious belief as inherent in human nature, and not hopeful of humanity being improved in any fundamental way. To think that it *could* be improved in such a way, he told Diderot, was 'a sweet error and beautiful chimera'; and, he might have added had he had the gift of prophecy, would remain so for the next 200 years.

2. Scotland: From Frazer to Hume

How much in the way of atheistic beliefs existed in Britain before the second half of the eighteenth century is hard to say. Certainly there are plenty of denials of it which suggests there was more of it about than people were prepared to admit although, as in France, no one was prepared to commit himself to print for fear of prosecution and imprisonment. The standard practice of those who publicly deplored it was to affirm that there were no atheists anyway but that if there were a few, they should be roundly condemned. As early as 1622 in his book *Atheomastix* Bishop Fotherby claimed in parts that there were no atheists and in others that there were many (yet even these had to be qualified):

> When we confess, *There be Atheists*, and dispute against them, we understand only such as deny there is a God rather by outward profession than by inward perswasion; or, if they have indeed any such inward perswasion, it is but only upon some sodaine passion; which vanisheth as sodainely as it was conceived fondly.

Two years later Lord Herbert of Cherbury was writing in the same vein:

> In reality there are no atheists; but because they have noticed that some people apply false and shocking statements to God, they have preferred not to believe in God than to believe in a God of such character. When he is endowed with true attributes, so far from believing in him, they would pray that such a God might exist, if there were no such Being.

In 1678 Ralph Cudworth published a massive treatise against atheism called *The True Intellectual System of the Universe*. In the preface he wrote: 'Some will be ready to condemn this whole labour of ours against atheism as altogether useless and superfluous upon this pretense, that an Atheist is a mere Chimera and there is no such thing found anywhere in the world' and went on to say that his book is not intended 'only for conversion of downright and professed Atheists (of which there is but little hope, they being sunk into so great a degree of sottishness) but for the confirmation of weak, staggering and sceptical Theists'.

And in the main body of his work he claims that atheists are not motivated by reason but by 'a certain blind and irrational impulse'.

Richard Bentley in the first of his 1692 Boyle lectures at Cambridge made a rather different point:

> What Government can be imagined without judicial Proceedings? And what methods of Judicature without a religious oath? which implies and supposes an Omniscient Being, as conscious to its falsehood or truth, and revenger of Perjury. So that the very nature of an Oath . . . is subverted by the Atheist.

This was understandable; for at that time in Scotland the oath in the Courts of Justice read: 'I swear by Almighty God *and as I shall answer to God at the great day of judgement,*[1] to tell the truth, the whole truth and nothing but the truth.' Taking an oath then was for most a solemn and frightening occasion and would, it was believed, deter the majority from lying; though in capital cases it could be assumed that an accused, whether theist or atheist, would take a chance on lying if it looked like sparing him the gallows.

It was also in Scotland, five years later and at the same time as the investigations into the Paisley witchcraft case, that the trial took place of Britain's first avowed atheist. His name was John Frazer, an Edinburgh merchant's apprentice, and he was charged with denying the existence of God, the devil, and the immortality of the soul and of ridiculing the divine origin of the scriptures, saying that 'they were only to frighten folks and keep them in order'. Asked about his religion, he said he had none but was 'just an atheist and that was his religion'.

Under Scottish law (which then, as now, is different from that of England) there were two Acts concerning blasphemy and atheism under which Frazer could have been charged. The first, the 1661 Act, was passed during the first Scottish parliament of Charles II, and prescribed the death penalty for anyone who, not being insane, 'shall rail or curse upon God or any of the persons of the blessed Trinity'. A second Act passed in 1695 confirmed the terms of the first in greater detail but the penalties were milder. On the first occasion the offender would be imprisoned 'and give public satisfaction in sackcloth to the Congregation within which the scandal was committed, on the second he should be fined and on the third he should be executed as an obstinate blasphemer'.

It was under this Act that Frazer was indicted and, confronted with the charges against him, at once recanted, proclaiming his belief in Christianity and pleading that he had merely been repeating views that had been expressed in *The Oracles of Reason*, a book published in London three years earlier by the deistic writer Charles Blount. The charges were proved and he was duly sentenced to be imprisoned and to give satisfaction for his misdemeanour in sackcloth, it being a first offence. He was released from prison in February 1697.

But hot on the heels of his conviction came that of another, a twenty-year-old Edinburgh University third-year arts student named

Thomas Aikenhead who had been left an orphan at the age of eleven. It was clear from the evidence that Aikenhead had had access in the university library and in the town's bookshops to works by such doubters as Hobbes and Spinoza, as well as Blount and Toland and G.C. Vanini,[2] and of course Aristotle for the world as eternal and Epicurus for the denial of providence and the immortality of the soul, all of which he needed for the ethics section of his degree: this embraced the relationship of the divine and the natural law and the morality of human actions.

Here was the indictment against him: that he had called theology 'a rapsidie of faigned and ill-invented nonsense, patched up partly of the moral doctrine of philosophers and partly of poetical fictions and extravagant chimeras', that he had 'ridiculed the holy scriptures by claiming them to be stuffed with madness, nonsense and contradictions', that the Old Testament was a set of fables and the New 'the history of the Imposter Christ who had learned magic in Egypt and in Judea had picked up a few ignorant, blockish fisher fellows [where] he played his pranks, as he had blasphemously termed the working of his miracles'. He had dismissed Moses ('if there ever was such a man') as cavalierly as he had dismissed Christ. He had declared the Trinity to be not worth any man's contradiction and the idea of Christ being both God and man was as great a contradiction as the mythical goat-stag or squaring the circle. He had called the doctrine of redemption by Jesus a presumptuous device and that the inventors of it were damned 'if after this life there be neither reward or punishment'. He claimed that the notion of a spirit was also a contradiction and that God, the world and nature were one thing, and the world was from eternity. Finally he said that he preferred Mahomet to Jesus and hoped (as Baron d'Holbach was to hope) for the extirpation of Christianity by the year 1800.

This was strong stuff, expressed in extravagant language, and because of it the Scottish Privy Council chose to prosecute him under the 1661 rather than the 1695 Act, the penalty for the former being death. None the less five of the nominated jurors summoned to try him refused to do so. Four of Aikenhead's fellow students whose views on religion Aikenhead claimed were similar to his gave evidence against him. One, Mungo Craig, testified that he had heard Aikenhead boast of 'the above mentioned ridiculous Notions' that had appeared in the Indictment, coupled with his claim to have converted to his views 'a certain Minister of the Gospel'.

Like Frazer before him, Aikenhead recanted too but with insufficient conviction to persuade the Privy Council of his sincerity, and when the time came for them to consider his petitions for clemency, one of the grounds being that he was still a minor, they rejected it by a single vote: many of the council were strict Calvinists and had been deeply shocked by the profanities he had uttered. On 8 January 1697 he was taken from the Tolbooth prison to the gallows green on Leith Walk and there, Bible in hand, was hanged by the neck until he was dead. The Rev. Alexander Findlater who witnessed the execution said he thought God would be glorified by such an awful and exemplary punishment.

Before he died, however, he left what was called his *Cygnea Cantio* or swan-song which survives to this day and in which, in contrast to the language he was accused of in his indictment, he made a much more reasoned statement about his beliefs. He had reached the conclusions he had, he said, because from an early age he had had 'an insatiable inclination to truth'. He had not arrived at his disbelief to justify some immorality he had committed but because he believed what he had said to be true, and indeed one of his witnesses had testified that he was not an immoral person 'but extremely serious'. He also claimed, truly enough, that a great part of morality, if not all, was of purely human derivation. He argued convincingly in favour of natural as opposed to revealed religion, claiming that the doctrine of providence contradicted revelation. Lastly he wrote, as St Bernard had done before him, of his difficulties in accepting the Trinity which he saw as a kind of pantheism. 'These things I have puzzled and vexed myself in, and all that I could learn therefrom is that I cannot have such certainty in either natural or supernatural things as I would have. And so I desire all men, especially ingenuous young men, to beware and take notice of these things on which I have split.' Interestingly, says

Michael Hunter in his essay 'Aikenhead the Atheist', expressions of doubt about even the most fundamental Christian doctrines were at this time common among the highly devout.

So was Aikenhead a prophet before his time, or, as the Scottish courts had found, a profane blasphemer? Writing in his *History of England* 150 years later, Lord Macaulay called Aikenhead's execution 'a crime which has never since polluted the island' and taken in conjunction with the hanging of the so-called Paisley witches six months later, as 'two persecutions worthy of the tenth century'.

There were no laws against atheism or blasphemy in England to compare with either the 1661 or the 1697 Acts of Scotland; though doubtless there would have been had there been cases similar to those of Frazer and Aikenhead. In any case, in religious matters the English were far more tolerant than the Scots. Two draft Acts of parliament to suppress atheism and blasphemy were published in 1666–7 and again in 1677–8: the first was the milder of the two, the punishment if guilty being no more than a fine of fifty shillings, but the second made the offence criminal. 'If any person, *being of the age of 16 years or more*, not being visibly and apparently distracted out of his wits by sickness or natural infirmity . . . shall after the day whereon the Royal Assent shall be given by word or writing deny that there is a God . . . that person shall be committed to prison.' In the end neither reached the statute book: atheism was not such a threat as to cause concern, and was best met by ridicule or pretending it didn't exist.

In the light of Aikenhead's execution, however, a new 1697 Act was passed, by which it was a criminal offence 'to deny any one of the persons of the Holy Trinity to be God or . . . deny the Christian religion to be true or the Holy Scriptures of the Old and New Testament to be of divine authority'. The punishment was to be mild for a first offence, providing the accused recanted, but for a second offence it was to be three years' imprisonment. I can find no record of any prosecution taking place under the Act.

None the less attacks on atheism and denials that it existed continued throughout the eighteenth century, prelates and others fearing the threat it posed to their comfortable orthodox beliefs. Those who railed against it most were: in 1712 Henry Moore, a Cambridge Platonist ('I may safely pronounce that it is mere brutish Ignorance or Impudence . . . that can encourage any man to profess Atheism'); in 1734 the author of an essay in the *London Magazine* ('A contemplative Atheist is what I think impossible; most who would be thought atheists are so out of Indolence because they will not give themselves Time to reason, to find out if they are so or not'); in 1737 Thomas Broughton in his *Bibliotheca historica-sacra* ('There is room to doubt whether there have ever been thinking men who have reasoned themselves into a disbelief of a Deity'); in 1749 John Balguy, moral philosopher ('Atheism offers such violence to all our facilities that it scarce seems credible that it should really find any footing in human understanding'); in 1771 the author of an article in the *Encyclopaedia Britannica* ('Many people, both ancient and modern, have pretended to atheism . . . but it is justly questioned whether any man seriously adopted such a principle'); and in 1791 Edmund Burke ('Atheism is not only against our reason but our instincts and it cannot prevail long').

In some quarters, though, it had already begun to prevail. In 1699 Lord Shaftesbury, a pupil though not a follower of the philosopher Locke, published a book called *An Inquiry concerning Virtue and Merit*. Locke believed that man's sense of rightness and wrongness came from God, and that a disbelief in the existence of God dissolved the bonds of society. Shaftesbury thought the opposite true: religion follows from, or is grounded in, man's innate sense of morality. Similarly man's belief in justice must precede a belief in a just God. Rightness and justice must exist independently of God.

Shaftesbury also denied that the promise of rewards and punishments should influence behaviour. To do what we know to be right in the hope of favours later subverts our morality. The same goes for the man who breaks the law under threat of punishment. 'There is no more of rectitude, piety or sanctity in a creature thus reformed than there is of meekness and gentleness in a strongly chained tiger.' Shaftesbury saw God as being remote from men, in whose affairs he did not interfere. 'He can do nothing for us; we can do nothing for him.' Thus an atheist could be virtuous, for virtue does not depend on God.

Other thinkers of the time also challenged the attributions of justice, goodness, love and mercy to God. Two prelates were among them, Archbishop King and Bishop Browne. Surprisingly (for them) they declared that we could have no knowledge of God's attributes, King going as far to say that we can as little believe that God is good or wise as that he has arms and is occasionally jealous (or, said Voltaire, as that he is blue or square). If that was so, then it seemed that nothing was left of God but his name, with no meaning attached to it. Bishop Berkeley, the philosopher, said that this view tended towards atheism, as of course it did. It was left to another deistic writer, Anthony Collins, to sum this argument up, as recounted by David Berman:

> God is an immaterial being and his identity is like nothing we can conceive. What we cannot conceive is meaningless. Supposing however that we can conceive his attributes, then they are observed to be contradictory. As the conception of such a being is either meaningless or contradictory, that being cannot exist.

He might have added, except as an idea in the mind where it has always existed and maybe always will.

In 1724 Collins published his *Discourse on the Grounds and Reasons of the Christian Religion*, another polemic against Christianity. He argued, as I have done, that there was little direct connection between the Old and New Testaments because the principal grounds for thinking so were the Old Testament prophecies about the coming of the Messiah whom the gospel writers wrongly claimed to be Jesus.

Then in the second half of the eighteenth century the most ardently religious doubter of all appeared in the shape of the great Scottish philosopher David Hume. In his long life he produced a body of work, particularly *Dialogues concerning Natural Religion*, which found all religions wanting. The Greek Infidel was called an atheist by many, which he always denied; a thoroughgoing sceptic would be nearer the mark.

Like all philosophers, Hume's starting point was the nature and extent of human knowledge. There was a general assumption, he declared, that nothing that exists, exists without a cause. If everything had a cause, what was the cause of the world we live in? The popular belief was God (whom Hume called 'a riddle, an enigma, an inexplicable mystery', whose existence it was impossible to prove). To what degree could that belief be sustained? For if God was the cause and everything had to have a cause, what caused God? Likewise, what caused whatever it was that caused God? There was no end to that line of reasoning, and it only ended in absurdity.

Then there was the problem of suffering, not that which men inflicted on each other, but those arising from natural causes such as famine, plagues, earthquakes, floods. Christians claimed their God was all-knowing, all-powerful, all-good. If he was all-knowing, said Hume, he was aware of the suffering. If he was all-powerful and all-good, he could prevent the suffering but didn't. What kind of a god was that?

There were also those who relied on the design argument, that just as a watch had been designed by a watchmaker or a house by an architect, so the universe had been designed and governed by certain fixed laws to allow it to function as it did. Hume admitted the attractions of this argument, but the more he examined it, the more he distrusted it, there being an insurmountable gap between the natural world, of whose origins we are ignorant, and an artefact such as a watch or a house which we know to have been manufactured and by whom. Was not the universe more like an animal or a vegetable that regenerated itself rather than something manufactured?

In any case, he argued, why predicate that if the world was made by a god it had to be by one god? Why not polytheism, a collection of gods, indulging in teamwork as humans do, to build a house or a city? Adherence to one god bred superstition and fanaticism, conflict and war. Was not a world of many gods preferable to 'the implacable narrow spirits of Judaism, the bloody principles of Mahometanism, the grotesque intolerance of modern Christianity'? It was one thing to assume from the works of nature a Supreme Creator, but when you turned the medal over and surveyed the religious principles which prevailed in the world 'you will scarcely be persuaded that they are anything but sick men's dreams . . . or the playful whimsies of monkeys in human shape'.

While it was on belief in the so-called Father rather than the Son that Hume focused his criticisms, he did not hesitate like Cicero to point out the absurdity of miracles:

> A miracle is a violation of the laws of nature. Nothing is esteemed a miracle if it ever happens in the common course of nature . . . But it is a miracle that a dead man should come to life, because that has never been observed in any age or country . . . When anyone tells me that he saw a dead man restored to life, I immediately consider with myself whether it be more probable that this person should either deceive or be deceived or that the fact which he relates should really have happened.

Nor would Hume allow religion to be the source of morality and goodness. A thing was right or good because it was right or good, not because some authority such as the headmaster, the bishop, the king, the Bible, Jesus Christ, God, said so. Even if one allowed that a god or gods created the world, it was nonsense to claim for them human attributes such as mercy, justice, love. In what way, he asked, did the deity's mercy or benevolence resemble the benevolence and mercy of man? And if we allowed there to be a deity or deities, what confidence could we repose in them? The laws of nature were carried on by an opposition of principles, hot and cold, moist and dry, heavy and light. 'The truth is that the original cause of all things is entirely indifferent to all those principles and has no more regard to good above ill than to heat above cold or moisture over drought . . . We have no more reason to infer that the rectitude of the First Cause resembles human rectitude than his benevolence does.' And if one was going to equate the deity with human attributes, why not bestow on him the human form – eyes, a nose, a mouth, ears, etc.? Epicurus had said that no man had ever experienced reason but in a human figure.

But was not some religion, he was asked, better than none? Could it not be said to regulate the hearts of men, humanise their conduct, encourage temperance, order and obedience? No, said Hume, and cited the clergy who were always lamenting the universality of human wickedness and yet in the same breath, as it were, claiming that without religion society would fall apart.

> It is certain from experience, that the smallest grain of natural honesty and benevolence has more effect on men's conduct than the most pompous views suggested by theological systems and theories; and none but fools ever repose less trust in a man because they hear that . . . he has entertained some speculative doubts with regard to theological subjects.

Popular religion, said Hume, was based on man's hopes and fears, what was going to happen to him in this world and in what he believed to be the next; the same fears that had produced 'the tribal deities of primitive men' and led to what he called 'some grovelling notion of superior powers'. He went on: 'We incessantly look forward and endeavour by prayers, adoration and sacrifice, to appease those unknown powers whom we find by experience to be able to afflict and oppress us.' Yet in those moments when man is happy and successful, it does not occur to him to thank his god for it, at least spontaneously; 'he only calls for him in time of distress and terror'. Nor did man run any risk in rejecting the terrors and with them the worship of God. 'It is an absurdity to believe that the Deity has human passions and one of the lowest of human passions, a restless appetite for applause' (a sentiment which some worshippers might consider when belting out 'Praise my soul, the King of Heaven' or 'Almighty, Invisible, God only wise!).

The worst effect of organised religion, he said, was its subversion of sincerity and self-knowledge. Popular religious belief was a form of make-believe which became a chain of hypocrisy leading to fraud, dissimulation and falsehood. 'Hence the highest zeal in religion and the deepest hypocrisy, so far from being inconsistent, are often united in the same individual character.'

'To all the purposes of life,' concluded Hume, 'religion is useless . . . No new fact can ever be inferred from the religious hypothesis; no event foreseen or foretold; no reward or punishment expected or dreaded beyond what is already known by practice and observation.'

What makes Hume's views so remarkable is the dispassion with which he sets them out, examining the phenomenon of religion as a scientist might examine a specimen under the microscope. He had no proselytising desire to urge people to deny God, which he himself was careful not to, admitting (his reasoning being all of a piece) that it was as impossible to prove that a god didn't exist as to prove that he did. His reasoning was entirely academic in that he did not expect it to influence practice. He knew that whatever he said, people would go on believing that the order they sought in their own lives came from the same source that had created order in the universe. Indeed, he advised one young sceptic who was in doubt about taking holy orders to go ahead, on the grounds that it didn't do to care whether the vulgar thought him a sceptic or not.

He was also quite indifferent to his critics. In his autobiography he tells of Reverends and Right Reverends bringing out rejoinders to his views two or three times a year, and that he could cover the floor of a large room with books and pamphlets written against him, 'to none for which I ever made the least reply, not from Disdain (for the authors of some of them I respect) but from my desire of ease and tranquillity'.

In 1775, when sixty-four, Hume fell ill with what was thought to be cancer of the liver. It gradually worsened, and in his autobiography written the following year he said he expected a speedy dissolution. He suffered little pain, his spirits and love of study were unaffected and he told his friends that he did not regret the loss of a few years of infirmity. 'It is difficult,' he added, 'to be more detached from life than I am at present.'

This philosophical approach to death was not what the pious thought proper or expected, the reflections at this time of those dying being concentrated on what awaited them in the great beyond, and trusting that their lives had been an adequate preparation for it. Dr Johnson, when he heard of Hume's calm at the approach of death, refused to believe it. A few years earlier, when discussing with him the question of death, Boswell mentioned that Hume had told him that he was no more uneasy to think that he *should not be* after this life than that he *had not been* before it; to which the orthodox Johnson replied, 'Sir, if he really thinks so, his perceptions are disturbed; he is mad. If he does not think so, he lies.' Such was the wisdom of the times.

Friends came to say goodbye, including Boswell. For all his philanderings he was as much a conventional believer as Johnson, and he left a wonderful and much-quoted account of his last visit to the Great Infidel.

> On Sunday forenoon the 7th of July 1776, being too late for church, I went to see Mr David Hume, who was returned from London and Bath, just a-dying. I found him alone, in a reclining posture in his drawing-room. He was lean, ghastly and quite of an earthly appearance. He was dressed in a suit of grey cloth with white metal buttons and a kind of scratch wig. He was quite different from the plump figure he used to present. He seemed to be placid and even cheerful. He said he was just approaching to his end. I think these were his words.
>
> I had a strong curiosity to be satisfied if he persisted in disbelieving a future state even when he had death before his eyes. I asked him if it was not possible that there might be a future state. He answered it was possible that a piece of coal put upon the fire would not burn; and he added that it was a most unreasonable fancy that we should exist for ever. That immortality, if it were at all, must be general; that a great proportion of the human race has hardly any intellectual qualities; that a great proportion dies in infancy before being possessed of reason; yet all these must be immortal; that a porter who gets drunk with gin by ten o'clock

must be immortal; that the trash of every age must be preserved, and that new universes must be created to contain such numbers. This appeared to me an unphilosophical objection, and I said, 'Mr Hume, you know spirit does not take up space' . . .

I asked him if the thought of annihilation never gave him any uneasiness. He said not the least. 'Well,' said I, 'Mr Hume, I hope to triumph over you when I meet you in a future state; and remember you are not to pretend that you was joking with all this infidelity.' 'No, no,' said he. 'But I shall have been so long there before you come that it will be nothing new.' In this style of humour and levity did I conduct the conversation.

Perhaps it was wrong on so awful a subject. But as nobody was present, I thought it could have no bad effect. I however felt a degree of horror, mixed with a sort of wild, strange, hurrying recollection of my excellent mother's pious instructions, of Dr Johnson's noble lessons, and of my religious sentiments and affections during the course of my life. I was like a man in sudden danger eagerly seeking his defensive arms; and I could not but be assailed by momentary doubts while I had actually before me a man of such strong abilities and extensive inquiry dying in the persuasion of being annihilated.

When Boswell reported to Johnson that Hume was quite easy at the thought of annihilation, the doctor, who was terrified of death, confirmed what he had said earlier. 'He lied. He had a vanity in being *thought* easy. It is more probable he lied than that so very improbable a thing should be as a man not afraid of death . . .'

On the day of Hume's burial, Boswell went along to inspect the open grave, and hid behind a wall to watch the mourners pass, fearful that the grave might be desecrated by religious zealots. That it was not desecrated was due, at least in part, to the presence of two guards whom the family had hired to watch it.

Even then there was no ending to the controversy over Hume's beliefs. His friend Adam Smith wrote a tribute to him in a letter to William Strahan, which was subsequently published. After praising

Hume's gentleness, generosity, good humour, depth of thought, independence of mind, modesty and frugality, he concluded: 'I have always considered him, both in his lifetime and since his death, as approaching as nearly to the idea of a perfectly wise and virtuous man as perhaps the nature of human frailty will admit.'

Although this sort of fulsomeness was standard practice for obituaries of the time, it caused outrage among the devout. 'A single and, as I thought, a very harmless sheet of paper which I happened to write concerning the death of our late friend Mr Hume,' Smith wrote after publication of his great work *The Wealth of Nations*, 'brought upon me ten times more abuse than the very violent attack I had made upon the whole commercial system of Great Britain.'

But Hume's reputation continued to be enhanced as time went on. Sir Leslie Stephen, Hume's biographer in the *Dictionary of National Biography* wrote of his influence on Kant, Adam Smith and Bentham, and concluded, 'He may be regarded as the acutest thinker in Great Britain of the eighteenth century.' Even Einstein, in our own century, is on record as saying that Hume's writings had helped him in his discovery of the principle of general relativity.

3. England: From Turner to Holyoake

Although Hume himself did not openly assent to atheism, his influence on eighteenth-century thinking led to the publication in 1782 of Britain's first unequivocally atheistic book. It was called *An Answer to Dr Priestley's Letters to a Philosophical Unbeliever*, and according to David Berman the preface and postscript were written by one William Hammon, of whom little is known, and the main text by his friend Dr Matthew Turner. Turner was an interesting man, a Liverpool surgeon, anatomist and chemist, a pioneer in establishing ether in medical treatment, a friend and colleague of Josiah Wedgwood the potter, a classical scholar and ready wit.

In his preface Hammon boldly declares, 'As to the question

whether there is such an existent Being as an atheist, to put that out of all manner of doubt, I do declare upon my honour that I am one.' To avoid falling foul of the blasphemy laws he inserted a disclaimer that as revealed knowledge (i.e. Christianity) was not criticised, Christians had no need to take offence. One critic described this as base equivocation, another as disingenuous, but Hammon knew it was far less dangerous to doubt the existence of God than, say, Christ's miracles and resurrection. Another critic scoffed at Hammon's declaration by questioning, 'What doth he swear by? Whom doth he appeal to? Not to God, for he believes there is none. And as he thinks he can swear by nothing greater, he swears by his HONOUR!' But Hammon was resolute. 'We are so proud in our singularity of being atheists that we hardly open our lips in company for fear of making converts.'

Hammon's preface made several good points: 'If upon sick beds or in dying moments men revert to their old weaknesses and superstitions, their fall may afford triumph to religionists; for my part I care not so much for the opinion of sick and dying men as of those who at the time are young and healthy.' He went on: 'My faith is in reasoning. I have a right to truth and to publish truth, let society suffer or not suffer by it. That society which suffers by truth should be otherwise constituted.'

In the main text Turner is convincing when he poses the question to believers whether if, as he assumed, they were to become convinced that God did not exist, they would still behave morally? If they would continue thus, then why should they maintain, as the faithful did, that morality required a belief in God?

As for God's existence, Turner denied Priestley's 'unsupported and unjustifiable' premise that the universe is an effect requiring a divine cause, especially as Priestley himself had admitted that it made no sense to speak of an uncaused Being. 'Is not that admission by Priestley,' Turner asked, 'alone an argument of there being no such thing?' A universe seen as cause rather than effect made much more sense. Elsewhere Turner's thoughts are those of Hume and d'Holbach. Where was to be found that benevolence of the Supreme Being which Christians claimed? Religion was not only unnecessary but dangerous to morality, which was best served by human laws. 'To support still the efficacy of religion in making men virtuous is to oppose metaphysical reasoning to the truth of fact; it is like the philosopher denying motion and being refuted by one of his scholars walking across the room.' A plurality of deities made more sense that one deity; and a series of finite causes being carried back *ad infinitum* made no sense at all.

When published, the book made very little stir which Berman finds odd, considering how greatly atheism had been feared and derided in the past. 'One possible explanation,' he says, 'is that whether consciously or unconsciously, believers felt that the best way to damn such a book was by silence or faint abuse. They bared their teeth not in an angry cry, but in a more effective yawn.'

Hammon and Turner having broken new ground, others began to follow. One of the most interesting views expressed was contained in a little-known pamphlet called *An Investigation of the Essence of the Deity* which was published in London in 1797. Its author called himself Scepticus Britannicus and that is all we know about him. Like Hammon and Hume, he was activated by a search for truth, and traditional beliefs were apt to conflict with truth: 'Man receives as little comfort from a persuasion that he has followed a like system of opinions with his forefathers as the unfortunate culprit who, under the gallows, is told that many others have suffered the same fate before him.'

The traditional beliefs of the faithful were that the deity was alleged to be 'omnipotent, incomprehensible, invisible, immaterial, and immutable'. This could not be right. If God was omnipotent, he could have prevented all sorts of unfortunate things happening, starting with Adam and Eve sinning. If God was omnipresent, why did he distance himself from the world he was said to have created? If he is incomprehensible why do his followers claim so much for him? And if immaterial, how could he possibly create a material world? Finally if God is immutable, is it not ridiculous to pray to him to alter his intentions? Such views of God, Scepticus held, were inconsistent and contradictory.

Not only, said Scepticus, did God not create the world but it was not created by chance either: 'We are of the opinion that . . . it never had a beginning and that it will never have an end, but that it exists necessarily.'

On rather shakier grounds Scepticus thinks that man invented a power superior to nature so as to account for the creation of his soul, so that the wish to believe in the immortality of the soul is a cause rather than an effect of belief in God. I say shakier grounds because, as I have said before, I do not know what people mean by the word 'soul'.

He concludes, not by committing himself to atheism but showing empathy with it. D'Holbach's definition of it seemed to him the greatest philosophical honour man could have bestowed on him. 'An atheist,' d'Holbach had said, 'is a man who destroyeth chimeras prejudicial to the human race.'

Nor were some of the English poets far behind. Rochester in the seventeenth century and Pope ('The proper study of mankind is man') in the eighteenth paved the way for Shelley in the nineteenth century, the most virulently atheistic of them all.

Brought up in a Christian household, Shelley went first to Eton at the age of twelve where he already began to express doubts, and six years later, in 1810, to University College, Oxford. At this time, like many radical-minded young men, he called himself a deist, i.e. a subscriber to a belief in natural but not revealed religion (i.e. Christianity). Two years later, in a letter to a friend, he expressed reservations about Christianity:

> The first doubts which arose in my boyish mind concerning the genuineness of the Christian religion, as a revelation from the divinity, were excited by the contemplation of the virtues and genius of Greece and Rome. Shall Socrates and Cicero perish, whilst the meanest minds of modern England inherit eternal life?

What propelled the young Shelley to progress from deism to atheism occurred during his first year at Oxford when he fell in love with his cousin Harriet Grove whose family, like his own, were Christians and deeply upset by contrary views. When Harriet rejected him because of these views, he was both angered and hurt. 'Oh! I burn with impatience for the moment of Christianity's dissolution. It has injured me; I swear on the altar of perjured love to revenge myself on the hated cause.'

And revenge himself (though with unforeseen consequences) he did, by writing and circulating to heads of colleges and bishops a printed pamphlet entitled *The Necessity of Atheism*, and signed it, 'Thro' deficiency of proof AN ATHEIST'. The consequence was that both he and his friend Thomas Hogg, who had admitted contributing to the pamphlet, were expelled from the university.

Shelley now committed himself wholeheartedly to his atheistic beliefs and during the next three years extended his thinking by adding to what he had written in *The Necessity of Atheism* two further works on the subject, *Queen Mab*, described as 'A Philosophical Poem' and in which the phrase 'There is no God' appears three times, and *The Refutation of Deism* in the form of an exchange of dialogue.

Shortly before the publication of *The Necessity*, says Berman, Shelley had already expressed in a letter the grounds for his atheistic beliefs: (1) Reasonable people do not require religious belief. (2) Christianity is unreasonable and incredible. (3) The most famous non-Christians were noted for the strictest morality. (4) Irreligious periods in history have been most peaceful. (5) The truth, and especially that contained in (2) above, has never been known to be prejudicial to the best interests of mankind. (6) Religion is likely to have a negative effect on reasonable men by fettering a reasoning mind with the very bonds which restrain the unthinking one from mischief. (7) Shelley's own moral principle which he often reiterated: that Mind cannot create, only perceive, and because belief is passive and involuntary, no merit or demerit should be attached to it: by this he hoped to pre-empt the possibility of prosecution. He had lit on the phrase, 'Mind cannot create, it can only perceive', on the fly-leaf of a copy of Bishop Berkeley's works belonging to a friend of the Poet Laureate Robert Southey, with whom he was staying.

Shelley also expressed the view that, as I have shown earlier, belief in God was not universal; but even if it was, he said, that was no reason for accepting it, as many false beliefs (e.g. the sun went round the earth) had once been widely held.

Berman pays tribute to Shelley and his principle when he says that it enables one to understand 'how a youth of 19 years, even though precocious, could assert something so novel, so potent and so hedged around with stigmas and taboos that throughout the whole of the British Enlightenment only a handful of writers had the courage to assert it'.

Yet even so, even after Shelley had categorically stated that, like d'Holbach, he considered himself an atheist and the existence of God a chimera, many simply refused to believe him, particularly early twentieth-century critics who felt that his avowals of atheism somehow conflicted with the beauty of his poetry. His friend Edward Trelawny in his book *Records of Shelley, Byron and the Author* (London, 1887) endeavoured to put the record straight: 'The Shelleyan writers, being Christians themselves, seem to think that a man of genius cannot be an Atheist, and so they strain their faculties to disprove what Shelley asserted from the earliest stage of his career to the last day of his life.'

The Roman Catholic Church meanwhile continued to indulge its perennial preoccupation with sex, its views, despite radical shifts in medical, psychological and social thinking, remaining as rigid and static as their view of planet earth before Copernicus and Galileo. The eighteenth-century divine, Alphonso de Liguori, held that a woman who had been raped was not entitled to remove the sperm from her uterus, even if she could, on the grounds that it would be 'an injustice to nature and the human race whose reproduction would be impaired'. Thus, says Ranke-Heinemann, 'the rapist's semen had been promoted to the status of a quasi-person: it enjoyed the same protection that a peaceful citizen would'.

There was some easement among Catholics with the coming of the Reformation when scores of Catholic priests abandoned the burden of celibacy by getting married. (Interestingly Luther himself was a reluctant bridegroom, calling marriage 'a hospital for sick people' which gave sex a veneer of respectability which God 'winked at' and concluding that we were driven to sex against our better instincts!) Yet for Catholics who did not convert the doctrines of continence and decrees against *coitus interruptus* and contraception continued.

During the nineteenth century the Holy Fathers were much exercised by the widespread habit of youthful masturbation. In 1842 a Dr Debreyne who was both a physician and a monk declared that masturbation led to palpitations, weakened vision, headaches, dizziness, tremors, cramps (in my youth the bogey word was blindness), and other doctors believed that it dried out the brain so that it was heard to rattle in the skull. The doctor noticed that one of his patients, a boy, had developed strange alterations in the shape of the back of his head. It turned out that he had been masturbating for several years and had almost non-stop erections. 'This habit lengthened the diameter of his head in such a way that his mother had difficulty in finding a hat that would fit him.' For compulsive masturbators a remedy was invented in the shape of wires or clasps being inserted into the foreskin and at night metal rings with points placed round the penis.

Although procreation without sperm was an impossibility, in women the clitoris played no part in procreation and existed only for orgasmic pleasure. This was a sin, and in France and England some doctors adopted the practice of cauterising the clitoris with a white-hot iron. 'It can be readily seen,' wrote Dr Zambuco, 'that after children have lost feeling through cauterisation, they are less liable to sexual excitement and less inclined to touch themselves.' This cruel and unnecessary procedure is still practised, and for the same reasons, among some fundamentalist Moslem sects.

Anyone reading the history of the Catholic Church in sexual matters must wonder how celibate priests in the confessional were so well informed about the highways and byways of sexual practice. The answers would seem to be twofold. In their probing questions to penitents, they would receive answers which enlightened them on practices of which they had had no previous knowledge (and which no doubt led to a certain smacking of lips and even clerical erections, in the box); and alternatively or additionally they themselves had already become men of the world as a result of secret liaisons with concubines.

Following Shelley and the Enlightenment several other atheists felt it safe to pop their heads above the parapet. One was George Grote, co-author with Jeremy Bentham of the pseudonymous *The Analysis of the Influence of Natural Religion on the Temporal Happiness of Mankind* (London, 1822). Grote was a historian, sometime MP for the City of London and governor of his family bank in Threadneedle Street; i.e. a respected establishment figure whom few would have suspected of holding unorthodox views. Bentham was a philosopher and social reformer who founded University College, London, where his clothed skeleton is still on public view. He was also an associate of John Stuart Mill who read *The Analysis* in manuscript and was greatly impressed by it.

The most significant feature of *The Analysis* is the argument that we endow God with moral and intellectual perfections such as goodness and wisdom because we are intimidated by his imagined power:

> Suppose that any tyrant could establish so complete a system of espionage, as to be informed of every word which any of his subjects might utter. It is obvious that all criticisms upon him would be laudatory in the extreme, for they would be all pronounced, as it were, in the presence of the tyrant, and there no one dares to express dissent.
>
> The unlimited agency and omniscience of the Deity is equivalent to this universal espionage. He is conceived as the unseen witness of everything that passes our lips – indeed even our thoughts. It would be madness therefore to hazard an unfavourable judgement of his proceedings, while thus constantly under his supervision.

Recently a cache of letters from Grote to his wife's sister, Frances Lewin, has come to light, and show an even greater commitment to disbelief than that expressed in *The Analysis*. On 10 October 1822 he writes to her: 'I do truly hope that it may be my lot to see you emancipated [from religious beliefs] which disguise . . . the true path conducting to happiness.' His wish must have been granted, for fifteen months later he is telling her: 'It is scarcely more than a year since you fully shook off the Jug' (Grote's and Bentham's euphemism for Christianity), adding, 'At your age I was beset by all the miserable phantoms of Jug.'[3]

In another letter he says:

There cannot be a benevolent God who suffers pain and evil to exist. And if there be a god of any other character, who does not design the happiness of mankind then all I can say is, that I shall prefer serving and benefitting my fellow countrymen and take the risk of his displeasure. But all these superstitions are really altogether on a fictitious basis. There is exactly as much reason to believe that there are ghosts, as that there is a God; indeed there is not so much evidence for the latter, inasmuch as his reputed attributes are thoroughly incompatible and contradictory.

And again:

If you say that the good part of Nature comes from this benevolent Being and the bad part by itself and without his agency, then I ask you why, if one part of Nature can exist without this cause, the other part could not exist also? If the bad part of Nature could exist uncaused, so could the good.

Besides, you would have just as good reason to say, that the good part of Nature came by itself, and that the bad part was superadded by some malevolent being, as you would have to say that the bad part came by itself and the good from some benevolent being. Take the doctrine as you will, the supposition of such a cause is both useless and contradictory.

Another important atheist to appear on the scene was the writer and publisher Richard Carlile. His own reasons for dissent were much the same as those of previous dissenters: for example, if God was immaterial as theologians taught, how could he create a universe out of nothing, and if he was incomprehensible, as theologians also taught, how could we know anything about him at all? The onus was on them to prove that the material world is an effect needing a divine cause. 'It is not fair to call on me,' he addressed the theists, 'to prove a creation out of nothing when it is quite impossible for anyone to conceive of the world not existing: the proof rests with you.'

Yet it is less as a writer propagating atheism than as a publisher of atheistic and other radical works, and the sufferings that he and his family had to endure because of it, that he deserves a footnote in history. A fervent admirer of the deist Paine whose *Age of Reason* had been published at the end of the eighteenth century, he reprinted it in 1818. He also reprinted *Answer to Dr Priestley's Letters to a Philosophical Unbeliever, Watson Refuted* (in which a Dr Francis had attacked Bishop Richard Watson for his strictures on *The Age of Reason*), Shelley's *Queen Mab* and Grote's and Bentham's *The Analysis* and excerpts from d'Holbach's *Système de la Nature*.

By 1819 Carlile had six indictments standing against him and in November of that year after trial, he was fined £1,500 and sentenced to three years' imprisonment in Dorchester prison.[4] Unable to pay the fine he was obliged to serve an additional three years in lieu. The fact of his incarceration however in no way affected his campaigning and between 1819 and 1825 he produced the first twelve volumes of his periodical the *Republican*. In 1821 his wife was arrested for helping to publish this and other dissenting works and joined him in the room allocated to him in Dorchester prison for two years' imprisonment; and the following year his sister Mary-Anne was incarcerated there too for publishing his New Year's *Address to the Reformers of Great Britain*, although she also had her own sleeping quarters. In addition the King's Bench sheriff and his men made two raids on his house at No. 55 Fleet Street and seized furniture and books that were his stock-in-trade: these were supposed to raise money for the £1,500 fine but, it was said, not a penny went towards it.

After release Carlile returned to Fleet Street where a further stream of pamphlets and periodicals flowed from his pen. Because what he cared for most was freedom of speech, he hired the Rotunda in Blackfriars Road for a series of public meetings to press for a relaxation of censorship, particularly in religious and medical matters (the Church and the establishment regarded dissection, so urgently needed by doctors, and birth control, which Carlile was also advocating, as not fit subjects for debate). 'Most of the public men out of London attended the discussions,' says one biographer, 'and a liberty of speech never before known in England was permitted.'

Later 55 Fleet Street was assessed for Church rates. Carlile's response was to take out the two front windows and in their place display effigies of a distraining officer and a bishop, to which he added a devil linked arm in arm with the bishop. When he refused to pay the rates, he was ordered to give sureties to the court for his good behaviour for the next three years; and when he refused, 'he entered,' says his biographer, 'with his accustomed spirit into three years more imprisonment', this in addition to a further ten weeks' imprisonment for refusing to pay the rates.

When he was finally released, after a total of nine years and four months spent in prison between 1819 and 1835, he returned once again to Fleet Street and carried on as before his business as writer, publisher and bookseller. To avoid further prosecution he devised an ingenious method of selling dissenting books by inventing a machine with a dial on it, rather like the modern vending machine. The customer dialled the publication he wanted, put in his money, and out came the book. There was a brisk demand for these books, as there always is for what is forbidden, and at times the shop was making a profit of more than £50 a week. But propagating his own particular gospel of free speech was an expensive business and overall Carlile had difficulties remaining solvent; though he was gratified by the praise heaped on him by public men for doing what they would have liked but did not dare do themselves.

During the last years of his life Carlile undertook a series of speaking engagements in the Midlands and North. His subjects were all aspects of working-class reform: universal suffrage, a land tax, the emancipation of women, a fairer justice system. 'More than anything else,' writes Joel Weiner in his biography of him, 'he believed that the overriding reform necessary as a prelude to all others was the destruction of Christianity in its traditional form.' In setting out his beliefs Carlile pulled no punches. 'Witchcraft, priestcraft, kingcraft and devilcraft,' he declared, 'have been one and all built on the ignorance, fear and credulity of mankind.'

None of these speaking tours could be considered a success. For a start Carlile had always been a more effective pamphleteerist than orator and found it hard to kindle an audience's response. Attendances in some towns were poor, and Carlile was beginning to find that nearly ten years of prison had severely affected his health. He was still only fifty-three when he died, practising what he had preached by leaving his body for dissection to St Thomas's Hospital. After his death it was said that he had done more during his life to bring about freedom of the press than any other Englishman of his time.

Shortly before his death Carlile had abandoned atheism for what Berman calls a confused form of mystical theism. In the field of publishing his place was taken by Charles Southwell, the youngest of numerous siblings and a former actor who in 1842 published *The Oracle of Reason or Philosophy Vindicated*. This was a virulently atheistic and blasphemous publication for which Southwell was, after trial, sentenced to a year's imprisonment.

The editorship of *The Oracle* was then taken over by G.J. Holyoake who later wrote: 'I had not become [an atheist] till after the imprisonment of Mr Southwell which led me to inquire into the grounds of religious opinion more closely than I had done before, and it ended in my entire disbelief.' In May 1842 he expressed his disbelief in a lecture at Cheltenham in Gloucestershire and in August was indicted at Gloucester Assizes. The indictment read in part:

... disregarding the laws and religion of the realm, and wickedly and profanely ... intending to bring Almighty God, the Holy Scriptures and the Christian religion into disbelief and contempt ... maliciously, unlawfully and wickedly, did compose, speak, utter, pronounce and publish with a loud voice of, and concerning Almighty God, the Holy Scriptures and the Christian religion these words, 'I do not believe there is such a thing as God. I would ... place Almighty God on half pay.'

Holyoake was found guilty both of atheism and blasphemy. Sentencing him to six months' imprisonment, Mr Justice Erskine said: 'You have been convicted of uttering these words with improper levity. The arm of the law is not stretched out to protect the character of the Almighty; we do not presume to be the protectors of our God, but to protect the people from such indecent language.'

Ten years after his conviction Holyoake wrote a book about his experiences with the law: *History of the Last Trial by Jury for Atheism*. It included this extraordinary exchange of dialogue between Holyoake and the prison chaplain:

CHAPLAIN: Are you really an atheist, Mr Holyoake?

HOLYOAKE: Really I am.

CHAPLAIN: You deny that there is a God?

HOLYOAKE: No, I deny that there is sufficient reason to believe that there is one.

CHAPLAIN: But if the atheist has so much on his side, why does he not make it known?

HOLYOAKE: Is it generous of you to taunt him with lack of evidence, when you are so prepared to punish its production?

CHAPLAIN: The reason is that your principles are so horrible; as Robert Hall l said, 'Atheism is a bloody and ferocious system.'

HOLYOAKE: And, my dear sir, has it never occurred to you that the language of the Christian is shocking to atheistical feeling?

CHAPLAIN: Atheists have a right to their opinion, I allow, but not to publish them.

HOLYOAKE: I shall think you speak reasonably when you permit the same rule to be applied to the Christian.

CHAPLAIN: But you really cannot be an atheist?

HOLYOAKE: And you say this who have been a party to imprisoning me here for being one! If you believe yourself, go and demand my liberation.

Convincing or otherwise to modern ears as were these avowals of early nineteenth-century atheism by such as Shelley, Hammon and Turner, Grote and Bentham, Carlile, Southwell and Holyoake, they were as pinpricks in the sides of the religious establishment, if indeed they were even aware of them. For Christianity at this time in England was riding high with the emigration of country people into the cities following the Industrial Revolution, among them the crowds that had gathered to hear the Wesleys preaching in the fields, and new churches to supply the needs of new congregations were going up in their hundreds. Sunday schools too were booming and every week little people were taught to give voice to such emollient verses as these.

> All things bright and beautiful,
> All creatures great and small,
> All things wise and wonderful,
> The Lord God made them all.
>
> Each little flower that opens,
> Each little bird that sings,
> He made their glowing colours,
> He made their tiny wings.
>
> The rich man in his castle,
> The poor man at his gate,
> God made them high or lowly,
> And ordered their estate.

And so on.

But a blow to all this mindless romanticising and to Christian belief generally, one as fundamental and destructive of it as the scientific findings of Copernicus, Galileo and Isaac Newton, was about to surprise the world. In 1859 Charles Darwin published *The Origin of Species by Means of Natural Selection*.

Chapter Nine

DARWIN AND AFTER

1. The Origin of Species

No one can begin to understand the impact that *The Origin of Species* made on the beliefs of the people of mid-Victorian England without knowing what their beliefs were. For 1,800 years, more or less, Christians had believed that the universe in general and our world in particular had been created by God, though just how this was done they had never been able to explain. God had also created, as hymns and psalms constantly proclaimed, everything in it. The source of this belief was the Book of Genesis which they had all read or had read to them countless times:

> And God created great whales and every living creature that moveth which the waters brought forth abundantly after their kind and every winged fowl after his kind; and God saw that it was good.
>
> And God blessed them saying, Be fruitful and multiply and fill the waters in the seas, and let fowl multiply in the earth.
>
> And God said, Let the earth bring forth the living creature after his kind, cattle and creeping thing, and beast of the earth after his kind; and it was so.
>
> And God said, Let us make man in our image, after our likeness;

and let them have dominion over the fish of the sea and over the fowl of the air, and over the cattle, and over all the earth, and over every creeping thing that creepeth upon the earth.

So God created man in his own image, in the image of God created he him; male and female created he them.

From this, contemporary Christians concluded that all creatures that on earth do dwell, the West Highland terrier, duck-billed platypus, giant sloth, humble maggot, ant and bee, lumbering rhino, Moray eel, creeping caterpillar, scavenging vulture, laughing gull, Komodo dragon and man himself had originally all been plonked down on earth, as it were ready-made; and that generation after generation had produced replicas of themselves without variation or change.

As a result of Adam and Eve's fall, 'God' was angered by the wickedness of man, and decided to destroy him: 'both man and beast and the creeping thing and the fowls of the air'. Noah was excepted, told by God to build an ark of gopher wood and to people it with his own family and his sons' families and two of every living thing of all flesh, one male and one female. All of which Noah did. And God made it rain for forty days and forty nights and everything on earth was destroyed. And Noah, who by now was 600 years old, and his family and sons' families and all the beasts and birds floated on the waters for 150 days until the waters dried up and the ark came to rest on Mount Ararat. And God told Noah to disembark with all his family and the animals and birds and go forth and multiply which they did.

To us at the end of the twentieth century all this is poetic myth of a high and compelling beauty. What it is not is history as the Christians of mid-Victorian times ardently believed. So that when in 1859 Darwin's *Origin* was published, it was, for many clergy especially, like a slap in the face with a wet fish; almost overnight they were obliged to accept that one part of their belief system was untrue: God had no place in the new equation of the history of species that Darwin was offering.

In the course of a five-year voyage that Darwin made in HMS *Beagle* and in which he explored the relics of flora and fauna along the coasts of South America and elsewhere, he made an important discovery, or, to be accurate, built on the discoveries previously made by such as Lamarck and Buffon and Lyell and Darwin's own grandfather Erasmus Darwin; this was that the ancient fossils of extinct animals bore only a faint resemblance to their living descendants, and that therefore in the course of time species had evolved. One reason for this was that climatic changes or shifts in land masses over thousands of years had meant that in order to survive species had had to adapt to new environments. Those that failed to adapt perished.[1] With his own eyes he saw proofs of it. In the isolated Galapagos group of islands, he found giant tortoises and lizards not only markedly different from those of the same species on the South American mainland but different too from tortoises and lizards living on other islands in the group; also that the commonest trees in the Galapagos were sunflowers which elsewhere in the world grew no larger than shrubs. Another example of how species adapt to their environment was to be seen in the even more isolated Hawaiian group of islands where no fewer than 82 per cent of the local species were found to be unique. No less remarkable was the history of the camel which first came into being in North America. From there, the majority made their way across the land bridge that then existed between North America and Asia (now divided by the Bering Straits) and so came to the deserts of Arabia and North Africa. But a branch of the species travelled south to South America, and there adapted themselves to the local environment by evolving into llamas.

Darwin had also been much impressed by the famous *Essay on Population* by an Anglican cleric, Thomas Malthus. This stated that living creatures multiply at a rate that exceeds the capacity of the environment to maintain them. Thus Darwin:

> Every being which during its natural lifetime produces several eggs
> or seeds, must suffer destruction during some period of its life
> . . . otherwise on the principle of geometric increase, its numbers

211

would quickly become so inordinately great that no country could support the product. Hence, as more are produced than can possibly survive, there must in every case be a struggle for existence, either one individual with another of the same species, or with the individuals of distinct species, or with the physical conditions of life.

Nature had a variety of ways of controlling population: by scarcity of food in some areas, by predators, by inability to adapt to changed climatic conditions, or by natural disasters such as fires and floods: in the face of these dangers, how was the preservation of species to be achieved?

I think it would be a most extraordinary fact if no variation ever had occurred useful to each being's own welfare. But if variations do occur, assuredly individuals thus characterised will have the best chance of being preserved in the struggle for life; and from the strong principle of inheritance they will tend to produce offspring similarly characterised. This principle of preservation I have called, for the sake of brevity, Natural Selection.

In future editions of *Origin* Darwin preferred Herbert Spencer's phrase, 'the survival of the fittest', an expression which the generality of the population immediately understood.

The more that Darwin worked backwards in time to reach a conclusion about the origin of life itself, the more he became persuaded that all creatures, however modified, are descended from a single original, protozoan. 'All living things have much in common . . . therefore I should infer from analogy that probably all organic beings which have ever lived on this earth have descended from one primordial form into which life was first breathed.'

From this one primordial form, Darwin thought, had emerged in the fullness of time all species on earth, each of which must have had its own originator; man's was probably some ape-like creature leading eventually to *homo erectus*, while the dog family owed its existence to some prime wolf and bitch whose ultimate assorted progeny in the shape of chow, spaniel, poodle, beagle, rottweiler, etc., are with us today, the fruit not of natural selection but of artificial selection by man.

Publication of *Origin*, writes Jonathan Howard, 'produced an instant reaction from the public and from the scientific community. An intemperate battle began in newspapers, magazines and scientific assemblies.' Most noticeable on the side of Darwin was the brilliant young naturalist T.H. Huxley,[2] and against him the active and ambitious Bishop of Oxford, Samuel Wilberforce, elder son of the reformer who helped to abolish the slave trade. The two met at a meeting of the British Association for the Advancement of Science held in Oxford the year after *Origin* was published. Wilberforce, eager to *smash* Darwin, as he put it, spoke first and, wrote Darwin (who was not present):

> spoke for a full half an hour with inimitable spirit, emptiness and unfairness. Unfortunately the Bishop, hurried along on the current of his own eloquence, so far forgot himself as to push his attempted advantage to the verge of personality in a telling passage in which he turned round and addressed Huxley: I forget the precise words and quote from Lyell. 'The Bishop asked whether Huxley was related by his grandfather's or grandmother's side to an ape.'

Huxley turned to his neighbour and said, 'The Lord hath delivered him into mine hands,' and after correcting Wilberforce on the few scientific observations he had made, delivered the *coup de grâce*:

> I asserted that a man has no reason to be ashamed of having an ape for his grandfather. If there were an ancestor whom I *should* feel shame in recalling, it would be a *man*, a man of restless and versatile intellect, who not content with an equivalent success in his own sphere of activity, plunges into scientific questions with which he has no real acquaintance, only to obscure them with an aimless rhetoric, and distract the attention of his hearers from the

real point of issue by eloquent digressions and skilled appeals to religious prejudice.

When he heard of Huxley's triumph, Darwin sent congratulations. 'I honour your pluck,' he said. 'I would have soon as died as tried to answer the bishop in such an assembly.'

Darwin always was and remained a very private man. Because his wife was a Christian, he never publicly expressed his own beliefs. But in an autobiographical sketch published after his death, he let it be known what they were:

> Disbelief crept over me at a very slow rate, but was at last complete.
> The rate was so slow that I felt no distress and have never since
> doubted even for a single second that my conclusion was correct.
> I can indeed hardly see how anyone ought to wish Christianity
> to be true; for if so, the plain language of the text seems to show
> that the men who do not believe, and this would include my
> Father, Brother and almost all my best friends, will be everlastingly
> punished.
>
> And this is a damnable doctrine.

The author of *Victorian World Picture*, David Newsome, writes:

> If the impact of Darwinism after 1859 was to rock the boat
> of orthodoxy more alarmingly than anything before, it was
> because the revelations of *The Origin of Species* were already
> being challenged, ironically by calling into question that very
> aspect of Victorian religious teaching that had been so confidently
> regarded as the most essential message to be absorbed and put into
> practice by all Christians; the moral content of the Word of God
> in the Scriptures.

And the Word of God that most dissenting Victorians took issue with was that part of the Athanasian Creed (Matthew 25:46) which the current liturgy required them to recite each Sunday: the prophecy of Jesus that sinners would go away into everlasting punishment but the righteous would inherit eternal life; prophecies which at best were highly contentious, at worst quite meaningless. In the previous century Charles Wesley had called this doctrine of salvation or damnation a hateful, horrible decree, while both Blake and Coleridge were shocked by the doctrine of the Atonement, whereby God and man were reconciled by the death of Jesus on the cross. Now in the nineteenth century and amid huge strides in scientific achievement, biblical cruelty became even more unacceptable. James Anthony Froude in *The Nemesis of Faith* found it incomprehensible that anyone could worship a God who had sanctioned Joshua's massacre of the Canaanites; while the Bishop of St David's was equally appalled by God's command to Abraham to make a human sacrifice of his son Isaac. Individuals who lost their faith reacted differently. The Rev. (later Sir) Leslie Stephen, the father of Virginia Woolf, found his faith so far gone that he could no longer bring himself to officiate as a priest and never did so again. 'I now believe in nothing,' he said, 'but I do not the less believe in morality. I mean to live and die like a gentleman, if possible.' T.H. Huxley invented the word *agnostic* and, like many of his contemporaries, became one. At the funeral of his little son, he had been what he called 'inexpressibly shocked' to hear the officiating priest say, 'If the dead rise not again, let us eat and drink, for tomorrow we die.'

Probably the most militant of all the dissenters was John Stuart Mill, the philosopher and social reformer. Unable to equate God's alleged goodness with his promise to consign sinners to hell-fire, he said in a famous passage: 'I will call no being good who is not what I mean when I apply that epithet to my fellow creatures; and if such a being can sentence me to Hell for not calling him so, to Hell I will go.'

Such bluntness greatly shocked middle-class Victorian susceptibilities, but there were others who welcomed it. John McTaggart, the Cambridge philosopher and atheist, said that it formed one of the great turning-points in the religious development of the world, while Viscount Morley said of it: 'Probably no English writer has done as much as Mr Mill to cut at the root of the theological spirit.'

Other dissenters objected to the fears imposed on children by Christian teaching, for instance, hymns with verses like this:

> There's not a sin that we commit,
> Nor wicked word we say,
> But in thy dreadful book 'tis writ,
> Against the judgement day.

And this from a book called *The Child's First Tale* and entitled 'The Bad Boy':

> There is an hour when I must die,
> Nor do I know how soon 'twill be,
> A thousand children, young as I,
> Are called to death to meet their doom.

And, on the same lines and worst of all, a book called *The Sight of Hell* by the Rev. Joseph Furniss and which is said to have been a bestseller. It was published in Ireland in 1889, ten years after the birth of my father.

Furniss envisaged hell as a place filled with streams of burning pitch and sulphur where tormented souls shrieked, hissed like serpents, howled like dogs or wailed like dragons. There were six dungeons in hell, each of which sponsored a different torture: a burning place, a red-hot floor, a boiling kettle, a red-hot coffin and a red-hot oven.

> The little child is in the red-hot oven. See how it screams to get out; see how it turns and twists itself about in the fire . . . God was very good to this little child. Very likely God saw it would get worse and worse and never repent and so it would have been punished more severely in Hell. So God in his mercy called it out of the world in early childhood.

Beliefs which people had held all their lives were now in the melting-pot. 'No one knows what to believe,' said one observer, 'and most people believe nothing.' The theologian Owen Chadwick has described the national mood as Doubt with a capital D.³

Then, to compound the turmoil, came criticism from another quarter, the 'form' criticism of the Bible by a succession of German scholars. Until this time in the western world the scriptures and the gospels were widely considered to be beyond criticism; they were the word of God, and to the Church and only the Church belonged the right of interpreting them. But in 1779 the German theologian Johann Gottfried Eichorn became the first of a whole line of scholars who regarded the stories in Genesis about the Creation and the Flood as being of the same nature as other similar stories in classical literature, for example Ovid's Creation story and Flood. Until then, suggests Don Cupitt in *The Sea of Faith*, 'the biblical Creation and Flood were regarded as revealed truths and all non-biblical Creation and Flood stories were merely heathen fables'. After Eichorn it became increasingly common to use the word 'myth' of both, myth being (according to him) the style of thinking found among peoples in the earliest stages of their history. The people of that time believed and would continue to believe, some up to the present day, that Genesis was a record of fact but, says Cupitt, for Eichorn:

> A biblical story of God appearing and speaking was not actually a case of God's appearing and speaking but merely evidence of a fascinating period in the early development of human consciousness when people had thought in such terms . . . like everything else in the Bible God was a product of human thought in a particular period of human history.

In other words God, like Hamlet, was, and still is, a fiction.

Yet the man who, next to Darwin, caused the most havoc to English orthodox belief in the nineteenth century was another German, not Eichorn but David Friedrich Strauss.

Born at Ludwigsburg in Swabia in 1808, he was the son of a businessman who was also a poet and scholar of languages. At the seminary where he began his formal education at the age of thirteen, he was one of only five pupils to gain the highest final marks. One of his tutors at the seminary was Ferdinand Christian Baur who founded and became the leading light of the Tübingen University school of theology and who greatly influenced Strauss. It was at Tübingen that Strauss received his doctorate of theology and to which he returned later to take up a tutorship in theology and philosophy and to make a start on his great seminal work, *Leben Jesu* (*The Life of Jesus*). His sources were the Old and New Testaments in their original languages, and he had meticulously studied the commentaries on them by the most important theologians and philosophers from the earliest times. He had, says Daniel O'Hara, 'a boldness of spirit that placed the claims of truth, clarity and honesty above the demands of tradition and conformity to ecclesiastical orthodoxy'.

The *Life* took Strauss three years to complete by which time he was still only twenty-seven – for one so young an astonishing feat. The book came out in two volumes running to 1,500 pages, and was later translated into English by the novelist George Eliot.[4]

In Germany publication caused a storm of protest, for the book asked people to read the Bible in a quite different way from before; and it finished Strauss's career, for he was never given an academic post again. In his biography of Strauss published in 1973 Dr Horton Harris explains why:

> What shocked the orthodox believer most of all was the frank and open repudiation of the historical veracity of the Gospels. What had previously been accepted as irrefutable and invulnerable to attack was now set in doubt. The mighty fortress had now been undermined and appeared to be about to collapse in ruins. It was not merely that the Christian faith had been repudiated – Voltaire and the French *philosophes* had poured out their vitriolic scorn on Christianity without causing any great theological commotion [but while] Voltaire and his friends had merely denied the traditional doctrines, Strauss had destroyed the foundations on which those doctrines stood . . . [He] had remorselessly exhibited the discrepancies, contradictions and mistakes in the

Gospel narratives, and made the supernatural explanations appear
weak and untenable.

Events in the gospels, impossible to believe as facts, such as the
miracles, Strauss (like Eichorn before him) called myths; and said
they were more easily understood as fanciful interpretations of the
Old Testament by suggestible members of a first-century Messianic
sect. Nor did he find any room for divine intervention.

In England the theologian Edward Pusey thought that Strauss's
theories were suitable for a learned discussion but trusted they would
never reach the ears of the common people. Others were more
generous. Albert Schweitzer, author of *The Quest of the Historical
Jesus*, called it 'one of the most perfect things in the whole range
of learned literature'. Dr Horton Harris described it as 'the most
intellectually reasoned attack ever mounted against Christianity',
while more recently Daniel O'Hara has said that its arguments have
never been effectively answered.

Strauss wrote other books during his life but nothing to match his
Life of Jesus. He died on 22 February 1874, and it is worth recalling
part of the address that the freethinker Moncure Daniel Conway gave
at the commemorative service given for him at South Place chapel in
London two weeks later. Some years ago, said Conway of Strauss, as
he walked with him by the banks of the Neckar,

> he declared to me that the motive he had in publishing his *Life of
> Jesus* was hardly less political than religious. 'I felt oppressed', he
> said, 'at seeing nearly every nation in Europe chained down by
> the allied despotism of prince and priest. I studied long the nature
> of this oppression and came to the conclusion that the chain which
> fettered mankind was rather inward than outward . . . The inward
> I perceived to be superstition, and the form in which it binds the
> people of Europe is Christian Supernaturalism. So long as men
> will accept religious control not based on reason, they will accept
> political control not based on reason. The man who gives up the
> whole of his moral nature to an unquestioned authority has suffered

a paralysis of the mind, and all the changes of outward circumstances in the world cannot make him a free man . . . I believe when I wrote that book, in striking at supernaturalism, I was striking at the whole evil tree of political and social degradation.'

Following on Darwin and Strauss, the latter part of the nineteenth century turned out to be a battleground between dissenters and believers, the latter now clearly on the ropes but not yet ready to throw in the towel.

The dissenters included G.W. Foote, editor of the *Freethinker*, sentenced to a year's imprisonment under the common law for blasphemy for publishing some anti-religious cartoons. He didn't enjoy prison but saw himself as another Heine: 'A soldier in the army of liberation is to persevere, to fight to the end, is to live (even if unknown) in the future of humanity.' Then there was the publication of *Essays and Reviews*, articles by a number of doubting clergymen, one of whom, the Rev. Rowland Williams, wrote that 'in Germany there has been a pathway streaming with light from Eichorn onwards!' He and another contributor who rejected the doctrine of eternal punishment were prosecuted for heresy and found guilty: on appeal however Lord Westbury (in the words of a contemporary wit), 'dismissed hell with costs and deprived the convicted clergymen of their hope of everlasting damnation'. In the wider world there was Nietzsche, one of the first to declare that God was dead, and Marx who said that religion was the opium of the people, and Freud who in my estimation said the truest things of all: Karen Armstrong in her *History of God* says that he

regarded God as an illusion that mature men and women should lay aside . . . A personal god was nothing more than an exalted father-figure: desire for such a deity sprang from infantile yearnings for a powerful protective father, for justice and fairness and for life to go on forever. God is simply a projection of these desires, feared and worshipped by human beings out of an abiding sense of helplessness. Religion belonged to the infancy of the human race; it had been a necessary stage in the transition from childhood to maturity. It had promoted ethical values which were essential to society. Now that humanity had come of age, however, it should be left behind.

2. Charles Bradlaugh, MP, Winwood Reade, and Ernie

But the most famous and outspoken of all nineteenth-century English atheists was Charles Bradlaugh, MP, founder of the National Secular Society, and after whom today's *Freethinker*'s headquarters, Bradlaugh House, has been named.

Born in the east end of London where his father never earned more than two guineas a week, Bradlaugh in early life became a dedicated social reformer. Malthus's theory of population explosion, which had led Darwin to formulate his theory of the origins of species, Bradlaugh saw in domestic social terms. Aware of an English population which had doubled in the thirty years 1801–31 with the ensuing poverty and misery of the slums, families with perhaps fifteen children living in a handful of rooms redolent with damp and decay and where to make ends meet perhaps one of the daughters had taken up prostitution, he became a fierce supporter of birth control, a subject which at that time was almost unmentionable.

In other social matters Bradlaugh was also in advance of his time. He was a republican who believed that government subsidies paid to Queen Victoria should be reduced ('that disgraceful man', the Queen later called him), wanted the courtesy titles given to the children of noblemen to be abolished and that the noblemen themselves should be required to pay the local tradesmen promptly instead of the common practice of remaining in debt to them for years. Again before his time he wanted a federal system for the United Kingdom with separate parliaments for Ireland, Scotland and Wales. Above all he was a committed atheist. 'Righteousness and benevolence,' he wrote in *Is there a god?*, 'are two of the words of description included in the definition of this creator and governor of nations. But is it righteous and benevolent to have created men to govern nations so that the men act criminally and the nations seek to destroy one another in war?' On a more practical level, he deeply resented the Lord's Day Observance laws which banned Sunday street trading, this being the only day when the masses of working poor could buy provisions and cheap clothes.

Hearing that there was to be a demonstration in Hyde Park one Sunday against these restrictive laws, Bradlaugh made his way there. He was a big, strong, handsome man who was not the least afraid of physical combat. Seeing a small man being hit with truncheons by several policemen, he ran over and threatened to knock down the next policeman to hit him. The police were so astonished they put away their truncheons and led the small man away. Later Bradlaugh himself was prodded with a truncheon. He faced his assailant and said, 'Do not do that, friend, you have no right to do it and I am stronger than you are.' The man called up two colleagues. Bradlaugh said to the first, 'If you attempt to touch me, I will take one of those truncheons and knock you down with it.' At this point some supporters of Bradlaugh came over and bore him away, and the police, preferring discretion to valour, disappeared.

Bradlaugh's atheism was radical. His friend and associate J.M. Robertson said that on many occasions he declared that to deny the existence of God was meaningless: 'I do not deny God because that word conveys to me no idea . . . I cannot war with a non-entity.' And, *pace* Shelley, he added, 'To suppose that any belief or unbelief can either be a virtue or a crime or any man better or worse from belief or unbelief, is to assume that man has a faculty which we see and feel he has *not* . . .'

Bradlaugh's atheism was unique in two respects. Although there were by this time in England many atheists and agnostics in high places, most kept their beliefs to themselves. Bradlaugh, on the other hand, says his biographer David Tribe, was a proselytising atheist who, 'if he did not shout his unbelief from every housetop in the realm, certainly used most of the town halls and market squares'. He was also (and refuting those who believed that morality stemmed from religion), puritanical in his atheistic beliefs. Referring to the National Secular Society, which he had founded, he said: 'Let no man remain a member who is habitually a drunkard or who ill treats his wife or neglects his children or who is guilty of immorality.'

Told once that it was always easy to pull down religion, but what was he going to put in its place, he gave a typically forthright reply: 'Tell the backwoodsman who, with axe in hand, hews at the trunks of sturdy trees, that his is destructive work, and he will answer, "clear the ground, that plough and reaping hook may be used by and by".' He added that capacity for human progress was being hindered, 'grated in by prison bars, priest wrought and law-protected': the good wide field of common humanity was overcrowded with fraudulent creeds, the outgrowth of ancient mythologies; and he concluded, 'Atheist, without God, I look to humankind for sympathy, for love, for hope, for effort, for aid.'

What made Bradlaugh notorious to many and a hero to others was his being denied taking the oath on several formal occasions in both court and parliament. The first time this occurred was when he was defendant in a civil action in a court at Wigan in 1861. Since 1854 it had been open to witnesses who regarded the oath as contrary to their religious beliefs to affirm instead. But as soon as Bradlaugh entered the witness-box, counsel for the plaintiff asked Bradlaugh if he believed in the religious obligations of the oath. Bradlaugh objected to answering any questions without first being sworn. The judge overruled this and said, 'You won't answer the question?' Bradlaugh replied that he was not bound to answer any question that might incriminate himself.

JUDGE:	You will not answer my question. Do you believe in the existence of a supreme God?
BRADLAUGH:	I object that the answer, if in the negative, would subject me to a criminal prosecution.
JUDGE:	Do you believe in a state of future rewards and punishments?

BRADLAUGH: I object that—

JUDGE: Then I shall not permit you to give evidence at all, and I think you escape very well in not being sent to jail.

Such was the deep-rooted bigotry of the times; and in a travesty of justice the judge declared the action undefended and gave judgement for the plaintiff.

In 1880 Bradlaugh was elected as junior Liberal MP for Northampton and on presenting himself at the bar of the House asked the Speaker if rather than swearing an oath which required him to pledge allegiance to the Queen and her heirs and successors and concluded with the words, 'So help me, God', he could, under the Evidence Amendment Acts of 1869 and 1870, affirm instead.[5] It was a simple enough request which only, and legally, required an affirmative answer. But this was the first time that a self-proclaimed atheist member had been elected, and cravenly the Speaker decided to refer the issue to the whole House. They decided to appoint a committee. The committee consisted of nineteen members, nine Conservative and nine Liberal but the chairman, who was a Tory, gave his casting vote against. The matter was then referred to a select committee which concluded that Bradlaugh was not entitled to take the oath but should be allowed to affirm. The member who had spoken most vehemently against Bradlaugh taking the oath was Lord Randolph Churchill, younger son of the seventh Duke of Marlborough (and father of Winston) who was furious with Bradlaugh's campaigning to end the £4,000 a year perpetual pension his family still enjoyed as a result of the first duke's victories over the French. He spoke of Bradlaugh as an avowed atheist and professedly disloyal person and was supported by Henry de Worms, an apostate Jew who had found Christ, who urged the House to prevent an avowed atheist from swearing a lie 'on the holiest of books'. After a two-day debate a vote was taken of the whole House as to whether Bradlaugh should be permitted to affirm and was defeated by forty-five votes. Bradlaugh then expressed himself willing to take the oath.

Next day, after Bradlaugh had made his maiden speech without notes at the bar of the House, saying that he would appeal to a higher court than parliament, the electors of Northampton, the Tory leader, Sir Stafford Northcote, proposed a motion for Bradlaugh to withdraw, and this was passed by 286 votes, many of his fellow Liberals having ganged up with the Conservatives. What had particularly riled the whole House had been Bradlaugh's admission when seeking to affirm that to him the words of the oath were 'of idle and meaningless character' and 'far less solemn to me than the affirmation I would have reverently made'. The meaningless words to which Bradlaugh referred were no more than the words 'So help me, God', but the House inferred that he had found the whole oath meaningless and would therefore be prepared to break it whenever it suited him. Pious Christians most of them, they felt deep offence had been given to God and Queen, and when Northcote's motion was voted on, they reacted as one body. Some said that had he agreed to take the oath in the first place, and without any of the reservations he had expressed, no one would have tried to stop him. So to some degree he had brought his troubles on himself.

They were troubles which, though he could hardly have foreseen them, were to be long-lasting. Three times during the next four years the House of Commons refused to allow him to take his seat, three times the electorate of Northampton returned him. Between debates that ended in motions to expel him, he went barnstorming around the country, and at meetings in town halls and market-places his oratory, now honed to a fine art, stirred his audiences. 'He winged off into the air of verbal magic,' wrote David Tribe. 'He was speaking for the rights of the little man against authority, of the constituencies against big government, of the provinces against London, of justice against bureaucracy . . . It was Us against Them and those who had no sympathy with his politics or philosophy found murmurs of assent leaping to their lips and their hands shooting up in support.'

His worst moment in the House came on 3 August 1881 when he again tried and failed to take his seat. After the Speaker and his retinue had processed into the chamber, the Deputy Sergeant-at-Arms, David Erskine, closed the door behind them. Bradlaugh, standing tense in the lobby, in immaculate frock-coat and silk topper, advanced towards him. Erskine said, 'I have the instructions of the Speaker to prevent you from entering the precincts of the House.' Bradlaugh replied that while he was ready to obey any lawful orders of the House, he was there in obedience to the mandate of his constituents and would not yield to what was illegal. Bradlaugh tried to push Erskine aside, but one of the ushers seized him. Bradlaugh grasped at his throat, saying, 'If anyone dares to hinder me . . .' Ten policemen did dare, seized the struggling Bradlaugh and propelled him down the steps into Westminster Hall; there were cries of 'Kick him out' from government supporters, and in the fracas Bradlaugh's new top hat was knocked from his head, his coat ripped from his back and he was flung into Palace Yard. Later that day he made a speech in the Hall of Science, still in a state of shock: 'Violence would only be justified,' he told the audience, 'if I had meant revolution. I did not mean revolution and I hope I never may.'

When on one occasion Edward Marjoribanks proposed an Affirmation Bill, it was defeated by fifteen votes to scenes of great jubilation, proving that the House, composed principally of Anglicans, Methodists, Roman Catholics and Jews, did not want an atheist among them at any price. Two of the most virulent of the anti-Bradlaughites were again Randolph Churchill, patronisingly upper class, and the Jew de Worms who told the House with glee that politically an atheist was as disabled as a felon, a lunatic or a woman. In contrast Bradlaugh's colleague as senior Liberal MP for Northampton, Henry Labouchere, likened the oath to 'the same superstitious incantations as the trash of any mumbo-jumbo among African savages'. (Laughter and cries of Oh, Oh!) The member for Dewsbury made a good point when he said that to profess to allow a man to think for himself and then to annex disabilities to his opinions, was to destroy religious liberty altogether. It was left to Gladstone as Prime Minister to articulate the mood of the majority. 'I have no fear of atheism in this House. Truth is the expression of the Divine Mind, and however little our feeble vision may be able to discern the means by which God will provide for its preservation, we may leave the matter in his hands.'

But once again God was a loser, and for another eighteen months Bradlaugh languished in the wilderness. He bore the humiliation with exemplary patience and good manners, yet never ceasing to remind members that right was on his side. 'The House, being strong, should be generous . . . but my constituents have a right to more than generosity. The law gave me my seat. In the name of the law I ask for it.'

The *dénouement* finally came with a change of government, the Liberals going out and the Conservatives coming in. The new Speaker of the House was A.W. Peel, a Liberal, son of the man who had given the country its first policemen (known as Peelers). He was of a different stamp to those who had gone before and determined to end the farce. When the new House assembled on 11 January 1886, he said, 'I know nothing of the Resolutions of the past. They are lapsed, they are void, they are of no effect in reference to this case. It is the right, the legal statutable obligation of members when returned to this House to take the oath prescribed by statute.' Members were handed copies of the oath and a Bible, Bradlaugh among them. In front of an assistant clerk he read the oath and kissed the Bible and, having shaken hands with the Speaker, took the seat that by rights he should have taken more than five years before.

This episode of the members of the British House of Commons barring its doors against a fellow member because of his religious beliefs or lack of them was one of the most shaming in its history. It showed above all, and despite Darwin and Strauss, how deeply conservative and hostile both Liberal and Conservative members then were to any system of belief that did not tally with their own. They knew (but shut their eyes to it) that Bradlaugh was just as moral a man as the rest of them, indeed compared to some members rather more so. It was fear that beset them; fear that underpinned their misconceived belief that it was the Christian religion that held society together and that any departures from that belief would spell anarchy or even revolution. It was a belief that persisted for years and took many more years to die out.

★   ★   ★

Although the last quarter of the nineteenth century marked the beginning of the Anglican Church's long, slow decline from which it is unlikely to recover, it was still amazingly resilient. Despite its senior members saying some shrill and silly things, such as Newman dubbing Strauss's *Life of Jesus* a historical impossibility, and calling the four gospels '*pure and unadulterated history*' all written before 70 CE; Matthew Arnold's claim that it was 'the enduring power not ourselves that makes for righteousness', showing himself unaware that we had created the enduring power and then bestowed righteousness on him; on the same lines R.H. Hutton saying that human trust did not create God, nor could distrust annihilate him, which is just what both did do; and Pusey saying of backsliders that fear of God would soon drive people back to God, which became less and less true.

Nor was the Church averse to telling deliberate fibs when it thought it might help its cause. In 1885 the Rev. J.E.C. Welldon, later to become Bishop of Calcutta and who thought the British Empire divinely ordained, was foolish enough to say in the hearing of the Cambridge University Librarian, Henry Bradshaw, that the spread of unbelief among the undergraduates had led to a loss of morality. Bradshaw, who was on familiar terms with the undergraduates, knew this to be untrue. So in his own time he gave Welldon a little lesson on morality. 'Well, Welldon,' he said, 'you lied; and what is more, you knew you lied.'

Yet Newman and others did what they could to make the best of a bad job, latching on to Darwin's own words that he saw and intended nothing atheistical in his theory of evolution and the survival of the fittest. 'It does not seem to me to follow that creation is denied,' said Newman, 'because the Creator, millions of years ago, gave laws to matter . . . Mr Darwin's theory need not be atheistical be it true or not; it may simply be suggesting a larger idea of Divine Prescience and Skill' (i.e. God himself brought about the evolution of species and the survival of the fittest, and then let Darwin discover it); there was nothing in the world that God was unaware of. Or, as the essayist Aubrey Moore put it: 'Darwinism appeared and under the guise of a foe, did the work of a friend. Either God is everywhere present in nature or He is nowhere.' Thus some degree of renewed belief was restored to doubters who in any case had immortal longings for the hereafter, for them a certainty which neither Darwin nor Strauss nor anyone else could shake.

Unfortunately much of the ground regained was in danger of being lost when a symposium of beliefs edited by Charles Gore, sometime Bishop of Oxford, and entitled *Lux Mundi* (*The Light of the World*) was published in 1889. One major theme of *Lux Mundi* which was mentioned in all the essays was that of the doctrine of the Incarnation, what was known as *kenosis*, 'the self-emptying of God's omnipotence and omniscience into the person of the Son'. David Newsome called this, 'when properly understood, the most elevating and exhilarating revelation of God's purposes for man. God,' he goes on, 'by becoming man in the person of His Son, had ennobled his own creation.'

Readers who have kept with me so far will know that I regard 'God' as no more than an idea in the mind – though to many a very powerful idea – and therefore to claim that an idea in the mind can somehow empty itself into the person of Jesus Christ is nonsense. It only makes sense, or half sense, if you still cling to the old-fashioned idea of God as an independent father figure who thinks and acts like a human but is essentially 'divine'. Even then it is a notion hard to grasp, as many have found. In the writings of late Victorian England I have found no evidence of a welcome mat being laid out for it, apart from those by clerics. And yet, says Newsome, 'The doctrine of the Incarnation came very soon to be the dominant tone of Anglican theology, lasting for some three decades into the twentieth century.' It was not until the middle of the twentieth century that another group of clerics came to discard it.

During my lifetime two books on religion have greatly influenced me. The first, from which I have quoted extensively in earlier chapters, is *The Age of Reason* and was written when its author, Thomas Paine, was in prison in Paris towards the end of the eighteenth century. In other books he also praised the French and American Revolutions. I discovered Paine by chance when I was in Newfoundland during the war. At some dinner party I found myself next to the wife of a local businessman who, to my surprise (for religion in those days was not considered a suitable subject for dinner-party conversation) shared my doubts about the claims of Christianity. 'Have you ever read *The Age of Reason*?' she asked, and when I said I hadn't, she said she would lend me her copy but to guard it with my life for, she said, it was one of the most precious books in her possession.

It arrived one evening a few days later. I took it to bed with me, and kept the light on until I had finished it. Written in sharp, lucid, almost conversational prose, articulating truths which I had always felt but had never dared to say, to me it was a revelation and when I went to New York on leave a month later, I bought a copy which has been with me ever since.

The other book which came my way when I was back at Oxford after the war was *The Martyrdom of Man*. It was written by a young man called Winwood Reade, a nephew of the more famous Charles Reade, author of *The Cloister and the Hearth*. Published in 1872, the *Martyrdom of Man* offended Victorian religious feelings even more than Strauss's *Life of Jesus* (which in any case was less widely read). After first publication it went into twenty-two impressions, was republished by the Rational Press Association in 1924 and between then and 1968 sold another 140,000 copies.

If *The Age of Reason* had impressed by the impact of its literary skills and outspokenness of its anti-Christian stance, *The Martyrdom of Man* was an essay in seduction, a work no less forthright than Paine's in its dismissal of orthodoxy but written in a prose style of a strange beauty and power. H.G. Wells was greatly taken with it and Winston Churchill said, 'Reade was right but wrong to say it: the human race must be allowed to keep its illusions' (a somewhat contentious proposition) while Michael Foot in his introduction to a later edition wrote: 'Single sentences linger in the memory like verses learnt in childhood and the whole resembles an epic poem.'

In his own introduction to the original edition, Reade wrote that his publisher and several literary friends had urged him to tone down certain passages on religion which they thought would provoke public anger. His response was to say that in the matter of religion he listened to no remonstrance. 'I acknowledge no decision save that of the divine monitor within me. My conscience is my adviser, my audience and my judge. It bade me write as I have written, without evasion, without disguise; it bids me to go on as I have begun, whatever the result may be.' If, he said, his religious opinions were condemned by every reader of the book, it would not make him regret having expressed them, and it would not prevent him expressing them again. 'It is my earnest and sincere conviction that those opinions are not only true but also that they tend to elevate and purify the mind . . . It has done me good to write this book, and therefore I cannot think it can injure those by whom it will be read.'

Here are some of the things that Reade said:

(*The Day Before Yesterday*)
Among savages it is not love which can excite the imagination and deceive the sense but reverence and fear. The great chief is dead. His vision appears in a half-waking dream; it threatens and it speaks. The dreamer believes that the form and the voice are real, and therefore he believes that the great chief still exists. It is thus that the grand idea is born. There is life after death.

The gods were not abstract ideas to our ancestors as they are to us but *bona fide* men differing only from men on earth in their invisibility and magic powers. Their characters are human and are reflected from the minds of those who have created them. They are in all countries and at all times made by man in his own image. A god's moral position, his ideas of right and wrong, are those of the people by whom he has been created. It is evident that as men become developed in morality, the character of their gods will also be improved.

In the period of thing-worship, as it may be termed, every brook, tree, hill and star is itself a living creature, benevolent or malignant, asleep or awake. In the next stage, every object and phenomenon is inhabited or presided over by a genius or spirit

231

and with some nations the virtues and the vices are also endowed with personality. As the reasoning powers of men expand, their gods diminish in number and rule over larger areas, till finally it is perceived that there is unity in nature, that everything that exists is part of a harmonious whole. It is then asserted that one being manufactured the world and rules over it supreme.

(*Yesterday*)
The Bible is simply a collection of Jewish writings. The miracles in the Old Testament deserve no more attention from historians than the miracles in Homer. The miracles in the gospels are like the miracles in Plutarch's *Lives* – they do not lesson the value of the biography, and the value of the biography does not lessen the absurdity of the miracles.

The current fancies respecting the approaching destruction of the world, the conquest of the Evil Power and the reign of God had fermented in [Jesus's] mind and had made him the subject of a remarkable hallucination. He believed that he was the promised Messiah or Son of Man who would be sent to prepare the world for the kingdom of God, and who would be appointed to judge the souls of men and reign over them on earth.

(*Today*)
Theology is an excellent nurse but a bad mistress for grown up minds. The essence of religion is inertia; the essence of science is change. It is the function of the one to preserve, it is the function of the other to improve.

It is as foolish to pray for the healing of a disease or for daily bread as it is to pray for rain or a fair wind. It is as foolish to pray for a pure heart or for mental repose as it is to pray for help in sickness or misfortune.

One fact must be familiar to all those who have an experience of human nature – a sincerely religious man is often an exceedingly bad man. Piety and vice frequently live together in the same dwelling, occupying different chambers but remaining always on the most amicable terms. Nor is there anything remarkable in this. Religion is merely loyalty; it is just as irrational to expect a man to be virtuous because he goes to church, as it would be to expect him to be virtuous because he goes to court.

(*Tomorrow*)
A day will come when the European God of the nineteenth century will be classed with the gods of Olympus and the Nile; when surplices and sacramental plate will be exhibited in museums; when nurses will relate to children the legends of the Christian mythology as they now tell them fairy tales.

Poetry and the fine arts will take that place in the heart which religion now holds.

To develop to the utmost our genius and our love – that is the only true religion. To do that which needs to be written, to write that which deserves to be read, to tend the sick, to comfort the sorrowful, to animate the weary, to keep the temple of the body pure, to cherish the divinity within us, to be faithful to the intellect, to educate those powers which have been entrusted to our charge and to employ them in the service of humanity – that is all that we can do.

In 1875, at the age of thirty-seven, Winwood Reade died of tuberculosis. The few extracts of *Martyrdom* presented above can give only a flavour of his thoughts on one subject; inevitably they lack the full range of his scholarship and the accumulative impact of his unique style. Few who have read *Martyrdom* would disagree with Michael Foot's summing-up. 'With such a style at his command and with a knowledge and imagination shared by few of his contemporaries, it is surely true that, had he lived, he would have become one of the most eminent of Victorians.'

233

I knew when I first read Paine and Reade, and today as I approach my four score years I know with even greater certainty, that the message they were preaching was true. Why then had I not been apprised of it earlier? Why, when at the age of fifteen the Bishop of Lincoln placed the wafer representing the body of Christ on my tongue in Eton's College Chapel, had not one of the masters there, and as much of a doubter as myself, taken me aside and whispered that there were other and better ways to self-fulfilment than this? *Eheu fugaces, posthume, posthume!* Oh, for the years that were lost to me, lost to me.

It so happened that during the two days that I was compiling those extracts from Reade's book I had to pay a visit to the local shopping centre. On the way I heard on the car radio a religious service broadcast by the BBC which was such an antithesis to everything Reade had been saying that I was moved to write to the BBC to ask for a transcript. The minister conducting the service is referred to in the script as Ernie, a shorthand for the Rev. Ernest Rae, the BBC's Head of Religious Broadcasting, and I print what he said without comment:

> With just over two weeks to go to Christmas we're well into Advent, the time of waiting for the coming of the Lord. That time when the glory of the Lord will be revealed and all flesh will see it together. So in expectation and faith we pray. Lord, you will come again as surely as summer follows spring; keep us steady when the world reels about us, and make us ready for the coming of your kingdom. Amen.
>
> What specifically do Christians mean when they talk about waiting for the coming of the Lord? Well, the one thing above all that we are saying is that history will surely arrive at its goal. There is a guiding purpose to life and in the fullness of time God's plan will be revealed and what is more we shall have a part in it. Now I know that this is a bold claim. We are nearing the end

of what many historians claim is the bloodiest century in history. It is sometimes difficult to discern any signs of God's activity, let alone that history is moving towards a climax.

But Advent declares that God is coming to us; in judgement, yes, but also in hope. Blaise Pascal once wrote that it is a glorious thing to ride upon a ship that may well be shaken by storms but which we know will arrive at a safe harbour. The message of the Bible begins with God breathing over the chaos and creating life; it ends with God's triumph, his purpose fulfilled and all things in subjection to him.

Chapter Ten

THE TWENTIETH CENTURY

1. Dr Margaret Knight

The three most notable atheists of the early years of the twentieth century were all friends and Cambridge University philosophers: G.E. Moore, John McTaggart and Bertrand Russell. All three were also members of the university society the Apostles, a radical group whose most notorious member in later years was the spy who became the Keeper of the Queen's pictures, Sir Anthony Blunt, who for his treachery was subsequently reduced to the ranks.

On the whole Moore was reticent about his beliefs though he did publish one essay on the subject entitled 'The Value of Religion' in the *International Journal of Ethics* in 1902. 'I am an infidel,' he wrote, 'and do not believe that God exists, and I think the evidence will justify my belief. But just as I think there is no evidence for his existence, I think there is also no evidence that he does not exist.'

Such equivocation is another example of how the weight of God-belief through 1,900 years of history was such that even so acute a thinker as Moore felt compelled to posit the possibility of 'God's' existence instead of concluding, as I have tried to do in these pages, that 'God' is not an external being but a projection of the human imagination.

Yet he did have one or two pithy comments. Religious belief, he said,

> gains much of its strength from the fact that [believers] think they ought to have it. They have a direct moral feeling that it is wicked to doubt of God's existence; and without this belief, which is a strong one, their direct religious certainty would offer but a weak resistance to scepticism. For such persons the final question arises, Are they right in thinking infidelity is wicked?

On which David Berman comments:

> The feeling that one ought to believe in God may arise from a conflation of two sorts of belief in the value of religion. The fideist may also be confusing the moral compulsion to believe with the religious or fideistic one. If so, the question becomes: how can it be wicked to believe the truth?

McTaggart was the first major British philosopher whose atheism was as committed and outspoken as Bradlaugh's; and yet, says Berman, he has seldom been acknowledged as such. One reason, Berman thinks, is the contradictory nature of some of his beliefs. He was a rationalist who was also a mystic; an atheist who was a believer in immortality and the non-existence of matter; a non-believer who was also a strong supporter of the Church of England; a dissident who disbelieved in the reality of time, yet who could laugh at the Irish for lacking a sense of it.

McTaggart set out the beliefs for this atheism in three books, *Some Dogmas of Religion*, *Studies in Hegeliam Cosmology* and *The Nature of Existence*. He was against religion on both general and particular grounds. On general grounds he claimed in *Some Dogmas* that no man was entitled to believe any religious dogma until he had investigated it himself.

> And since the investigation of dogma is a metaphysical process, and

religion must be based on dogma, it follows further that no man is justified in a religious attitude except as a result of metaphysical study . . . most people, as the world stands at present, have not the disposition, the education and the leisure for the study of metaphysics. And thus we are driven to the conclusion that, whether any religion is true or not, most people have no right *to accept* any religion as true.

Two of his particular reasons for rejecting Christianity were that if time was unreal, God could not have created a world subordinate to himself – an argument which G.E. Moore found incredible – and secondly a somewhat eccentric antipathy to Jesus himself.

> . . . if one were a Christian, one would have to worship Christ, and I don't like him much. If you take what he said in the first three gospels . . . it is a horribly imperfect and one-sided ideal. Would you like a man or a girl who really imitated Christ? I think most people I know are living far finer lives than anything you could get out of the gospels. The best thing about him was his pluck at the Crucifixion, and other people have shown as much.

The beliefs of the third member of this trio, Bertrand Russell, were far less sure than those of McTaggart, at times calling himself an atheist, at others an agnostic and, like Moore, allowing himself to posit the possibility of an independent all-seeing God as worthy of consideration. When in his eighties, he was asked at the end of a lecture what he would say to God if he met him after his death. '"God!" I would say [and I can hear the slightly querulous, high-pitched voice even now], "God, why have you made the evidence for your existence so insufficient?"'

It was a point that Bradlaugh took up in his *Plea for Atheism*:

> Every Theist must admit that if a God exists, he could have so

convinced all men of the fact of his existence . . . But as many
men have doubts, disagreements and disbelief as to God's existence
and attributes, it must follow that God does not exist, or that he is
not all-powerful or that he is not all-good.

During the 1920s Russell published two statements of personal
disbelief, *What I believe* and *Why I am not a Christian*. The latter
was reviewed in the *Criterion* in 1927 by the devout Christian and
American-born poet T.S. Eliot. Eliot had been a former pupil and
friend of Russell and must also, presumably, have had some respect for
his mind and philosophical achievements. His aggressively patronising
review of *Why I am not a Christian* therefore comes as something of
a shock:

> Mr Russell supposes that he is not a Christian because he is an
> Atheist . . . As we become used to Atheism, we recognise that it
> is often merely a variety of Christianity. In fact, several varieties.
> There is the High Church Atheism of Matthew Arnold, there is
> the Auld Licht Atheism of our friend Mr J.M. Robertson, there is
> the Tin Chapel Atheism of Mr D.H. Lawrence. And there is the
> decidedly Low Church Atheism of Mr Russell. For one only ceases
> to be a Christian by being something else definite – a Buddhist,
> a Mohammedan, a Brahmin. Just as Mr Russell's Radicalism is
> merely a variety of Whiggery, so his Non-Christianity is merely
> a variety of Low Church sentiment. This is why his pamphlet is
> a curious and a pathetic document.

It might be truer to say that of the two – *Why I am not a Christian*
and Eliot's review of it – it is the latter that more resembles a
curious and pathetic document, harking back as it does to the days
of the early eighteenth century when believers deemed atheism an
impossibility.

The first half of the twentieth century was dominated by two world
wars, which induced the combatants to offer up prayers to God for

victory for themselves and defeat for their opponents. Sir John Squire took the satirical view:

> God heard the embattled nations sing and shout
> *Gott strafe England* and *God Save the King*,
> God this, God that, and God the other thing
> Good God, said God, I've got my work cut out.

In England, after the end of the Second World War, social attitudes were found to be changing. The first upheaval occurred during the 1945 general election when to the surprise and disappointment of the middle classes, the electorate rejected the party led by the man who more than any other had won the war for them and, in a landslide victory, brought in Labour instead; and in that administration and a succeeding one reforms in health care, social security and education were introduced which are still with us today. Religious beliefs too continued to change, and in 1955 were brought sharply into focus by two talks given on BBC radio by an unknown lecturer in psychology at Aberdeen University by the name of Dr Margaret Knight. The title of the talks was *Morals without Religion*. They were to cause a sensation.

In a little book with the same title, published after the two broadcasts, Margaret Knight related the background to the talks. She began by saying that aside from the millions of frank unbelievers in the country, there were also large numbers of what she called half-believers 'to whom religion is a source of intellectual and moral discomfort'. She could appreciate their feelings, for they had been her own for many years:

> I had been uneasy about religion throughout my adolescence, but I had not had the moral courage to throw off my beliefs until my third year at Cambridge. Then . . . I made contact with the books and lectures of the philosophers Bertrand Russell, J.M.E. McTaggart and C.D. Broad. A fresh, cleansing wind swept thorough the stuffy room that contained the relics of my religious

241

beliefs. I let them go with a profound sense of relief, and ever since I have lived happily without them.

She went on to say how much she disagreed with the commonly held belief that Christian dogma and Christian ethics went together.

> It is specious for two reasons. First, the moral code we accept today is by no means wholly Christian. In its emphasis on justice and tolerance, rather than on the more passive virtues of long-suffering and meekness, it derives from Greece and Rome rather than from Christianity [which has] tacitly dropped the unacceptable features of Christ's teaching, such as the emphasis on hell-fire and the wrath to come. Secondly, there is no reason why we should not retain the valuable parts of the Christian ethic, such as its emphasis on love (a feature, incidentally, which it shares with most of the great world religions) while rejecting the belief that Christ was divine . . .

Her next comments reflected the climate of the times:

> It is difficult, none the less, for the ordinary man to cast off orthodox beliefs, for he is seldom allowed to hear the other side . . . Whereas the Christian view is pressed on him, day in and day out. Organised indoctrination begins at school, at the impressionable age of five; and the process is vigorously continued by the BBC which, besides its religious broadcast to schools, regularly devotes some ten hours a week to religious services and exhortations (such as 'Lift up your Hearts') and from two to six hours to talks with a religious flavour.

This high-powered propaganda, she said, had not made us a nation of believers, but had created strong deterrents to the expression of unbelief:

> In some cases the threat is financial; a teacher, for example, who is openly agnostic, finds his chances of promotion threatened. But

more subtle than the financial deterrent is the effect of mass suggestion – the feeling, sedulously fostered, that 'inability to believe' is a regrettable and slightly embarrassing condition, to which it is best not to refer. Thus many sceptics feel ashamed and furtive about their doubts; and all over the country perplexed and uneasy parents are creating similar conflicts for the next generation by teaching their children doctrines which they do not believe themselves.

Reckoning that a talk or talks on BBC radio would give her the widest possible audience for what she wanted to say, and aware that the BBC had previously announced that it was prepared to entertain affirmation for widely different beliefs as well as of unbelief (so long as such affirmations 'did not wound reasonable people or transgress the bounds of courtesy or good taste'), Mrs Knight submitted a draft script for the BBC's approval. 'It got into the hands of one of the Catholics who hold key positions in the BBC and was rather forcibly rejected.' A second draft met the same fate. But Mrs Knight was determined to be heard and went on badgering the corporation until they invited her to London for discussions.

Two talks were agreed on, and in preparing them, she said,

> My chief aim was to combat the view that there can be no true morality without supernatural sanctions. So I argued at length that the social or altruistic impulses are the real source of morality, and that an ethic based on these impulses has far more claim on our allegiance than an ethic based on obedience to the commands of a God who created tapeworms and cancer cells.

The reader will recall similar expressions being made by other dissenters in the course of this book, among them David Hume and the Rev. Leslie Stephen who, having abandoned the priesthood in the light of Darwin's revelations, declared that his future life would be no less moral and that he hoped to die like a gentleman. But, as we shall see, the British people as a whole were unaware of any alternative guide to conduct, and believed, or rather had been conditioned to believe, that 'God' and morality went hand in hand.

Knowing that after the broadcasts she would be asked what she advocated in place of Christianity, she answered unequivocally, 'Scientific Humanism', the essence of which was that it was not supernatural, was concerned with man rather than God and with this life rather than the next. 'The moral act, to the humanist, is the act that is conducive to human well-being, not the act ordained by God.'

She tried also in the talks, she said, to destroy the stereotyped picture of the non-Christian as seen by the Christian. There were two versions of him. One was the atheist, 'envisaged as a strident, loud-mouthed and wholly insensitive individual who equates "the good" with material goods and is always of course a Communist'.[1] Then there was the unbeliever. 'He is a gentler type, usually thought of as wistful, rootless and suffering from a deep sense of loss.' She added, 'The many, well-balanced, warm-hearted, cheerful and sensitive humanists most of us know, are ignored. I tried to suggest their existence.'

The press, as might be expected of it in those days, greeted the talks with outrage. The *Daily Express* came out with a banner headline: WOMAN PSYCHOLOGIST MAKES REMARKABLE ATTACK ON RELIGION, while the *Daily Telegraph*, as reactionary as always, called the talk 'one large slab of atheistical propaganda, offensive to public feeling', and called on God and the BBC to cancel the second broadcast. At the weekend the *Sunday Graphic* published a picture of Margaret Knight and alongside it in two-inch lettering THE UNHOLY MRS KNIGHT. 'Don't let this woman fool you,' an article on her began. 'She looks – doesn't she – just like the typical housewife; cool, comfortable, harmless? But Mrs Margaret Knight is a menace. A dangerous woman. Make no mistake about that. The misguided BBC have allowed a fanatic to rampage along the air lanes, beating up Christianity with a razor and a bicycle chain.' Increasingly hysterical, the piece concluded: 'Let's have no more of her twaddle. She's due to dish up a second basinful on Wednesday. The BBC should pour it down the sink.'

When Mrs Knight arrived at Broadcasting House a week later there were so many pressmen and photographers waiting at the entrance that she had to be smuggled in by a side door. The next day's papers kept up the barrage: MRS KNIGHT SAYS IT AGAIN: BISHOP CHECKS MRS KNIGHT: GODLESS RADIO REPEAT SHOCKS NATION: KEEP THIS WOMAN OFF THE AIR. Leading articles and interviews with clerics shared a common reason and phrases such as 'untrue and vicious propaganda', 'pernicious', 'irresponsible' and 'stale so-called rationalist patter' were a hallmark of many of the contributions. Leading churchmen were particularly severe. The Dean of Windsor thought the broadcasts should never have been made, Canon Mervyn (later Bishop) Stockwood resented the one-sidedness of her remarks while the Church Council of St Augustine's, Highbury, passed this resolution: 'We are shocked and horrified beyond anything that words can express, that a public responsible institution like the BBC would dare to violate all the laws of decency and Christian conduct by broadcasting the pagan views of Mrs Knight to the parents and children of Britain.'

Some of the personal letters Mrs Knight received were equally abusive. One, like most of them anonymous, said: 'You beast in woman's clothing. One day the God you scoff at and deny will judge you. I don't ask for mercy for you, you foul Communist Russian dupe.' Another was equally batty: 'Both you and the BBC speak and act solely in the interests of Jewish international Bolshevism.'

But as the days went by, Mrs Knight saw support for her views begin to gather strength. In a press interview Dr Donald (later Lord) Soper, President of the Methodist Council, expressed himself appalled by the hysteria aroused by the talks: 'Christians will do themselves a great deal of harm if they assume that the Christian faith is a sort of hothouse plant that must be protected against the weather.' The *Daily Mirror* came out in favour and the *News Chronicle* carried the headline, GIVE MRS KNIGHT THE FREEDOM OF THE AIR. But the calmest and most impressive comment came from the *Church of England Newspaper*:

There is only one way of dealing with people of different opinions;

answer them. We shall achieve nothing permanent by trying to prevent their speaking . . . If the Christian faith can only reply to such a person as Mrs Knight with personal abuse and can find no compelling answer, it deserves to fail and will in fact disappear . . . Those who share Mrs Knight's doubts about Christianity probably outnumber those who do not in Britain at the present time, and include large numbers of our most respected and highly responsible citizens.

Many of the 1,200 personal letters to Mrs Knight were also coming out more and more in her favour:

We listened to the talks with real excitement, feeling at last that someone is saying things we have felt for so long.

You have crystallised my own vague thoughts. You have given us courage.

It was like opening a dungeon door to admit the light.

From a parent
I am a father whose children are, willy-nilly, taught at school what I firmly believe to be rubbish. They come to me to resolve what even their immature minds perceive to be conflicts between what they are taught about God and what their science teachers say and what they themselves experience. It is difficult indeed for a parent not to increase their confusion.

From a headmaster, and typical of similar letters
My experience was that very many schoolmasters were unwilling to take scripture lessons, because they did not know what to say. In no subject in examination does one get such ridiculous answers as in scripture and this, I think, is because boys say what they think they are expected to say and not what they think.

From an O.A.P.

I am not only convinced that religion is not necessary for a sound morality, but I think it positively bad as a basis for it. At 93 I am more clear in my mind about it than when I was at 33, when I found it necessary for the sake of mental integrity to break with my profession as minister.

From a clergyman

Every single one of us knows perfectly that you can have morals without religion; we are doing our daily work among thousands of whom that is true.

Mrs Knight broke down the letters into six categories. Ignoring the Neutral and Deranged groups and combining the Favourable and Tolerant as Pro and the Unfavourable and Abusive as Anti, she found that the Pros numbered 661 and the Antis 382, a majority of more than three to two in favour.

In addition there were articles and letters from the United States, South America, Canada, Australia, New Zealand, South Africa, France, Germany, Holland, Belgium, Italy, Norway, Sweden, Denmark, Finland, Egypt, India and Burma. Mrs Knight particularly treasured a headline from *Paris-Presse* which read, LA BBC A LAISSE MRS KNIGHT DIRE QUE LE DIABLE N'EXISTAIT PAS and sub-titled *Consternation en Angleterre et violente campagne de presse.*

Among the general public the name of Margaret Knight and her fifteen minutes of fame have long been forgotten but the fact that she was speaking simultaneously to millions marked, in my view, a turning-point in British religious thought; one as seminal and far-reaching as that brought about by Strauss's *Life of Jesus* or John Stuart Mill's rejection of God in the nineteenth century. Before Mrs Knight, Britain had been a more or less Christian country; after her it became a more or less secular one.

I once heard Cardinal Hume, the Roman Catholic Archbishop of

Westminster, say that the Christian religion showed that goodness was achievable, the unspoken corollary being that without it, goodness was less likely. Margaret Knight had exploded that myth by revealing in the letters she received that very many irreligious people were leading very good moral lives, which most of us knew already. In any case, the time when clerics had found it necessary to exhort us, in the name of Father, Son and Holy Ghost, to strive for virtue and to eschew sin was long since past.

For many years now I have believed that all, or the great majority of us, share what I like to think of as the collective conscience. With a few exceptions we all know or think we know what is right conduct and what is wrong, and it is on that shared assumption that we establish our relationships, whether business or social. For instance the public stance of most heads of institutions as well as civil servants, service chiefs, publishers, lawyers, teachers, journalists and newspaper editors is a moral one; and while our moral guidelines are apt to shift from generation to generation, there are certain constants to which we all adhere. Papers which print stories of murder, rape, assault, burglary, fraud, do not do so to praise them, but to stress that they *are* aberrations deserving of notice and punishment (and thus allow the Jekyll side of some readers to become momentarily Hydes and enjoy a touch of *Schadenfreude* to know that there, but for the force of the collective conscience, go they). And to people who ask, as they surely will, from where do you think the morality of the collective conscience came but from 'God', I would reply, along with Feuerbach, that it was we humans who bestowed (and continue to bestow) that morality on the fictional God, not the other way round.

2. Bishop John Robinson

In the decade that followed Mrs Knight and the *Morals without Religion* furore, the Anglican Church was becoming increasingly worried. People were abandoning church services in droves, no longer able to subscribe to what clerics called the gospel message and finding most of the liturgy not only false but an irrelevance. Nor were the generality of the population impressed by Anglican spokesmen trying to salve something from the wreckage by telling us that while it was true that church attendances had fallen, there were still more people going to church on Sundays than to football matches on Saturdays.

An editorial in the religious magazine *PRISM* in September 1962 laid bare the heart of the matter:

> Whether it is true . . . that the *homo non religiosus* is in bulk a new phenomenon, I do not know. What certainly is true is that there are many men who find traditional religion and spirituality completely meaningless, and that you will find them among those who are completely committed to Christ as well as among those who are not.
>
> We have reached a moment in history when these things are at last being said openly, and when they are said, there is an almost audible gasp of relief from those whose consciences have been wrongly burdened by the religious tradition.

Twenty years earlier a German theologian named Dietrich Bonhoeffer had arrived at much the same conclusions. Bonhoeffer, like Strauss, had been educated at Tübingen and later in Berlin, but in 1933 he had left Germany for England in protest against Hitler's persecution of the Jews. But he returned to Germany two years later and became head of a seminary until it was closed down by the Nazis in 1937. During the war he became deeply involved in the anti-Hitler resistance movement and in 1943 he was arrested and imprisoned. In 1945, when he was thirty-nine, and only a week or two before the war ended, he was taken from his cell at Flossenburg and hanged. But before that he had set down his thoughts on the place of man in the Christianity of the mid–twentieth century, and these were later published under the title of *Letters and Papers from Prison*.

Man has learned to cope with all questions of importance without recourse to God as a working hypothesis. In questions concerning science, art and even ethics this has become an understood thing which one scarcely dares to tilt at any more. But for the last hundred years or so, it has been increasingly true of religious questions also; it is becoming evident that everything gets along without 'God' and just as well as before. As in the scientific field, so in human affairs generally, what we call 'God' is being more and more edged out of life, losing more and more ground.

   Catholic and Protestant historians are agreed that it is in this development that the great defection from God is to be discerned, and the more they bring in and make use of God and Christ in opposition to this trend, the more the trend itself considers itself to be anti-Christian.

Later he deplores the Church's opposition to man's coming of age, and it claiming that on the ultimate questions of humanity it is still only 'God' that can provide an answer. But what if one day these ultimate questions can also be answered without God?

The attack by Christian apologetic upon the adulthood of the world, I consider to be in the first place pointless, in the second ignoble and in the third un-Christian. Pointless because it looks to me like an attempt to put a grown-up man back into adolescence, i.e. to make him dependent on things on which in fact he is not dependent any more ... Ignoble because this amounts to an effort to exploit the weakness of man for purposes alien to him and not freely subscribed to by him. Un-Christian because for Christ himself is being substituted one particular stage in the religiousness of man.

How did Bonhoeffer see the way forward? If it was true, he said, that man no longer felt the need for a god to whom to give himself, a god in terms of whom to explain the world; if he felt he could get along perfectly well without religion, without any desire for personal salvation, without any sense of sin, did that mean that Christianity in the future was to be confined to no more than those with a sense of insufficiency or those who could be induced to have it? Bonhoeffer's answer was that in the mid-twentieth century 'God' was calling us to a new form of Christianity *which did not depend on the premise of religion*. This baffled me. What else was a sense of religion but the vehicle whereby people came to believe in God and Jesus Christ; though at least Bonhoeffer had retained some element of the old anthropomorphic God by stating that he was human enough to be 'calling us'. And when he said that he now saw God as 'the beyond in the midst of our life', where did that differ from the traditional way of regarding God as a Being 'out there'?

Man's sense of religion, Bonhoeffer went on, had made him look in his distress to the power of God in the world, to regard him as a *Deus ex Machina*:

> The Bible however directs him to the powerlessness and suffering of God; only a suffering God can help. To this extent we may say that the process we have described by which the world came of age was an abandonment of a false conception of God, and a clearing of the decks for the God of the Bible who conquers power and space in the world by his weakness. This must be the starting-point for our worldly interpretation.

This baffled me even more. If by using the word God in this extract, Bonhoeffer actually meant Christ who *did* suffer (the 'suffering servant' of Isaiah 53:12 and Philippians 2:7) it was a pity he didn't say so. If on the other hand he meant the Father, whom most Christians have always envisaged as all-powerful, *not* suffering, I have to say I find that a contradiction in terms. In any case, as I have claimed often enough before, all gods past and present and not excluding the Christian god are chimeras, mental fantasies, and as such can neither suffer nor exercise power.

Another German theologian who agreed with Bonhoeffer that for many the traditional interpretation of the word God was now meaningless was Paul Tillich. He had served as an army chaplain in the First

World War and had found the experience traumatic. Later he taught theology at Marburg, Dresden and Leipzig. But, like Bonhoeffer, he was an early critic of Hitler and in 1933, having been banned by the government from all German universities, he emigrated to the United States. Here he taught theology in New York, Chicago and Harvard, and in 1940 became an American citizen.

In a collection of some of Tillich's contributions to modern theology published in England in 1949 under the title *The Shaking of the Foundations* was a sermon called 'The Depth of Existence' and in it Tillich advocated an entirely new way of looking at God. God, according to him, was not the father figure we had all known since childhood but what he called 'the infinite and inexhaustible depth and ground of all being'.

> That depth is what the word God means. And if that word has not much meaning for you, translate it and speak of the depth of your life, of the source of your being, of your ultimate concern, of what you take seriously without any reservations. Perhaps, in order to do so, you must forget everything traditional you have learned about God, perhaps even that word itself. For if you know that God means depth, you know much about him. You cannot then call yourself an atheist or unbeliever.

I found this confusing; also a statement in which Tillich (like Jewish, Greek Orthodox and Moslem leaders before him) had asserted that God was 'not a Being at all'. What exactly did he mean by saying that 'depth is what the word God means'? Not in my dictionary it didn't, and if Tillich was claiming that this was what he *wanted* the word to mean, to others as well as to himself, he ought to have said so. Then again, why refer to God as 'him', the old anthropomorphic way of looking at God which Tillich was encouraging us to discard? And even if the old God was now outdated and irrelevant, what was so beguiling about this impersonal abstraction that Tillich was trying to put in his place?

Time to turn to a senior Anglican cleric, the Right Reverend John

A.T. Robinson, suffragan Bishop of Woolwich. Robinson had been born within the precincts of Canterbury Cathedral where his father was a canon and educated at Cambridge University where he had later returned to teach. For a long time he had felt that his Church had lost its way. He had read and been much impressed by the writings of Bonhoeffer and Tillich, also by a third German theologian, Rudolf Bultmann, who was much older than the other two (he was fifty-five when the Second World War began and lived until 1976). It will be recalled that a hundred years earlier David Strauss in his *Life of Jesus* had set about mythologising the New Testament to interpret events which, if taken literally, were impossible to believe. Now Bultmann saw as one object of his life's work the need to demythologise the Bible, as mythologising it tended to cloud the significance of Christ's life in the context of history.

In the early 1960s Robinson found himself confined to his bed for three months and made use of his enforced idleness by distilling the thoughts of Tillich and Bonhoeffer and to a lesser degree Bultmann into a book of his own which he called *Honest to God*. It was published in 1963, less than a decade after the *Morals without Religion* broadcasts and was an immediate runaway bestseller, being translated into twenty languages and having a worldwide sale of more than a million copies.

The reason for the book's success was (as with most successful books) its timing. Here for the first time, a bishop of the Church of England was telling his readers that what *they* were experiencing, *he* was experiencing, that the way they had all been brought up, to visualise 'God' as an external father figure 'up there' or 'out there' was no longer credible; and that if the Church continued to preach traditional orthodoxy, 'we shall find in all likelihood that we have lost out to all but a tiny religious remnant'. Indeed, *pace* Tillich, there was a case for giving up the word God altogether for a time, 'so impregnated has it become with a way of thinking we may have to discard if the gospel is to signify anything'.

He was even bold enough to call in aid the naturalist Julian Huxley, T.H. Huxley's grandson:

The God hypothesis is no longer of any pragmatic value for the interpretation or comprehension of nature, and indeed often stands in the way of better and truer interpretation. Operationally God is beginning to resemble not a ruler, but the last fading smile of a cosmic Cheshire cat.

It will soon be as impossible for an intelligent, educated man or woman to believe in a god as it is now to believe that the earth is flat, that flies can be spontaneously generated, that disease is a divine punishment, or that death is due to witchcraft. God will doubtless survive, sometimes under the protection of vested interests or in the shelter of lazy minds or as puppets used by politicians or as refuges for unhappy or ignorant souls.

Among his intelligent non-Christian friends, Robinson went on, there were many far nearer the kingdom of heaven than they themselves would credit, 'For while they have imagined they have rejected the gospel, they have in fact been largely put off by a particular way of thinking about the world which quite legitimately they find incredible.' He had to admit that when he heard a broadcast debate between a Christian and a Humanist, his sympathies were with the Humanist. He also admitted to having had personal difficulties in regard to prayer. It was this blunt admission of failure and being honest to God about it, that echoed what thousands, perhaps millions, were thinking in their hearts and led to the book's huge initial sales. The king is dead, long live the king, Robinson seemed to be saying. But what sort of king was he proposing to put on the old king's throne?

He knew the magnitude of what he had set himself. 'Every one of us lives with some mental picture of a God "out there", a God who "exists" above and beyond the world he made, a God "to" whom he prays and to whom we "go" when we die.' To ask people to give up the idea of such a god would seem to be an outright denial of God. 'For to the ordinary way of thinking, to believe in God means to be convinced of the existence of such a supreme and separate Being. "Theists" are those who believe such a Being exists, "atheists" those who deny he does.'

Like Tillich and Bonhoeffer he did not flinch from where his logic led him:

> Suppose that all that such atheism does is to destroy an idol and that we can and must get on without a God 'out there' at all? Have we seriously faced the possibility that to abandon such an idol may in the future be the only way of making Christianity meaningful . . . Perhaps after all the Freudians are right, that such a God – the God of popular theology – *is* a projection, and we are being called to live without that projection in any form.

So far, so good; but the morning which had broken so full of promise could not be sustained; for to laymen such as myself the answers as to how we should interpret God in the future neither illumined nor convinced. Robinson saw God as Ultimate Reality, whatever that might mean, but he also saw him as Love which was a regression to the old-type God he wanted us to abandon. Indeed in the latter pages of his book he seems to have forgotten how fired he had been by Tillich's theory of God no longer a Being by saying things like, 'Through Jesus Christ, God spoke and acted,' and that right and wrong were 'the commandments that God gave us'. Elsewhere he gets tangled up in what I can only call theology-speak, as when he says that 'prayers and ethics are the outside and inside of the same thing and could be defined as meeting the unconditional in the conditional in unconditional personal relationship'; yet in his chapter on prayer he never once poses the question whether prayer is speaking to oneself or to 'God' and if the latter, whether he is listening.

Nor were Tillich's God-no-longer-a-Being or Bonhoeffer's Christianity without religion any more intelligible or helpful. All three in my view were attempting the impossible: trying to persuade the world that the word God could be made to mean something other than what it had meant for western Christians and non-Christians for nigh on 2,000 years. What they were trying to achieve was the retention of the word God, even in another incarnation, at all costs.[2]

What they were trying to avoid was having to flush out the baby with the bathwater. What they refused to admit was that God was now an old, sick, wizened baby whose time was almost up and therefore ripe for flushing.

Whether I am right in this assessment, or not, it is for others to say. What I do know is that today, thirty-five years after publication of *Honest to God*, few people under the age of fifty and outside clerical circles will have heard of Bishop Robinson and his book – or of Tillich and Bonhoeffer and Bultmann. Mrs Knight in her broadcasts succeeded in shifting people's perceptions regarding morality and religion. Bishop Robinson and Co. put their fingers in the dyke to try to stem the flood, and failed.

The publication of *Honest to God* caused almost as much furore as Mrs Knight's two broadcasts. In the first three months after publication the bishop received more than 1,000 letters and there were reviews and comments in all the media, many of which were subsequently collected in a SCM paperback edited by Dr David Edwards and called *The Honest to God Debate*.

Some of the letters were dismissive or actively hostile. A rural dean thought the best way the bishop could be honest to God would be to resign his office and leave the Church of England, while an archdeacon told him his book was deplorable. Most letters however were favourable, many people, especially women, thanking the bishop for giving them the means of renewing their faith ('I would like to tell you that your radical reinterpretation is just what is needed to make Christian religion dynamic and viable').

Some of the reviews were as critical as some of the letters. Alasdair Macintyre, a Fellow of University College, Oxford, opened his review in *Encounter* by declaring that first and foremost the bishop was an atheist.

Many of the critics spoke of their difficulties with Tillich's phrase about God being the ground of our being. Sir Julian Huxley called it 'semantic cheating and so vague as to be practically meaningless', while a lecturer at Lincoln College said that to talk of Love being exercised by an abstraction said nothing at all. John Lawrence asked how the ground of our being could be transcendent and another critic wondered how you could pray to it.

One of the most trenchant reviews came from a cleric who believed in the old-type external, distinctive God who had created man, provided for him, judged and redeemed him. 'What really matters in this view,' he concluded, 'is not what the Bishop thinks about God, but what God thinks of the Bishop.'

During succeeding decades, the Church of England began giving up more and more ground, approving such innovations as permitting divorced people to be remarried in church, lifting the ban on the ordination of women (a ban which most lay people had always found incomprehensible), welcoming gays among the clergy (Dr Hope, Bishop of London, who later became Archbishop of York, publicly confessed to his sexual orientation being in 'a grey area'), and blessing both gays and lesbians among the congregations. In the decade that followed the *Honest to God* debate, a group of senior theologians published a booklet called *The Myth of God Incarnate*, believing that the doctrine of Jesus being the second person of the Trinity, 'fully God and fully man', was now impossible to take literally, weakened the impact of his earthly ministry and was an insult to Hindus and Moslems in his saying that no one could come to the Father except through him. A year later this was countered by another group of fundamentalist theologians with another but wholly unconvincing booklet, *The Truth of God Incarnate*.

A decade later the controversial Dr David Jenkins, a leading biblical scholar, was appointed Bishop of Durham. Before his consecration in York Minster, he took part in a television programme in which he declared unequivocally that he did not consider the virgin birth, the resurrection or the miracles to be historical facts; thus blatantly contradicting what a former Archbishop of Canterbury, Dr Michael Ramsey, had told me in the 1950s, that the physical resurrection of Jesus Christ was the core of Christian belief, and that without it, as Paul had said, Christianity was nothing. In another programme Dr

Jenkins told his interviewer that he did not think that God *would have allowed* (my italics) Jesus to walk on the water. He also declared that the story of the Star of Bethlehem and the three wise men was mythical, and indeed that nothing said in the New Testament could be regarded as certain. This brought a sharp retort from the then Archbishop of Canterbury, Robert Runcie, who said that this was not the time to raise divisive issues but for all Christians to remember that 'what unites them in wonder is the Incarnation of our Lord' – another piece of delusional whimsy. Two days after the bishop's consecration York Minster was struck by lightning and damaged by fire, which some simple souls took to be God's response to his heretical opinions.

Following Dr Jenkins's doubts, a poll was taken of the country's thirty-one diocesan bishops. Two out of three agreed with another of the bishop's views, that it was not necessary to accept the divinity of Christ to be a Christian (almost like saying you didn't have to be a soldier to join the army). Half agreed they had similar doubts about the miracles, and one out of three denied a belief in the virgin birth and the physical resurrection. Fifty years earlier this sort of talk would have been regarded as the grossest heresy, in Europe 500 years earlier it would have meant breaking on the wheel or burning at the stake; yet when an ordinary parish priest in Sussex, the Rev. Anthony Freeman, expressed similar views, his bishop removed him from his living. With friends and colleagues such as these, the new Archbishop of Canterbury, George Carey, must have wondered, who needed enemies?

Indeed in Britain there were numbers of practising Anglicans and Episcopalians, both clergy and laity, who were so appalled by their own Church's flight from orthodoxy in the matter of the ordination of women that they sought refuge in Rome which they saw as the only true faith, unchanging and uncompromising, the rock, as the hymn said, of ages past. And yet that Church too, and its leader, Pope John Paul II, had their own problems. It was true that in the course of his pontificate John Paul had introduced some minor social changes, true too that he had travelled the world, kissed a score of airport runways and been greeted, as is the way with people seeking imagined leadership, by the cheers of millions.

Yet on certain fundamental matters he had been inflexible; and the most fundamental was his insistence on the doctrine of safeguarding the sanctity of life. One can understand his objections to abortion, which many regard as the lesser of two evils, but his decrees against contraception, which is also unsupported by biblical dogma, is harder to understand. Sophisticated Roman Catholic westerners can and do safely ignore it, but in Third World countries thousands of women have been condemned to half a lifetime of bearing children which they do not want and cannot afford. In greatly overpopulated Brazil, for instance, where the punishment for abortion is up to twenty-four years' imprisonment, it has been estimated that there are ten back-street abortions for every seven live births and that every year hundreds of Brazilian women die as the result of botched abortions. As a consequence many American Protestant missions with less restrictive attitudes have moved in to Latin American countries and made many successful conversions. And when forward-looking, compassionate Roman Catholic priests like Father Boff in Brazil and Gustavo Gutierrez in Peru introduced what became known as 'liberation theology' to improve the wretched conditions in which so many unfortunates were living, the Pope effectively silenced them.

In Calcutta, one of the most grossly overpopulated cities in the world, Mother Teresa did much during her long life to alleviate the sufferings of the diseased, deprived and dying, but it seems never to have occurred to her that by accepting contraception she would have found fewer on the streets in need of succour. Harry Stopes-Roe, a leading Humanist, once replied to her assertion that God loved every child, by saying, 'Yes, after they are born', to which Mother Teresa replied, 'No, from the moment of conception'. Stopes-Roe pointed out that St Thomas Aquinas had held that the foetus did not receive the soul until quickening, to which Mother Teresa said, 'I know no theology,' and walked away.

Not even in Uganda where more than a million of the country's 17 million inhabitants are said to have AIDS was an exception allowed to be made to the ruling on contraception, thus generating the further spread and consequent deaths caused by this dreadful, lethal disease, and the sanctity of *their lives* could be conveniently forgotten.

Nor did the sanctity of life extend to those condemned to death by due process, to whose executions the Pope made no demur, and there is a tradition of Catholic priests blessing the colours of soldiers about to kill each other in battle. It was the same with voluntary euthanasia to which the Pope has always been implacably opposed. 'Suffering,' he said in 1980, 'especially in the last stages of life, is part of God's saving plan for humanity.' It is difficult to fathom just what this means but it has always struck me as medieval in its thinking, and cruel in its lack of compassion.

One senior Catholic opposed to the Pope on this issue is Professor Hans Küng, the independent German Swiss theologian who first broke with the Pope on the contraception issue and was then barred from preaching or lecturing in any Catholic church or seminary. In a book on voluntary euthanasia Küng argues powerfully against traditional Catholic teaching that says it is for God, not humans, to decide how and when we end our lives. God, he avers, has given us the discretion to act as we think right, and we evade our responsibilities by shifting them on to him. He speaks of shattering letters he has had from Germany of old people complaining that no one will help them to die and some doctors wanting to talk them out of it.[3]

To sum up, the Protestant Church has given way to liberal reforms in a variety of areas and is now in decline because of it: the reactionary Catholic Church has stuck to the old dogmas and doctrines which are now seen as oppressive and because of them is also in decline. Whether either has any long-term future is anybody's guess.

Chapter Eleven

TOUCHING THE TRANSCENDENT

We all have to discover our own paths to spiritual truth. Some look for it in the east, in Confucianism, Buddhism, Zen Buddhism; many Americans in Christian Fundamentalism, others among the Mormons and Moonies, Jehovah's Witnesses, and Seventh Day Adventists; some in Hinduism or Islam among the Shiites or Sunnis, others in some of the hundreds of New Age cults which secularism has brought about, a diminishing few in orthodox Christianity. But their way is not my way.

First, let me sum up those aspects of the Christian religion which I find impossible to believe. Firstly they claim that their god is supernatural and not bounded by time and space. But we are: our thinking is conditioned by time and space, and this vale of joy and tears is the only one we know. Next, when Christians claim that their god made heaven and earth, we are entitled to ask, how? The heavens whose wonders science has opened up for us today is a much vaster affair than the one the Ancients knew, so vast indeed, with its billions of galaxies divided by billions of miles, that it defies mental attempts to formulate it. To say that 'God' created this immensity out of nothing insults the imagination and adds nothing to the store of human knowledge.

When Christians are asked to describe their god, they are usually at a loss for words. He is, they say, mysterious, ineffable, beyond human comprehension; so nebulous in fact that one wonders why they feel the need to worship him. Pressed, they will say that he is merciful and loving, though when asked to give examples, they are unable to do so. They also claim that as well as being all-loving he is all-powerful and all-knowing. In that case, you ask, why does he allow the humans he created to suffer from such 'God'-made disasters as floods, fire, famine and earthquakes, which he could prevent but doesn't? And they find that unanswerable too.

Finally, if he is as real to Christians as he would seem to be, why, as Bertrand Russell asked, doesn't he make himself known to the rest of us?

The only possible conclusion to draw from all this is that this god is so insubstantial a figure that he does not exist in any meaningful way and like all previous gods, therefore, must be an invention of the human mind, passed on unthinkingly from generation to generation. What happened, I guess, is that the early Christians who were all Jews had inherited from their Jewish past the great, roaring, vengeful, manipulative god they called Yahweh of whom they stood in great fear. At the time of Christ's birth Yahweh was, so to speak, the god in residence. But the characteristics the Israelites had bestowed on him were not those shared by the first Christians; the ones they wanted to admire in a god were those that Christ often preached: love and mercy, justice and compassion. So they ceased to worship Yahweh and began to worship 'God'; that is, a god on whom they bestowed the qualities they most revered. And in the course of time it came to be forgotten that this God, like all others, was a human invention, and with the help of generations of Popes and bishops and latterly with the likes of Jack Miles, took on an existence of his own.

And if that is so, then the whole elaborate, artificial structure of Christian theology that was built up over the centuries is pure moon-shine. These include what you might call the stations of God which I wrote about in Chapter 7: Pentecost, Advent, All Saints, Epiphany and so on; and to these must be added some of the arcane names (from the Greek) that theologians have dreamed up to indicate aspects of Christian belief: *Parousia* (the Second Coming); *Homoousion* (the Son the same essence as the Father); *Kerygma* (Preaching the Gospel); *Kenosis* (God's and Christ's self-emptying); *Agape* (the love of God for man); and, as part of private theology-speak, the creation of cosy, esoteric adjectives from the proper names of the Evangelists (Marcan, Lucan, Johannine, etc.). And at the apex of it all the wholly fictitious 'God', so that one can only marvel at the thousands of books and millions of words that have been written about this non-existent Being and his non-existent attributes: transcendent, immanent, numinous, thoughtful, purposeful, watchful, disappointed, loving, suffering, etc., all human attributes because it is only in human terms that he can be imagined. Twentieth-century scholars whom I admire such as Uta Ranke-Heinemann, Karen Armstrong, David Jenkins and Don Cupitt want to persuade us that we must cease to see God in these terms, rather envisage him and the gospel stories in terms of myth and metaphor. But for the generality of people, both Christians and dissenters, I believe this to be impossible. For most of us God is either a larger than life, separate, sentient Being or he is nothing. God as myth or metaphor, as existing within us or as ground of our being is beyond most people's understanding.

For early and later Christians, equally ignorant of science and the workings of the human mind, belief in a personal god was the only thing that gave meaning to their existence. But now that science has mapped out most of the earth and part of the heavens, and Freud and Jung have tried to explain how we come to think and act as we do, why the need to perpetuate it? I hesitate to criticise the clergy, if for no other reason that most are decent men living on inadequate incomes who have dedicated their lives to the service of others; but when in three-quarters empty churches (though there are exceptions) I hear them making supplications and incantations to 'the Lord', it seems to me that they are no better than their Palaeolithic ancestors, pleading for *their* 'lord' to guard them from wolves and bears, imploring him to bring rain to refresh their crops/prevent it from flooding their dwelling-places.

For some time now I have been collecting cuttings from papers like *The Times* and the *Telegraph* relating to current Christian beliefs. Here is what Dr Hope, the Archbishop of York, wrote in the Credo column of *The Times* in August 1997, headlined MARY'S GLORY PUTS EARTHLY AFFAIRS IN A HEAVENLY LIGHT:

> This feast of the Blessed Virgin Mary is so significant because before all else, it is about the abundant and amazing grace of God as set before us in the vocation and response of Mary herself. He 'looked upon the lowliness of the Blessed Virgin Mary and chose her to be the mother of His only Son'.

When I read paragraphs like these, I have to ask myself what a grown man like Dr. Hope thinks he is doing, peddling such fantasies as though they were historical fact.

And here is a news item, also from *The Times* and headed, STATUE CRIED.

> *Rome*: The Vatican rules that tears of blood shed by a statue of the Virgin Mary at Civitavecchia north of here two years ago were 'authentic' . . . The Vatican said that it had detected no sign of 'trickery'.

Other equally dotty stories are headlined ARCHBISHOP QUESTIONS EXISTENCE OF SOULS, POPE BUILDS TELESCOPE TO FIND GOD, and JESUIT ASSURES ATHEISTS OF A PLACE IN HEAVEN:

> Atheists who secretly worry that there might be an afterlife after all were yesterday offered comfort by a leading Jesuit theologian who declared that non-believers would also enter Paradise after death, 'provided they live and die with a clear conscience'.

When I read that medley of absurdities, I begin to wonder whether I am living towards the end of the first millennium rather than the second. For how much longer are men and women prepared to delude themselves with such feeble panaceas for their comfort: how much longer before they recognise they have come of age and it is time to put away childish things?

People say, as they did to Bradlaugh, well, if you want to discard religion, what are you going to put in its place? Bradlaugh replied that when a tree had outlived its usefulness, it became necessary to cut it down and prepare the ground for something else. But what?

Before he died, the Victorian poet Walter Savage Landor wrote this:

> I strove with none, for none was worth my strife,
> Nature I loved and next to Nature art,
> I warmed both hands before the fire of life,
> It sinks, and I am ready to depart.[1]

Ignoring the first line which is a little patronising, the thing that strikes me most about the poem is that there is no mention of religion among the things Landor loved, only nature and art. It does not surprise me. The Church has always assumed that they alone are the guardians of the spiritual, and that a sense of the spiritual plays no part in the make-up of non-believers. They are wrong. Like Landor I have gained more spiritual refreshment from nature and from art than any other single source.

As a boy I first discovered the benison that nature had to offer from the sea lochs and mountains ('I will lift up mine eyes unto the hills from whence cometh my help') of my native Scotland, and which it has continued to give me generously ever since. Here's what I wrote in my autobiography about going on a picnic to the battlefield of Culloden Moor, Bonnie Prince Charlie's nemesis, when I was eight or nine.

> As we were having our picnic, I heard a sound which was new to me and which, although I have heard it and variations on it many times since, I have never forgotten. It was the sound of a piper. It

was a distant sound. We could not see the piper who I think must have been on a different part of the moor. But when we heard it, we all stopped our chatter and listened.

At this distance I find it hard to convey the effect that sound had on me. Although unaware until that very afternoon that I had Scots blood in my veins, the sound roused in me some deep, atavistic emotion I could only dimly comprehend yet which instantly brought tears to my eyes. The piper, my mother told me, was playing a pibroch, a slow, melancholy lament, each long-held note leading inevitably to its successor; for me (and I suppose for the piper), it was a lament for all those on both sides who had died on the battlefield and of whose presence our pilgrimage had made me aware.

I have heard the pipes on many occasions since, and they never fail to move me. I know that many of my English friends find them risible, but when I see and hear a pipe band leading a column of marchers, it instils in me dreams of glory. When I dance a reel or strathspey to the beat of pipe music, I am filled with exhilaration. And when I see and hear again the pibroch, especially when played by the lone, floodlit piper on the ramparts of Edinburgh Castle on the conclusion of the tattoo, I am consumed by what Frank Adams has called 'the joy of grief'; not only grief for the millions of my countrymen who seem to have fallen in every war there has ever been, many for the English, many against, but for other people and things too: for the thousands dispossessed by the savagery of the Clearances and the empty glens whose ruined dwellings bear stark witness to them; for the overwhelming beauty of the mountains and moors of the Highlands and Islands; for the reed-fringed, water-lilied lochs and lochans that grace them and for the boisterous seas that flank them; but above all perhaps for the loss of our independence, our nationhood, our psyche. If I feel those things today more than ever, I am glad that the truth of them came to me, albeit subconsciously, on Culloden Moor nearly seventy years ago.

And this, twelve years later, about leaving Skye on 1 September 1939 after hearing that war had been declared:

> Next morning, in response to telegrams to rejoin their units, some members of the house party packed and left. As yet, I had no unit, but that afternoon, feeling that I too should leave the periphery for the centre, I joined the exodus. It was, I recall, a lovely summer's day, with a light wind stirring the roadside grasses and moving the shadows of the clouds over sunlit heather and bracken. All the way south, across blue water at Lochalsh and over the moors to Invergarry, by Loch Ness and Ballachulish to the great cleft of Glencoe and on to the bare uplands of Rannoch, my eyes and senses absorbed that marvellous country with a heightened awareness, seeing it as it were for the first time because – who knew? – it might also be the last. Passing through Stirling after dark I saw the shape of things to come. Not a light showed anywhere. The war had begun.

But no one has more movingly or more succinctly expressed his feelings and mine about Scotland than the poet Hugh MacDiarmid whose lines I can rarely utter without tears.

> The rose of all the world is not for me,
> I want for my part
> Only the little white rose of Scotland
> That smells sharp and sweet – and breaks the heart.

In 1941, when I was twenty-two, I became an officer in a fleet destroyer, and on several occasions experienced a sense of the spiritual which I found quite magical. It always took place after dark when I had one of the night watches. I was alone on the open bridge while most of the ship's company of some 250 slept below: their safety was in my hands. On summer evenings when the sea was calm, there was no movement except the gentle swaying of the foremast from side to side, like a giant inverted metronome, no sound but the swish of the bows as they sliced through the water and the tick-tick of the gyro compass repeat as it shifted in its gimbals. Stars, billions of miles distant, seemed ever close and protective, a watchful presence above my head. (Later, as navigator of another destroyer, one of them, Vega, would show me the way from Scapa Flow to Murmansk.) There were moments then when I felt that sky and sea and I were one, concordant and indivisible,[2] and I recalled Rupert Brooke's line about 'a width, a shining peace under the night'. For me it was both a glimpse of eternity and the peace that passeth all understanding, and on the four or five occasions it happened in the course of the war, I treasured every moment; and, when the watch ended, though tired after four hours' standing, went down to my cabin with lighter tread.

Wordsworth too experienced something similar when he wrote of a mood

> In which the burthen of the mystery,
> In which the heavy and the weary weight
> Of all this unintelligible world
> Is lightened . . .

And again when he spoke of

> A presence that disturbs me with the joy
> Of elevated thoughts; a sense sublime
> Of something far more deeply interfused
> Whose dwelling is the light of setting suns
> And the round ocean and the living air,
> And the blue sky, and in the eye of man:
> A motion and a spirit, that impels
> All thinking things, all objects of all thoughts
> And rolls through all things.

So did the nineteenth-century naturalist and writer, Richard Jefferies, in his book, *The Story of my Heart*. He had walked three miles from the farm near Swindon where he lived to the top of a hill:

I was utterly alone with the sun and the earth. Lying down on the sward, I first looked up at the sky, gazing for a long time till I could see deep into the azure. Then I turned my face to the grass and the thyme. I felt deep down into the earth under, and high above into the sky. Gradually entering into the intense life of the summer day, I came to feel the long-drawn life of the earth into the dimmest past, while the sun of the moment was warm on me. I was plunged deep in existence.

Beside the place where he had lain down was a 2,000-year-old tumulus:

Two thousand years! Two thousand times, the woods grow green and the ring-doves build their nests . . . Mystery gleaming in the stars, pouring down in the sunshine, speaking in the night, the wonder of the sun and of far space, for twenty centuries about this low and green-grown dome. Yet all that mystery and wonder was as nothing to the spirit I felt so close . . . Realising that spirit, recognising my own inner consciousness so clearly, I could not understand time. *Now, this moment, was the wonder and the glory.*

In the days when I used to go to church, I recall preacher after preacher saying that finding God was not always easy (though one or two quoted Pascal's dictum that he who seeks God has already found him). Christ had put it a different way: 'Watch therefore; for you know not what hour your Lord doth come' (Matthew 24:42). In the same way, I believe, if you want to attain the kind of mystical, experience of nature which Wordsworth and Jefferies and I and others have had the good fortune to enjoy, you must also open your heart to the possibility of it: the readiness is all.

The spiritual delights to be found in art are equally fulfilling and, among the people at large, increasingly popular. Since the end of the last war there has been a kind of explosion in the arts in the shape of concerts and plays, opera and ballet performances, art exhibitions, poetry recitals, audio-tape readings, televised competitions for the

269

BBC's Singer/Pianist/Musician of the Year, architectural competitions, success of Classic FM. So that Winwood Reade's prophecy of a hundred years ago that in the future art would take the place of religion looks like being fulfilled.

Of all the arts the one I cherish most is poetry which, like music, speaks directly to the heart. It has been a love of mine since childhood, having been weaned in Edinburgh on Burns and Scott and Robert Louis Stevenson's *Child's Garden of Verses*. Winning the Open Finals Contest in the English Festival of Spoken Poetry in 1953 enabled me and my wife Moira Shearer, after her retirement from ballet and theatre, to give joint recitals at festivals and other venues all over the country; and for the last ten years we have been accompanied by a tiny, brilliant blonde harpist, Gillian Tingay, whose playing is the perfect counterpoint to poetry.

The lines of some poems are etched in my mind for ever:

> daffodils
> That come before the swallow dares and take
> The winds of March with beauty.[3]

> O, but everyone
> Was a bird; and the song was wordless; the singing
> Will never be done.[4]

> Turn the key deftly in the oiled wards
> And seal the hushed casket of my soul.[5]

> There was a woman, beautiful as morning.[6]

> The woods are lovely, dark, and deep,
> But I have promises to keep,
> And miles to go before I sleep,
> And miles to go before I sleep.[7]

> Beauty is truth, truth beauty
> That is all
> Ye know on earth, and all ye need to know.[8]

I saw eternity the other night,
Like a great ring of pure and endless light.[9]

And of course:

Know then thyself, presume not God to scan,
The proper study of mankind is man.[10]

Nor, among my favourite poems, do I exclude what are called the metaphysicals, Donne, Herbert, Vaughan, Crawshay and, later, Blake. Indeed, and this may surprise you, one of the poems I love best is called 'Love' which I know by heart and at the drop of a hat will recite to anyone prepared to listen. It was written in the early seventeenth century by the Rev. George Herbert, parish priest of Bemerton in Wiltshire, author of many hymns which are still sung today.

Love bade me welcome; but my soul drew back,
Guilty of dust and sin,
But quick eyed Love, observing me grow slack
From my first entrance in,
Drew nearer to me sweetly questioning
If I lacked anything.

A guest, I answered, worthy to be here,
Love said, you shall be he.
I the unkind, ungrateful? Ah my dear,
I cannot look on thee.
Love took my hand, and smiling did reply
Who made the eyes but I?

Truth Lord, but I have marred them; let my shame
Go where it doth deserve.
And know you not, says Love, who bore the blame?
My dear, then I will serve.
You must sit down, says Love, and taste my meat:
So I did sit and eat.

For me the beauty and strength of that poem is that although the poet is addressing 'God', the word is never mentioned and the word 'Lord' only once. 'Love' as an abstraction enables the poem to be appreciated by Christians, Humanists, agnostics and atheists alike.

We live today in a multi-cultural, multi-faith society, both in individual countries and worldwide, and therefore the social cohesion which religious belief gave to so many societies in the past is missing. Has anything come to take its place? Two things: first sport, especially football, an appreciation of which people can and do share at city, county, country and international levels. The second is television itself which has become a common denominator for all of us, again at both local and worldwide levels, with the same news bulletins, documentaries, plays, wildlife programmes and sporting events being shown, some contemporaneously, in as many countries as broadcast television. Marshall McLuhan's assessment of the world as a global village has become truer with every day that has passed. And if a shift from a social cohesion based on religion to one based on sport sounds like a descent from the sublime to the ridiculous, I can only say that any conflicts that arise in the world of sport (mostly riots at football stadiums caused by fans without tickets) are mere bagatelles compared to the tortures, murders and massacres inflicted on dissenters by clerics of the medieval Church.

As one looks back at the nearly two millennia of Christianity, one can see the landmarks that led to its rise: the impact made by the extraordinary life of Jesus Christ and the impact of the novelty of what he is said to have said, and did; the bogus Old Testament prophecies which convinced early Christians and Gentiles that he was the Messiah chosen by God to liberate Israel; the missionary work of Paul, Peter and others; the adoption by Constantine of Christianity as the Roman Empire's official religion and its subsequent spread across Europe and the world. Equally one can see the landmarks that have led to its slow but inevitable decline: the Renaissance, the Reformation, Copernicus and Galileo, Newton and Darwin, Nietzsche and Freud. It cannot be denied that for many hundreds of years Christianity filled a need, though whether in the course of them it was an overall force for good or bad, whether the magnificent works of art that it engendered, the cathedrals of Cologne and Chartres and Canterbury, the paintings of Titian and Tintoretto, the music of Bach and Handel, Beethoven and Verdi, all the books of devotion and poetry that were created to praise it, outweigh the murders and massacres imposed on infidels and heretics, would be hard to say; though many would maintain that while the murders and massacres have been long forgotten, the beauty of the cathedrals and paintings and devotional music and poetry are still there, for us and our children's children to enjoy.

Yet I would add this. For a long time now the British press has been reiterating the view that the Church of England has somehow failed us, that it's entirely their fault that the pews are three-quarters empty and religious belief in general decline. I think that is unfair. It is not the Church's hierarchy which is found wanting, rather the doctrines they preach. The premise of an almighty, invisible, god only wise who 'fathered' an only begotten son who was born of a virgin, performed a number of astonishing miracles and then rose from the dead, is no more credible than the promise of rewards and punishments in some imaginary future state, from whose bourne, as Shakespeare and the Italian dissenter Commodo Canuove declared, no traveller returns.

As I said in an earlier chapter it has been man's innate curiosity and perennial asking of questions that has brought him from a creature in a bearskin wielding a club to the world of the Internet, cyberspace, and cloning. Some of the first questions to which man wanted answers were, how did the world begin, how did we get there and why? And one of the reasons that religions came into being was to answer them by saying that some god or gods, later 'God', made it and us. That would now seem an inadequate answer, so the question is asked afresh; and this time in truth we have to say we do not know and do not think we will ever know. Whether it came about as the result of a purposeful act, a physical evolvement or something accidental must remain a mystery beyond human comprehension. And when I am asked if human life has any meaning, I can only reply, such meaning as each of us individually can find in it.

In any case, I do not think that these questions demand either an answer or our keen attention. Today I believe that most people are content to accept the world as it is. It is less the distant past that exercises most people's imaginations than the future; the problems that unite us all are those that threaten the survival of life on the planet; the destruction of the rainforests and global warming leading to a dramatic rise in sea levels and unpredictable changes in climate; the population explosion; where energy is to be found and harnessed after the oil has run out; the inevitable spread of nuclear weapons; terrorist-inspired planting of bubonic plague or anthrax; assault by a meteorite of the force that killed off the dinosaurs 65 million years ago; an out-of-control global virus. The solutions to those problems, not where we came from but where we may be going, are the problems facing us now and require our urgent attention. And should we fail in any of our endeavours to avert disaster, and decimation or even extinction face us, I do not believe that this time we will be foolish enough to ask 'God' to come to the rescue. For, as I have tried to show in this book, atheism (or, as I prefer to spell it, a-theism) has had a long (400 years) and honourable history and is entitled to be taken seriously, not dismissed, by all thinking people.

One last thought. There was a time in the history of the Christian Church when the devil, Beelzebub or Satan, the king of evil, was as real and forceful a figure as for a diminishing number of people 'God' still is today; a creation of the Jews and early Christians to give substance in half-human, half-bestial form to the wickedness they saw about them. Later Christians came to recognise that this was a fantasy figure with no basis in reality and quietly discarded him. How soon or long before they come to recognise that God is a fantasy figure, like Satan an idea in the mind, and learn to discard him too?

Fifty years? A hundred? Five hundred? Never?

Notes

Introduction (Pages xiii–xvii)

1 Sir Isaiah Berlin, the distinguished historian and essayist, told me a few months before he died that, like Charles Bradlaugh in the nineteenth century, he was at a loss to know what the word God meant.

Chapter Two (Pages 15–27)

1 See Chapter 4.
2 Translated by Peter Heinegg (Penguin, 1990). Uta Ranke-Heinemann is a German Roman Catholic theologian appointed a lecturer at the University of Essen in 1969. In 1970 she became Professor of Catholic Theology but was subsequently dismissed from her post by John Paul II for interpreting the Virgin Birth theologically (as he had done in 1984) instead of biologically (i.e. he accepted it as a historical fact). Today Ranke-Heinemann is still at Essen and now holds the chair of the History of Religion.

Chapter Three (Pages 29–44)

1 One African legend had it that God distanced himself from a certain tribe because he was angry that they had taken bits out of the sky to put in their soup.
2 Bacchus to the Romans.

Chapter Four (Pages 45–81)

1 In a book entitled *The Jesus Papyrus* by Carsten Peter Thiede and Matthew d'Ancona published in 1996, it is claimed that a fragment of papyrus in the possession of Magdalen College, Oxford, proves that the gospel of St Matthew was written much earlier than previously thought, possibly not long after the crucifixion and certainly in the lifetime of those who had witnessed it. This claim however has been refuted by Graham Stanton in *Gospel Truth?* and by other biblical scholars.

2 'And when [Herod] had gathered all the chief priests and scribes of the people together, he demanded of them where Christ should be born. And they said unto him, in Bethlehem of Judaea: *for thus it is written by the prophet.*'

3 Mark's account of Jesus appearing once to Mary Magdalen, once to two unnamed disciples walking in the country and once to the eleven while they are eating dinner is given in verses 9–15 but these are a later addition and not in the original manuscripts.

4 Karen Armstrong writes: 'Ascension is a metaphysical way of saying that Jesus is now in a different place, a higher level of being.'

5 See his lecture, 'Jesus and the Revelation of God', delivered at the 1967 Annual Conference of the Modern Churchman's Union at Somerville College, Oxford, and subsequently published in *Christ for us Today* (ed. N. Pittenger, SCM Press, 1968), a collection of the papers given at that conference.

6 The American comedian W.C. Fields is reported to have said, 'Do unto others before they do unto you', while Bernard Shaw's contribution was, 'Do not do unto others as you would that they should do unto you. Their tastes may not be the same' (from the *Revolutionist's Handbook*, attached to the play *Man and Superman*).

7 Our former self.

Chapter Five (Pages 83–106)

1 At the time he wrote this (*c.* 240) it was a bit of an exaggeration. There were isolated pockets of Christianity then, but it wasn't until 596 that Pope Gregory sent Augustine to Canterbury as the first Bishop of England.
2 These perverted views remained the stock-in-trade of Catholic thinking for centuries and influenced Pope John Paul II when at a general audience in October 1980, and again in September 1984, he expressed similar bizarre views on the scenario of a husband committing adultery with his wife.
3 Modern man might wonder why penitents did not lie when confronted with such questions. A very real fear of God who, they believed, knew and saw all things, prevented it.

Chapter Six (Pages 107–149)

1 The German Crusaders believed that when they reached Jerusalem, Christ would return in glory, as he had promised, and that the Jews would welcome him, as St Paul had promised. To bring this about they offered the European Jews a choice between baptism or death.
2 The Moslem opponents of the Crusaders.
3 An exception was sometimes made 'to avoid fornication' (with others).
4 The late diplomat Sir Harry Luke wrote in one of his books how he and a companion were shown a stain on the floor of some Italian cathedral, said to be the blood of Christ. The companion, who must have been an expert on stains, knelt down and licked it. 'Bat's urine!' he declared. The Turin Shroud, in which some believed Christ to have been buried, was also thought to possess magical properties until proved by carbon dating to be a fake.
5 In 1962 in the cathedral of Bom Jesus in Goa, I was shown a box allegedly containing a toe of the Spanish missionary St Francis Xavier.

6 Purgatory is a place or state dreamed up by Roman Catholics as a kind of halfway house between heaven and hell. Here sinners not wicked enough to go straight to hell expiate their sins until such time as God permits them to enter heaven. 'The existence of Purgatory,' says John Haldane, Professor of Philosophy at St Andrews University, in the Credo column in *The Times* of 20 September 1997, 'is confirmation of God's mercy, not evidence of his desire to inflict punishment.'

7 For a fuller account of this extraordinary case, see the author's *In Bed with an Elephant* (Bantam Press, 1989).

8 Moloch. An ancient pagan god to whom children were sacrificed.

Chapter Seven (Pages 153–161)

1 'Sun, stand thou still upon Gibeon, and thou, Moon, in the Valley of Ajalon' (Joshua 10:12).

Chapter Eight (Pages 163–208)

1 This phrase fell out of use in 1976.

2 See page 165.

3 I.e. Juggernaut.

4 It was government policy at this time to incarcerate prisoners convicted of blasphemy or sedition in jails as far removed from London as possible.

Chapter Nine (Pages 209–235)

1 Interestingly d'Holbach too anticipated Darwin, when he wrote that while our experience was inadequate to answer precise questions about our origins, terrestrial diversity in plant and animal

(including human) life was due to environmental and climatic differences, and that if essential physical relationships changed, which they must, then forms of life unable to 'co-ordinate' with their surroundings would die out, and only varieties capable of that co-ordination would survive (Adam Charles Kors, *The Atheism of d'Holbach and Naigeon*).

2 Whose reaction on first reading *Origin* was, 'How extremely stupid not to have thought of that.' He was right: the evolution of species was a fact waiting to be discovered. At the same time as Darwin, and quite independently, another naturalist, Alfred Russel Wallace, living in Borneo, had written an essay which had come to exactly the same conclusions. He and Darwin subsequently corresponded.

3 I was brought up to believe that one should never commit oneself to any belief or course of action about which one had doubts, on the grounds of 'if in doubt, don't'. Yet during my lifetime I have rarely had talks with any clergyman who did not admit that there were times when he was beset by doubts.

4 The atheistic views of George Eliot (pen name for Mary Ann Evans) greatly shocked her father, a man of strong but conventional opinions. However, she came to a compromise with him by agreeing to continue to attend church, so long as he would allow her to think what she liked while there.

5 At this time neither oath nor affirmation was required in the legislatures of France, Germany and Sweden; there was an option in the Netherlands, Switzerland, the United States; no incantation to the Almighty ('So help me, God') was required of the oath in Belgium, Italy and Spain.

Chapter Ten (Pages 237–260)

1 This sounds ridiculous today but at that time, when the Cold War with Soviet Russia was beginning to hot up, to call someone a

Communist, with its veiled suggestions of anarchy and treachery, was considered the ultimate smear.

2 As per the Rev. Don Cupitt in *After God* (1997): 'I am proposing to show in due course both that one should now give up the idea that God "exists" and that we should nevertheless believe in God (or at least come to see that the idea of God is still of use in helping us to become ourselves).' But he doesn't convincingly (at least to me) explain how.

3 Doubtless because of fear of being contaminated with Hitler's terrible programme of *compulsory euthanasia* on Jews, gypsies, the handicapped, 'undesirables', etc.

Chapter Eleven (Pages 261–274)

1 When I was searching for a title for my autobiography (which in the end I called *On My Way to the Club*), my friend the novelist Angela Huth thought that the poem's last three words might do.

2 During the Margaret Knight controversy, a seventy-seven-year-old widow wrote to her as follows: 'It is only when we can lose our own identity and become not only part of the universe but immersed in it as a drop in the sea – that everything we do becomes spontaneous and intuitive, almost without thought and *right*, and the stresses and strains resolve themselves. It is at such times that life becomes exciting and wonderful, even ecstatic.'

3 Shakespeare.
4 Siegfried Sassoon.
5 Keats.
6 Shelley.
7 Robert Frost.
8 Keats.
9 Vaughan.
10 Pope.

Books Consulted

Armstrong, Karen, *A History of God* (London, 1994)
Ayer, A.J. and others, *What I Believe* (London, 1966)

Bainton, Roland, *The Mediaeval Church* (London, 1962)
Bainton, Roland, *The Penguin History of Christianity* (London, 1967)
Barnes, Ernest William, *The Rise of Christianity* (London, 1947)
Barnes, Jonathan, *Aristotle* (Oxford, 1996)
Barth, Karl, *Preaching through the Christian Year* (Edinburgh, 1985)
Berman, David, *A History of Atheism in Britain* (London and New York, 1988)
Bestermann, Theodore, *Voltaire* (London, 1969)
Blackham, H.J., *Humanism* (London, 1968)
Bonhoeffer, Dietrich, *Letters and Papers from Prison* (London, 1953)
Bronowski, J., *The Ascent of Man* (London, 1976)
Brooke, John Hedley, *Science and Religion* (Cambridge, 1991)
Brown, Raymond E., *Responses to 101 Questions on the Bible* (New York, 1990)
Bruce, F.F., *The Hard Sayings of Jesus* (London, 1983)
Buckley, George T., *Atheism in the English Renaissance* (New York, 1965)
Buckley, M., *At the Origins of Modern Atheism* (Yale, 1987)

Calthrop, Gordon, *The Future Life and Other Essays* (London, 1905)
Cantor, Norman, *A History of the Jews* (London, 1994)
Carol, Avedon, *Nudes, Prudes and Attitudes: Pornography and Censorship* (London, 1994)

Carpenter, Humphrey, *Jesus* (Oxford, 1990)

Chastel, André, *Art of the Italian Renaissance 1280–1580* (New York, 1988)

Cherrington, Bet, *Facing the World. An Anthology of Poetry for Humanists* (London, 1989)

Church, R.W., *Cathedral and University Sermons* (London, 1892)

Cupitt, Don, *After God* (London, 1997)

Cupitt, Don, *The Sea of Faith* (London, 1984)

Dahmus, Joseph, *The Middle Ages* (London, 1969)

Darwin, Charles, *The Origin of Species by Means of Natural Selection* (London, 1866)

Davie, Grace, *Religion in Britain since 1945* (Oxford, 1994)

Davies, Paul, *The Mind of God* (London, 1992)

Drake, Stillman, *Galileo* (Oxford, 1980)

Fernandez-Armesto, Felipe, *The Future of Religion* (London, 1997)

Foster, John, *Church History 2, AD 500–1500. Setback and Recovery* (London, 1974)

Foster, John and Frend, W.H.C., *Church History 1, AD 29–500. The First Advance* (London, 1972)

Frazer, J.G., *The Golden Bough* (London, 1976)

Freeman, Anthony, *God in Us. A Case for Christian Humanism* (London, 1993)

Gascoigne, Bamber, *The Christians* (London, 1977)

Gordon, Stuart, *The Encyclopaedia of Myths and Legends* (London, 1994)

Grant, Michael, *Myths of the Greeks and Romans* (London, 1962)

Green, Michael (ed.), *The Truth of God Incarnate* (London, 1977)

Gribbin, John, *The Future of Cosmology* (London, 1997)

Grigson, Geoffrey, *Painted Caves* (London, 1957)

Grote, George and Bentham, Jeremy, *The Analysis of the Influence of Natural Religion on the Temporal Happiness of Mankind* (London, 1822)

Hall, Maria B., *Colour and Meaning* (Cambridge, 1992)
Hardy, A. Lister., *The Biology of God* (London, 1975)
Hick, John (ed.), *The Myth of God Incarnate* (London, 1977)
Homer, *The Odyssey*, translated by Walter Shewring (Oxford, 1980)
Homer, *The Iliad*, translated by Robert Fitzgerald (Oxford, 1984)
Howard, Jonathan, *Darwin* (Oxford, 1982)
Hume, David, *Dialogues concerning Natural Religion* (New York, 1948)
Hume, David, *A Treatise of Human Nature* (London, 1987)
Hunkin, Oliver, *A World That has Lost its Way* (Lewes, Sussex, 1994)
Hunter, Michael and Wootton, David (eds), *Atheism from the Reformation to the Enlightenment* (Oxford, 1992) and containing essays by Nicholas Davison on Atheism in Italy 1500–1700, by Tullio Gregory on Pierre Charron, by Silvia Berti on the *Traité des trois imposteurs* and its debt to Spinoza's *Ethics*, by Michael Hunter on Aikenhead the Atheist, by David Berman on Charles Blount and John Toland, and by Alan Charles Kors on the Atheism of d'Holbach and Naigeon.

James, William, *Varieties of Religious Experience* (London, 1903)
Johnson, Paul, *A History of Christianity* (London, 1976)
Johnson, Paul, *The Quest for God* (London, 1996)
Jones, Peter, *Hume's Sentiments* (Edinburgh, 1982)
Jung, C.G., *Memories, Dreams and Reflections* (London, 1963)

Kahl, Joachim, *The Misery of Christianity*, translated by N.D. Smith (London, 1971)
Keller, Werner, *The Bible as History*, translated by William Neil (London, 1960)
Kennedy, Ludovic, *An End to Belief?* The Voltaire Memorial Lecture, 1984
Kennedy, Ludovic, *On My Way to the Club* (London, 1989)
Kennedy, Ludovic, *In Bed with an Elephant* (London, 1995)
Kenny, Mary, *Good-bye to Catholic Ireland* (London, 1997)
Knight, Margaret, *Morals without Religion and other Essays* (London, 1955)

Knight, Margaret and Herrick, Jim, *Humanist Anthology* (London, 1961)

Knight, Margaret, *Honest to Man* (London, 1974)

Kors, Alan Charles, *D'Holbach's Coterie* (Princeton, 1976)

Kors, Alan Charles, *Vol. I: Atheism in France 1650–1729* (Princeton, 1990)

Küng, Hans and Jens, Walter, *A Dignified Dying*, translated by John Bowden (London, 1995)

Lane-Fox, Robin, *The Unauthorised Version* (London, 1991)

Lang, Andrew, *The Making of Religion* (London, 1898)

Lofmark, Carl, *What is the Bible?* (London, 1990)

Mehta, Ved, *The New Theologian* (London, 1965)

Miles, Jack, *God: A Biography* (London, 1995)

Moore, Patrick, *Atlas of the Universe* (London, 1997)

Moorman, J.R.H., *A History of the Church in England* (London, 1954)

Newsome, David, *The Victorian World Picture* (London, 1997)

Paine, Thomas, *The Age of Reason* (Paris, 1794, 1795)

Pope John Paul II, *Crossing the Threshold of Hope* (London, 1994)

Ranke-Heinemann, Uta, *Eunuchs for the Kingdom of Heaven. The Catholic Church and Sexuality*, translated by Peter Heinegg (London, 1990)

Reade, Winwood, *The Martyrdom of Man* (London, 1968)

Reynolds, Alfred, *Jesus versus Christianity* (London, 1988)

Ridley, Matt, *The Origins of Virtue* (London, 1996)

Robinson, John A.T., Bishop of Woolwich, *Honest to God* (London, 1963)

Rousseau, Jean-Jacques, *The Confessions* (London, 1953)

Russell, Bertrand, *History of Western Philosophy* (London, 1946)

Russell, Bertrand, *Why I am not a Christian* (London, 1957)

Ruthven, Malise, *The Divine Supermarket. Shopping for God in America* (London, 1989)

BOOKS CONSULTED

Sanders, E.P., *The Historical Figure of Jesus* (London, 1993)

Schmidt, Wilhelm, *The Origin of the Idea of God* (London, 1912)

Schoeps, Hans-Joachim, *An Intelligent Person's Guide to the Religions of Mankind* (London, 1966)

Schonfield, Hugh, *Those Incredible Christians* (London, 1968)

Scruten, Roger, *Spinoza* (Oxford, 1996)

Seton-Williams, M.V., *Greek Legends and Stories* (London, 1993)

Sinclair, Andrew, *Jerusalem. The Endless Crusade* (London, 1996)

Smart, Ninian, *The Religious Experiences of Mankind* (London, 1982)

Smith, Edwin (ed.), *African Ideas of God* (Edinburgh, 1950)

Sobel, Dava, *Longitude* (London, 1995)

Stassinopoulos, Ariana and Beny, Rocoff, *The Gods of Greece* (London, 1983)

Storr, Anthony, *Jung* (London, 1973)

Storr, Anthony, *Feet of Clay. A Study of Gurus* (London, 1996)

Stott, John R.W., *Basic Christianity* (Leicester, 1958)

Taylor, John, *The Primal Vision* (London, 1965)

Thiede, Carsten Peter and d'Ancona, Matthew, *The Jesus Papyrus* (London, 1996)

Thomas, Keith, *Religion and the Decline of Magic* (London, 1982)

Thomson, Alan, *Church History 3, 1500–1800* (London, 1976)

Tillich, Paul, *The Shaking of the Foundations* (London, 1949)

Trelawny, Edward, *Records of Shelley, Byron and the Author* (London, 1887)

Tuck, Richard, *Hobbes* (Oxford, 1989)

Weiner, Joel H., *The Life of Richard Carlile* (Westport, Connecticut, 1983)

Wells, G.A., *Did Jesus Exist?* (London, 1975)

Wells, G.A., *The Historical Evidence for Jesus* (New York, 1982)

Wells, G.A., *Who was Jesus?* (La Salle, Illinois, 1989)

Wilson, A.N., *How Can We Know?* (London, 1985)

Wilson, A.N., *Paul: The Mind of the Apostle* (London, 1997)

Wilson, Ian, *Jesus: The Evidence* (London, 1984)

The Alternative Service Book 1980

The Book of Common Prayer

Dictionary of the Bible, eds T. and T. Clark (Edinburgh, 1963)

The Dictionary of National Biography

The Ethics of Belief. A Symposium, Vol. 2, No.1 (*The Journal for the Critical Study of Religion, Ethics and Society* (Amherst, New York, 1997)

The Holy Bible (King James's Authorised Version)

Oxford Companion to the Bible (Oxford, 1993)

Religious Education in the Basic Curriculum (Wiltshire County Council, 1992)

Scottish Record Office JC2/19; 588–90, 592–6 (Indictment of Thomas Aikenhead)

The World Christian Encyclopaedia (Oxford, 1982)

Index

INDEX

INDEX

Hawaiian group of islands, 211
Hawking, Stephen, 157
  A Brief History of Time xiv
healers, 33, 62–3, 86
Hebrews, epistle to the, 79
Heine, Heinrich, 220
Helen, 40
hell, 141–2, 164, 215, 216
Henri of Navarre, 146, 147
Henry VII, King, 36
Henry VIII, King, xv, 144, 145
Hephaistos, 40
Hera, 40
Herbert, Rev. George, 271
  'Love', 271–2
Herbert of Cherbury, Lord, 181
Hercules, 40
herm, 39
Hermes, 39
Hero, 40
hero, the, 40–41
Herod, King, xiv, 57, 69, 83, 84, 125
Hesiod, 43
  Theogony, 39
  Works and Days, 39
Hestia, 40
Hillel, 73
Hinduism, 261
Hippocrates, 102
Histoire des Ouvrages des Savans, 174
Hitler, Adolf, 249, 252
  Mein Kampf, 146
Hobbes, Thomas, 29, 146, 161, 179, 183
Hogg, Thomas, 198
Holbach, Paul Thiry, Baron d', 149, 175–80,
  183, 195, 197, 199
  Système de la Nature, 177–80, 203
Holland, 145, 169
Holocaust, 99, 112
Holy Communion, 5, 6, 7–8, 98
Holy Ghost/Spirit, 5, 30, 58,
  67, 70, 77, 83, 87, 96, 98, 149
Holy Lance, 112, 123
Holy Land, 116, 126
holy oil, 37
Holyoake, G.J., 205–7
  History of the Last Trial by Jury for Atheism,
  206–7
Holyrood monastery, 140
Home, Lord, 22
Homer, 43, 232
  Iliad, 38–9, 40
  Odyssey, 39, 41
Homeric Hymns, 39, 42

Homoousion (the Son the same essence as the
  father), 262–3
homosexuality, 24, 257
Hope, Dr, Archbishop of York, 257, 264
Horus (sun god) Egypt, 34
Hosea, 57, 79
House of Commons, 224–7
Howard, Jonathan, 213
Howitt (a traveller), 32
Huguenots, 146–7
Huitzilopochtli (corn god), 38
human sacrifice, 34
Humanism, 15, 17, 18–19, 21, 22, 164,
  254, 259
Hume, David, 75, 149, 174, 176–7, 187–94,
  195, 196, 243
  Dialogues concerning Natural Religion, 187
Hunt, Derek, 15
Hunter, Michael, 161
  'Aikenhead the Atheist', 185
Huss, John, 128, 129, 130
Hutton, R.H., 228
Huxley, Sir Julian, 22, 253–4, 256
Huxley, T. H., 213–14, 215, 253
hymns, 4, 21, 216, 271

Icarus, 40
Ignatius of Antioch, Bishop, 89
Ignatius of Loyola, 70
Ilium, 38
immaculate conception, 99
immortality, personal, 164, 165
incantations, 35
Incarnation, 159, 229, 258
Incas, 34, 35
incense, 37, 100
incubus, 133
Independents, 148
Indian Ocean, 33
indulgences, 36, 129, 143
Industrial Revolution, 175, 207
infidels, xiv, 109
Innocent II, Pope, 118
Innocent III, Pope, 116, 126
Innocent IV, Pope, 114
Innocent VIII, Pope, 133
Inquisition, 102, 117–18, 131–2, 146, 155,
  164, 165, 166, 169
International Journal of Ethics, 237
Internet, 273
Inti (Inca sun god), 34
Ireland, Catholic priests' celibacy, 22–3
Irish Times, 23
Isaac, 53

293

INDEX